THE CURSE OF THE TURTLE

THE TRUE STORY OF THAILAND'S "BACKPACKER MURDERS"

SUZANNE BUCHANAN

WILDBLUE
PRESS

WildBluePress.com

THE CURSE OF THE TURTLE published by:
WILDBLUE PRESS
P.O. Box 102440
Denver, Colorado 80250

WILDBLUE PRESS is registered at the U.S. Patent and Trademark Offices.

ISBN 978-1-952225-99-4 Trade Paperback
ISBN 978-1-952225-98-7 eBook

Book Cover/Interior Formatting by Elijah Toten
www.totencreative.com

THE CURSE OF THE TURTLE

This book is dedicated to all of those who lost their lives in Koh Tao, their loving families, and those wrongfully convicted for crimes they did not commit.

THAILAND'S DEADLIEST ISLAND – KOH TAO – THE CURSE OF THE TURTLE

Preface

My name is Suzanne Buchanan. I am a British citizen and the exiled former owner and editor of the Samui Times *online newspaper. There is a warrant out for my arrest in Thailand because of articles I have published in the* Samui Times. *I am no longer able to live in the country that was my home for over 20 years. I have no access to my house in Thailand. Through my investigations into backpacker murders in Thailand, I have been forced to leave the country for my own safety. This is my story and the story of two Burmese men wrongfully sentenced to death for the murders of two British backpackers in 2014. It is also the story of the families of other backpackers who lost their lives on a tiny island in the Gulf of Thailand called Koh Tao, AKA Turtle Island AKA Death Island, which is purportedly owned and run by the infamous Thai mafia.*

Author's Note | The term "mafia" in this book, as well as other publications, is used to describe powerful local families who control various aspects of commerce and are the go-to people when you have a problem. It is a term that is commonly used by locals and the media. It is not used here to insinuate the families on Koh Tao participate in "organized crime" as "mafia" is interpreted in other parts of the world.

CHAPTER 1 – THE BRUTAL MURDERS OF HANNAH WITHERIDGE AND DAVID MILLER ON KOH TAO

Like many other ex-pats in Thailand, it was SCUBA diving that initially took me to the Gulf of Thailand. In 1999, I started my journey on the tiny island of Koh Tao, a diving mecca only accessible by speed boat. Koh Tao is neighbored by Koh Phangan, an island known for its infamous Full Moon Parties. After two years in Koh Tao, I moved to the third and largest island, Koh Samui, which is the closest of the three to the mainland.

By 2010, I began to tire of diving and started writing restaurant reviews for a friend's local magazine. I was later hired by two Philippine-owned-and-run bi-monthly newspapers to write articles on local events, sports, and happenings around the island. Seeing a gap in the market for a daily newspaper in 2013, I developed my own online news publication called the *Samui Times*. The *Samui Times* was catapulted into global view on the 15th of September 2014, when two backpackers were found dead on the island of Koh Tao. Overnight, my online publication became the contact for global news stations as they hungered for information on one of the biggest stories to ever leave Koh Tao, and indeed Thailand. The story dominated tabloid headlines around the world, as did the subsequent deaths of more backpackers on the tiny island of Koh Tao.

Prior to 2014, I had investigated many deaths and murders in Thailand where it is very easy to enter crime scenes, so easy it can be a bit unsettling. The local rescue teams, who are always the first to arrive, are well known for posting graphic photographs of the victims of crime and accidents to social media and are happy to tip off journalists to a story for a couple of quid. While I don't profess to be a forensic expert, my experience in reporting and investigating crimes has allowed me to build up a reasonable picture of most situations I have been faced with.

The 15th of September 2014, started out as an uneventful day. I had no idea when I woke up that it was a day that would change my life forever. The only notable part of that day, prior to getting the news, was the discovery that my dog had developed tick fever so a trip to the vet's office was required. It was while driving to the vet, around 3 p.m., that my phone rang.

The caller was a Thai friend of mine who had good connections with the local police. When you run a local newspaper, it's vital to have friends in all of the right places and this particular friend always had her finger on the pulse of what was going on. My friend told me that a *farang* couple had been found dead on the beach on Koh Tao. *Farang* is the Thai word for anyone who is not a Thai national. The slain couple had been found on Sairee Beach, an area thought of to be owned and operated by what the locals call the Koh Tao mafia. My mind immediately started racing with questions about who the dead couple were and where they came from and how they met their end on Sairee Beach in Koh Tao.

In 2014, smart phones were not commonplace, so as soon as the vet had finished with my dog, I raced home to fire up my laptop to start my investigation.

My phone rang again as I drove. This time it was a fellow British ex-pat, "Su, what is going on? A British couple has been found dead on the beach on Koh Tao. It looks like murder". As usual, news was spreading fast around Koh Samui.

I fired up my laptop and went to the rescue organization's social media pages. In my early days of reporting on crimes and visiting crime scenes, I had been appalled to see graphic photographs of the dead and injured victims of crimes: discarded newborn babies, suicides, bodies found weeks after they had died; but over the years I had become icily desensitized to them. I am not sure what I was expecting when I started this investigation but as the images loaded my jaw dropped and I gasped.

The crime scene was horrific; I had never seen such brutality. I was first faced with the corpse of a young white girl lying dead and spread-eagled on the beach. Her injuries were so severe my immediate thought was that she must have been shot in the face with a sawn-off shotgun. Her lower clothes had been pushed up around her waist, her underwear had been removed, leaving nothing to the imagination; the top half of her body was also exposed. Her face, utterly misshapen and distorted, was crimson with blood; her lower teeth were as black as coal. She looked very petite, physically fit, suntanned, and very, very young.

The man who had tragically died with her was also photographed. He was floating in the ocean, his injuries were not immediately apparent; however, I knew he had been there for a while as his right arm was stiff and poking out of the water like a flagpole; rigor had set in. He had typical death pallor, his lips were white, as were his fingers and toes, and oddly, he was naked other than one black sock. I could hardly believe what I was seeing. Who could have done this to two young travelers? And who were they? The following day, the victims' passports were posted onto the rescue site; I discovered the two victims were British and named as Hannah Witheridge, 23, and David Miller, 24. Despite what was being published in newspapers around the world, I discovered they had not been a couple but had met on Koh Tao where they had shared the same resort.

The brutality of the attack on Hannah left me gobsmacked. I had seen many photos of people who have been murdered but nothing like this. It was a frenzied attack from somebody who must have been utterly enraged, deranged, and possibly on psychotic drugs. The police said her injuries had been caused by a garden hoe. My mind filled with images of a man who was very large and very strong, and capable of creating that much damage with a garden implement. Examining photographs of her lifeless corpse it occurred to me that there were no injuries to her body, only her face. I shivered as I began to imagine what might have happened to her.

The concept of 'Face' (better known to Westerners as embarrassment) in Thailand is a huge part of their culture. Saving face and not losing face is an obsession with Thai people. I had come across many a crime scene where somebody had paid the ultimate price for causing another Thai to lose face. In this instance, it looked as if Hannah had quite literally lost her face.

I felt queasy wondering what on earth she could have gone through in the final few moments of her fragile young life and pondered what on earth could have caused her to end her days in such an unimaginable way on a tiny island that, on the surface, is paradise? Who had she upset? Who would have done this to her? Why in such a public place and in an area of the beach known to be owned and run by the local mafia? I thought the perpetrator had to be, or be linked to, powerful people, to create this kind of mess on mafia turf. It was insanity. In Koh Tao, many fear the mafia more than the police as they have a great deal more power. I came to only one conclusion, and it scared me.

CHAPTER 2 - KOH TAO

Koh Tao, or Turtle Island in English, started off life as a virgin island in the Gulf of Thailand. It is part of the Chumphon Archipelago on the western shore of the Gulf of Thailand. The Island is 21 square kilometers and covered in coconut trees. Historically, it was only visited by the occasional fisherman from neighboring islands looking for a break in his journey or perhaps to shelter from a tropical storm.

Despite being utterly undeveloped, the island was visited by King Chulalongkorn on the 18th of June 1899. Evidence of this visit can be seen with his monogram on a huge boulder at Jor Por Ror Bay next to Sairee Beach, a stone's throw away from where Hannah and David met their horrific demise.

In 1933, the island was used as a political prison. Khuang Abhaiwongse, who was the prime minister in 1947, pleaded and received a royal pardon for all prisoners on the island. Everybody was shipped off the mainland and Koh Tao was left uninhabited once again.

Legend has it that later in 1947, Khun Uaem and his brother, Khun Oh, arrived on the island from neighboring Koh Phangan on a traditional boat. This would have been a long and dangerous journey. Despite the island being under royal patronage, the two claimed a large chunk of Sairee Beach and made it home. Sometime later their families joined them, and they began to cultivate the rich soil and became the first generation of the present-day community.

Travelers from around the world started to arrive on Koh Tao's tropical shores in the early 1980s and by the 90s, it was a mecca for divers who joyfully explored the delights of this tropical paradise below its shores. When these first travelers came seeking adventure, Koh Tao was an unspoiled paradise offering rustic, and very affordable, huts on the beach along with a handful of bars made largely out of driftwood. Small, thatched restaurants popped up offering cheap but delicious local fare. There were a few motorbikes available to hire and the odd massage station could be found on the pristine beaches that were home to a few scabby dogs and the odd beach chair.

As time went on, the main town and port of Mae Haad developed. Concrete shops went up and the island, once powered by noisy and expensive generators, was provided with basic electricity that failed as often as it worked. With power available, an ice factory was built. Several hotels went up, two of which had hot water. A money exchange was put at the end of the pier. More diving operations were established. More ferries were laid on to transport backpackers to the island from the neighboring islands of Koh Samui and Koh Phangan and from the towns of Surat Thani and Chumpon on the mainland. A couple of basic nursing stations were established to tend to the burst ear drums and coral-scraped legs of clumsy divers, as well as food poisoning, insect stings, and other minor ailments. Electricity crept around the island and hundreds of coconut trees were felled to make way for more and more resorts. Koh Tao was cashing in on tourism and expanding at a rather alarming rate, but the guests kept arriving and the pockets of the locals swelled.

CHAPTER 3 - MY INVESTIGATIONS BEGIN

Having spent the latter part of my day investigating the most horrific crimes I had ever come across, I decided to go out and see if I could gather information from the local police, many of whom frequented ex-pat bars and played in local pool leagues, one of which I ran at the time.

The police in Koh Samui were a great source of information, especially after a few beers and if you were buying. In Thailand, the idea of confidential information does not exist, and it is possible to get any information you like if you are not hard up for cash. I drove down to an area called Soi Reggae. The word *soi* in Thai means 'street'. This particular Soi was a strip of 'girlie bars' where locals and foreigners drink and frequent with scantily clad women and pick up prostitutes for either an hour in a 'short time room' normally found at the rear of the bar or for a night back at their house or hotel. At the end of the Soi is a large bar/nightclub called Reggae Bar that gives the Soi its name. The bars are always packed in this part of town, mainly by locals and ex-pats but many tourists find their way there too. The murders were obviously a hot topic of conversation, nobody seemed to be talking about anything else. I made my way to a bar known to be frequented by local police and started to listen in on their conversations. The talk on the street indicated that the murders were the work of a gang on the island, local mafia who liked to take drugs and pick on tourists. A few people who had lived in the area for a long time were familiar with talk of a rape gang on the island who had been preying on young women as long ago as when I first arrived in Thailand and lived on Koh Tao in 1999. The consensus seemed to be that the woman had in some way caused a Thai chap, who was part of, or connected to, a powerful local family, lose face by refusing his advances. He had then drugged her drink before taking his revenge on her.

I overheard police and locals theorizing this whole event would be covered up and some Burmese migrant workers would be blamed while the real culprits walked free. This is a story I did not find hard to believe.

When I first arrived on the paradise island of Koh Tao, I was blown away by its beauty. Clear, blue waters gently lapped the golden sands of utterly unspoiled beaches swathed with palm trees gently swaying in the hot, summer breeze. Only accessible by speedboat, and deliciously secret, this idyllic paradise captivated me. It was as if my wildest dreams came true just by living there.

However, it was not long until I realized that this incredibly beautiful island had a dark side. When I first arrived, like thousands before me, I was keen to get my PADI (Professional Association of Dive Instructors) license and spend my days above and below the waves enjoying the tropical sunshine while getting paid for the privilege, so I paid to be herded through the PADI system and popped out the other end with my teaching certificate in hand. That was the easy part—getting a job on an island saturated with fledgling newbie dive instructors was something more of a challenge. It very quickly became apparent to me that it was all about who you knew and which part of the island you hung about on. Many believed that the island was run by five main families, presumably descendants of the original inhabitants who had all claimed their own patch and, as Koh Tao developed, became richer and richer on the proceeds.

One of the biggest families and owners of the biggest dive school on Sairee Beach were the Ban family. Having the best accommodation and, at the time, one of the only swimming pools where confined water diving training for those taking their first course to learn to be SCUBA divers took place, they took the lion's share of the diving custom on the island. Mr. Ban was a man large in both stature and personality and seemed to be the friendliest and most accessible headman of the five in charge.

Another influential family, headed by a man named Mon, resided on the other side of the island; they owned Buddha View, another large dive school located in Chalok Baan Kao.

A third influential family called Jetsin ran a smaller patch of the island but were known for having owned the first petrol station in the main town and port of Mae Haad.

A fourth family owned a big resort called Sunset Buri notable for being the first resort to install a swimming pool.

By far the most influential and richest family was, and still is, the Toovichien clan. Known and feared by many on the island, they were the proud owners of what is probably now the most notorious bar and resort on the island, called AC1, that was built prior to their second resort, AC2. Ironically, AC2 is where I first lived when I arrived in Thailand. Of course, then I had no idea who I was renting from, or how they would change the entire course of my life. This family owns more businesses on Sairee Beach than anyone else on the island.

Two events stick out in my mind from my days in Koh Tao when the island was predominantly Thai, unlike today when it's packed with Burmese. At the time, for a few quid a day, you could hire a Thai to do just about anything: drive you around the island on a moped, lug scuba tanks, paint a wall, carry luggage, grab you some lunch, clean your boat; no task was too menial. However, even back then, Burmese migrant workers had started to drift in and were more than happy to undercut the going rate for a handyman for the day. They were very much resented by the Thai people, many of whom considered themselves far superior to their Asian neighbors and were treated very badly. Despite many warnings not to hire them, for financial reasons, many dive schools employed the help of the Burmese.

I first obtained paid employment as an underwater videographer for Samui Sports Divers on Koh Tao. Samui Sports Divers was owned by a rebellious British chap called Simon. Simon employed a Burmese handyman called Ali who, while being very pleasant, never seemed able to relax as he ducked and dived around our organization. It soon became apparent why. I had not really been on the island long enough to know 'who was who', so I can't tell you who was driving, but I do remember a pick-up truck pulling up outside our dive shop and an angry looking Thai guy coming in and demanding we all take a look in the back of his truck. To my horror, the back of his truck contained the body of a Burmese man who had had his throat cut from ear to ear. This is what would happen to any Burmese we employed, the man told us, before driving to the next dive shop.

I looked for Ali but he was nowhere to be seen. I don't know what stopped me packing my bags and leaving that day. I had never seen anything like that before in my life and I can only assume amid the bright sunshine and the coconut trees swaying in the light ocean breeze I just put it out of my mind and carried on regardless. I have often looked back on that day and pondered why it didn't result in me leaving as fast as my legs could carry me.

The second incident came a year or two later. I was now the manager of the dive school as well as videographer and instructor. We were small fry compared to Bans, but having passed my IDC (Instructor Development Course) at Bans, I was friendly with the staff and the owner, Mr. Ban who spoke English and had a great sense of humor.

He had a passion for gambling with Mr. Mon from Buddha View. One night they were playing for big stakes. The local butcher, who had borrowed a lot of money, was playing too. Mr. Ban won what I can only assume was a vast amount of money as a few days later he was shot in the head in broad daylight. A friend of mine, who had been sitting next to him at the time he was brutally murdered, flew into my house covered in brain matter, spluttering, "Mr. Ban is dead! He was shot"! I was in total shock. It turned out the butcher, unable to repay his gambling debts, was given the unenviable task of shooting, at that time, the richest and most powerful man on the island. He is in prison now. I am told he is well looked after, and he and his family receive generous payments every month.

Oddly enough, I put this incident to the back of my mind, too. There was something about Koh Tao. It was only reachable by boat, there was only one internet shop with a computer that seldom connected to the outside world, we had no mobile phones, and rarely contacted anybody outside the island. It was a different time and a different place that none of us wanted to leave, or acknowledge anything untoward about. In our minds, it was paradise. I think we all wanted to keep it that way and shoved any idea there was a dark side way out of our minds. And if it was not completely out of our minds, it was certainly going to stay in our minds as not sharing Koh Tao's secrets with the outside world was an unwritten rule that was never to be broken.

CHAPTER 4 - POLICE INVESTIGATION INTO THE MURDERS OF HANNAH AND DAVID

From what I first gathered, the bodies of Hannah Witheridge and David Miller had been found very early in the morning by the daughter of a Burmese man who oversaw the cleaning of the beach. She immediately told her father what she had found and is believed to have called Montriwat Toovichien, whose family owns AC1 Resort and In Touch Resort. Montriwat is also the brother of Worapan, the headman of the island. It is the Toovichien family who own and run this part of the beach. Montriwat, known to locals as Mon, told Tom Stone, who conducted a documentary for Channel 4 which aired in April of 2016, "My worker was in shock and panicking. She quickly ran to my room and woke me up. I came down together with my worker and saw two dead bodies. I am the first Thai who saw the dead bodies".

From the crime scene pictures I saw, I know Mon would have been faced with a section of beach covered in blood with clothes strewn all over it. Mon continued, "I never want to see that scene again. It is a scene that brings me no happiness at all".

Sergeant Major Apichet Cherdguea, a rather young and inexperienced police officer, is widely believed to have been the first police officer to arrive at the scene. He told Tom Stone's crew, "When I arrived at the scene, I was taken aback by what I saw. There was a lot of blood and personally I felt it was just too violent". He went on, "This area is surrounded by temples. I hope God will punish the person who committed this crime".

Despite his wish that God should hand out the punishment, the Royal Thai Police opened a murder investigation. But with only six officers on the island at the time, they did not get off to a good start. They made little to no effort to secure the crime scene and strangers were seen wandering all over the beach taking photos of the dead bodies and posting them on social media. Social media sites were now drenched with pictures of the victims. News of this reached Bangkok fairly quickly. The news did not go down well; the shoddy handling of the case and the social media storm threatened to embarrass Thailand.

The Commissioner of Metropolitan Police Bureau, Suwrat Janggodsuck, was ordered to direct operations and apologized to David's family for the information that had leaked out, particularly the photographs that he acknowledged would have caused great trauma for the victims' families. With little clue where to start, the police focused on the forensic evidence and tests were run on some cigarette butts found on the beach, a used condom, the murder weapon (a garden hoe), and David's and Hannah's bodies, which were wrapped in blue plastic and sent to Bangkok. The police said they had found the DNA of two Asian men. As time went on, the DNA evidence would become one of the most contentious parts of the investigation as the police were accused of corruption and covering up evidence and being heavily influenced by the mafia.

CHAPTER 5 - MONTRIWAT AND NOMSOD TOOVICHIEN SUSPECTS IN THE CRIMES

Over 60 police were drafted onto Koh Tao along with Police Lieutenant General (Pol. Lt. Gen.) Panya Mamen who oversaw the investigation into the brutal murders of Hannah Witheridge and David Miller. He and his team quickly suspected a link to the crimes to the notorious Toovichien family who, in light of Mr. Ban's departure, had business interests that now ran the length of Sairee Beach. The investigations eventually hit the press.

A report by a Thai news publication called *Thai PBS* on the 23rd of September 2014, stated that the police had arrested a suspect in the murders of Hannah Witheridge and David Miller and it was none other than Mon. While police Command Commissioner Pol. Lt. Gen. Panya Mamen identified the first suspect as Mon, he was also seeking the arrest of Nomsod, Mon's nephew, who it was believed had fled the island. He is also known as Worat. Pol. Lt. Gen. Panya Mamen announced that both suspects had been captured on CCTV and there was enough evidence to implicate them both in the murders. He went on to say that the southern police were coordinating with the metropolitan police to track Nomsod down. He then reassured the public that no scapegoats would be used in this case as it was gaining the attention of the world. In the article, he dismissed any suggestion that local mafias or influential people could twist the investigation and promised that local influence would pose no obstacle to the police and stated that instead the police would eliminate the mafia. It ended by saying anyone who helped the suspect to escape would also be arrested. An article on the *Asia One* website on the 24th of September 2014, suggested that Worapan's son, Nomsod, had left the island very early after the morning of the murders and arrived on the mainland at Surat Thani before disappearing.

Ten days after the murders Pol. Lt. Gen. Panya Mamen reassured the press that he was expecting DNA results from the crime scene to yield results within 48 hours. "The world has been watching the case and the police force has been doing what it can to ensure that the evidence obtained is strong and tight enough to arrest the killers", he said.

While I had no trouble believing the reports suggesting Montriwat and Nomsod were responsible for the crimes, as I had heard it being said from day one, I found it interesting that a press release by the head Pol. Lt. Gen. would include the reassurance that no scapegoats would be used. Why would he need to do that? Did he have a reputation for using them in the past or was it a Freudian slip? Was he being told to use scapegoats and publicly proclaiming he would not in an act of defiance? Also, very interestingly he once again went on to say, "The investigation would not be influenced by reports that some influential persons on the island might try to obstruct police work". It was not difficult, for anybody who had the first clue about how the islands were run, to figure out to whom he was referring.

In the meantime, reporting for the BBC, Southeast Asian correspondent Jonathan Head said that the police believed three people were involved in murders and that two murder weapons had been identified: a garden hoe and a piece of wood. He reiterated in the report that one of the murderers, the headman's son, had left the island and was still at large. The BBC correspondent said attention had focused on one of the most powerful families on the island. He went on to say in his reporting that the police had questioned the bar owner where Mr. Miller and Ms. Witheridge were reported to have been involved in an argument shortly before their deaths, that both apprehended men had given DNA samples, but had not actually been charged, and that the police were still trying to locate the man who had fled the island shortly after the crime took place. A reward of £4000 was then offered for any information that might lead to an arrest.

By the 25th of September 2014, the story had changed, the police had ruled out the son of the village headman as a suspect in the murders as he had provided evidence that he was elsewhere at the time of the crime. The evidence was CCTV footage that caught Nomsod at university in Bangkok during the time of the murders. However, online sleuths soon established that the footage came from his apartments in Bangkok, the time stamp was wrong, and the appearance of the lobby had changed prior to the date on the images so it was widely speculated that this 'evidence' had been doctored.

With members of the Toovichien clan out of the frame, the police changed the focus of their investigation to foreign tourists and migrant workers. In 2014, Thailand was under military rule following a coup. Thailand's Junta, Prayuth Chan-O-Char, made a statement to the press announcing, "Nobody Thai could have committed a crime like this". Although I was not surprised, as Thailand had a reputation for blaming anyone but their own citizens for crimes, it was a rather stupid statement to make, especially when it came to light that a copycat crime had taken place on the mainland and two Thai men were tried and found guilty of killing a woman with a garden hoe.

The police announced they were going to focus on who had left the island in the hours and days after the crime in the hope of identifying new suspects. Media outlets had reported that the ports of Koh Tao had immediately been closed after the gruesome discovery of the bodies, but this was not true as tourists were openly observed arriving and departing on the various ferry and catamaran services unabated.

Pol. Lt. Gen. Panya Mamen quickly excluded Worapan Toovichien, 49, from his suspect list. I did not find this at all surprising. A successful businessman, he was seldom on the island and known to be involved with very wealthy businessmen including the owner of Bangkok Airways who was rumored to be a good friend of the King Bhumibol Adulyadej. What I did find surprising was news reports emerging that Worapan had offered one million baht to anyone who could prove members of his family were involved in the murders of the two British backpackers. Why on earth would he offer a reward to anyone who could prove his brother was involved? Surely, it would have been better to offer the reward to anyone who could find information leading to the arrests of the culprit or culprits. I concluded it was a veiled threat, and not particularly well veiled.

At this point, there were no witnesses to the crime, apparently no CCTV footage of the crime or suspects, nobody seemed to have a motive, and all the police had to go on was two samples of DNA from Hannah's body that belonged to Asian men. Pol. Maj. Gen. Suwat Jaengyodsuck, acting chief investigator of the Metropolitan Police Bureau (MPB), was sent to help the local police investigate the murders and told the press that the police had collected over 200 DNA samples from migrant workers on the island in a bid to find clues but none of the samples matched those collected from Ms. Witheridge or the condom or cigarette butts found on the beach. The mass collection of DNA samples was criticized for infringing on human rights but Pol. Maj. Gen. Suwat, reportedly one of the MPB's best investigators, told the press that the mass testing of foreign workers was an essential part of the probe to find the killers. The police were now focusing on finding Asian men around 170 centimeters tall (5ft 7) with a size 40 (UK7) shoe based on surveillance camera footage and footprints found on the beach. I found the footprint aspect of this quite surprising as the first images released of the victims showed the tide had been in so any footprints that may have been found on the beach were unlikely to be those of the killers. Interestingly, the two Asian men, who were later arrested and charged with these crimes were nowhere near 170 centimeters tall.

The next twist in the tale came when Mon accused a British man of being covered in blood on the night of the murders and stated that an employee named Jok helped him wash the blood off. The British man was named Sean McAnna and he later accused Mon of threatening to kill him.

CHAPTER 6 - SEAN MCANNA

Sean McAnna, also known as 'The Candy Man', due to rumors that he was the island's drug dealer, had been living on Koh Tao and working as a DJ for some time before his Leeds University friend, David Miller, arrived on the sun-kissed shores. There is little information as to how much time they had spent together in-between David's arrival and his untimely death. However, I did get an interesting insight into Sean McAnna from public posts on his Facebook page. One day after David Miller and Hannah Witheridge were found dead, he took to social media to make comments relating to the death of his university friend.

Sept. 16, 12:30 p.m.: Sean posts on David's Facebook page; *"Nah man. Please tell me it's not you"*

Sept. 16, 1 p.m.: again on David's FB page: *"I loved you so much brother. I know you tried to save her. You are the most honorable guy I've ever met. From getting mauled by a honey badger, giving out sleeping bags to homeless people, to just partying like there's no tomorrow. I will miss you terribly. I'm sorry I didn't come out with you that night. Really my heart is breaking. The legend that is Dave Miller "*

Later on, Sean started posting on the public wall of his own Facebook page that anyone with access to Facebook could see:

"I'm here on the rock my friend died near. I'm looking at Koh Tao. I can see it all. It's not the island I used to know" (sic)[1]

Then later,

"I'm fucking devastated right now and I have a lot of anger. But I know Koh Tao will continue to be the paradise island it always was. Especially now I've spoken to girls who are heart-broken about this but have said that nothing will stop them living the free island life. And fair play to them, this has been the first westerners killing in a decade and will be the last, hopefully"

"It's a life we know and always attempt to strive for"

"It's a life my friend tried to seek out"

"I'm gutted he died on that endeavor, but from the evidence it shows that he died the way he lived"

"In my first message I said that I knew he tried to save her. That was a guess, but now I've seen that that he didn't leave with that girl and he must have stumbled upon what happened and tried to fight them off"

"That's the Dave I knew and loved. That's the Dave we all expected him to be"

"If nothing happens from this all I wish is that everybody takes tomorrow by the grip of their hands and tries to find the best thing they can do. For the least close person they can find. Buy two English breakfasts and go meet a homeless person, then share them, or go save someone from being lonely"

"I'm sure he could have thought up better plans than this, but I'm not as amazing as Dave was, so I can only try Please, do something nice for someone tomorrow in Dave's honor"

---

1. Quoted material is being presented verbatim as it is said or written, sometimes by non-native English speakers.

While I found Sean's posts interesting, he was wrong about one thing; this was not the first western death in a decade, and it would certainly not be the last.

CHAPTER 7 - BEN HARRINGTON

When Sean McAnna boldly announced to the world on his Facebook post that the Hannah and David murders were the first western killings in ten years, he may have thought he was correct, but it was certainly not the first suspicious death.

Only two years prior to the Miller and Witheridge murders, in August 2012, Ben Harrington, a 32-year-old British IT consultant, was on holiday in Koh Tao with his brother, Mark, and another friend when he lost his life.

Ben Harrington was born on 9th of July 1980 in Redhill Hospital in Surrey. Along with his two brothers, Mark, born in 1984, and Luke, born in 1988, he enjoyed life to the fullest and was always in demand with his friends, of which he had many, conversations about what a great guy he was were commonplace. No matter where he was in the world, he would always make sure he was home for his mother's birthday, Mother's Day, Christmas Day, and other family special occasions.

Ben was a popular student attending St Joseph's Primary School and then Starhurst School, leaving at age 16. He took his first job at age 14 working in a butcher's shop on Saturdays. When he left school, he worked at a local kennel. Ben absolutely loved working with animals; his gentle and kind nature made him the perfect companion for animals of all shapes and sizes. Ben went on to have many jobs, including one at Gatwick Airport. Having explored many career options, he settled down to become an IT consultant, a role in which he became very successful. Exceeding expectations, Ben was always top among his colleagues and earned big rewards as well as the respect of all of those who worked with him.

Ben loved to travel and explore the world. Once a year, he would go on holiday with his family to enjoy quality time with them. He also enjoyed trips abroad with his friends; it was during one of these trips that tragedy struck.

Ben had planned to visit Thailand in 2011, but due to unforeseen circumstances he was unable to make the trip. In August 2012, however, Ben arrived in Bangkok with his brother, Mark, and another friend. After six days in the nation's capital, the trio travelled to Koh Tao.

The travel companions booked a villa on the beach on Koh Tao; however, Ben knew a QPR supporter who was working at a bar in town who advised the men to move to a different area on the island. In order to facilitate this, the 'island based' friend organized a moped for the men so they could get around the island. The new accommodation was on the Toovichien-owned and-run Sairee Beach.

Far from being the paradise vacation all 20-somethings dream of, the trip ended up in tragedy on their first night when Ben, eager to go and enjoy a cold beer, asked his brother, Mark, and their other travel companion to join him. Mark, feeling weary after his trip from Bangkok, decided to stay at the villa. Ben and his friend left the villa to go for a beer. It is unclear why, but Ben returned to the villa to try to persuade Mark to join them. Once again Mark declined the offer. Ben once again left the villa to join his friend at the bar. He never arrived.

Later that night, Ben was found dead at the side of the road. Ben's mother recalls receiving the call that all mothers dread at 4 a.m. on the 30th of August 2012. It was Mark's voice at the other end of the phone. Pat recalls Mark crying and repeating, "Sorry, Mum, but Ben is dead".

The police were called to the scene and recorded the incident as a roadside collision that took place at 12.30 a.m. on the 30th of August 2012. On the face of it, it seemed that he had somehow crashed his motorbike into an electricity pylon pole. He was alone at the time. What made this death suspicious was that when Ben's body was discovered on this dark and lonely road, both his cash and his wallet were missing.

After his death, the Thai people were very keen to rapidly cremate his body. His mother Pat refused, wanting to bring her son home. In order to facilitate this, she was charged £500 to store his body in a refrigerated coffin at the temple on Koh Tao until arrangements could be made to fly his body home. This is a startling figure for a service that costs locals between nothing and ten pounds a day. Ben's brother Mark, however, paid the fee and stayed on the island for a week before accompanying his brother's body home.

Ben's funeral took place 3 weeks later. The church was packed. So many mourners attended that many had to stand outside to pay their last respects.

Ben's mum, Pat, was told by the Koh Tao police that a roadside postmortem was performed and established that Ben's head was turned around facing backwards and that he had died of a broken neck. However, the postmortem that was performed in the UK told a different story. Pat, who works in the medical profession, recalls that when she went to see Ben in the UK, she found no ligature marks around his neck, something that would have been evident if his neck had indeed been broken. Toxicology tests were unable to be performed in the UK due to the embalming process that had taken place back in Thailand. The UK coroner refused to classify Ben's death as an accident and said that it would be very difficult to get witnesses to come forward. After the inquest back on British soil, the coroner gave a rather ambiguous conclusion saying, "I am not going to put on record that it was an accident because I don't feel I have got sufficient evidence to be satisfied it was definitely an accident, but clearly it was a collision of some sort. We only have limited information. That is quite often what happens when you have a death abroad".

Despite the Thai police trying to quickly wrap this case up, Ben's mother, understandably, never believed the story and has spent years looking for information from the authorities regarding her son's death. Sadly, she has been unsuccessful with Freedom of Information requests to the Foreign and Commonwealth Office.

To this day, Pat Harrington continues her mission to find out what actually happened to her son. She, along with the families of other victims of Koh Tao, has formed a group on Facebook called Grieving Together We Want Justice. This astonishing group of bereaved families takes comfort from each other and offer help and advice to new families who join the group at an alarming rate as more and more travelers to Thailand lose their lives in suspicious circumstances. What is also alarming is the chilling repetitive nature of each tragedy, botched and careless police investigations, lack of information provided, lack of support and help from the British Embassy and the Foreign Office, contradictory information, UK postmortems offering conflicting evidence to that handed out in Thailand, and all of the families being left with more questions than answers and no sense of peace or closure. However, as time went on, it turned out that Pat and her group did far more than simply offer each other love and support.

Ben Harrington was not the only British man to have died in suspicious circumstances prior to the horrific murders of Hannah and David.

Another family who knows exactly what it means to lose a family member in Koh Tao are the Pearsons.

CHAPTER 8 - NICK PEARSON

In December 2013, Nick Pearson was looking forward to ringing in the New Year on the paradise island of Koh Tao with his family from Derby. Nick's brother, Matt, was working on the island at that time so it was a great opportunity for the family to spend some quality time together. The family went out for a meal and celebrated the arrival of the New Year on Sairee Beach before Nick's dad, Graham, walked him back to his room in the resort where they were staying. The resort Nick was staying in is perched about 50 feet up on the rocks overlooking the ocean. Nick had a drink and needed a hand getting to bed. His brother, Matt, said that Nick was limping from an infected knee he acquired from falling a few days prior to his death. Graham says that Nick took off his shoes and shorts and got into bed before saying goodnight to him.

The following morning, New Year's Day 2014, the family called to his bungalow to find no answer. They raised the alarm and later on the police recovered his body from the water below his bungalow and suggested he had fallen 50 feet and drowned in the sea. However, Nick's room was locked, and it would be impossible to fall into the sea from his bungalow as the route down to the ocean involves a very steep path of steps that meander and slink around huge granite boulders. Brother Matt wondered if it had been possible for Nick to have sleepwalked but having taken a look at the path down to where he was found deduced this would be impossible. The family considered if he had walked down and then slipped into the water and drowned but again this is a highly unlikely scenario. Nick was found wearing the same underwear that he wore to bed, so it is also highly unlikely that he got out of bed and went out for another drink.

Nick's family does not believe the police did a thorough investigation. They told me that the police did not visit Nick's room and did not interview anybody with regards to his death. Nick's mother Tracy said to me he had been chatting to a Thai girl the night before his death. There was speculation that the woman was the girlfriend of one of the locals.

The police in Koh Tao ruled that Nick had drowned and gave no explanation as to how he could have fallen into the ocean from his room without sustaining a single broken bone. The family told the press in the UK that they were taken to see Nick at the temple to identify him and he had a large gash in his head. It was also rumored that his brother, Matt, was warned that there were "powerful people on the island", and the family should leave rather than stirring up trouble.

Back in the UK, pathologist Dr. Michael Brigs told the hearing that there were many injuries to Nick's body, including his head, limbs, and face. However, he went on to say that these would have been present prior to his death and that he could not rule out the possibility that Nick had been attacked.

Nick's mother, Tracy Pearson, told the Derby and South Derbyshire Coroner's Court she had a gut feeling there was foul play.

Derby coroner, Louise Pinder, said there was not enough evidence to say how he died and recorded an open verdict.

CHAPTER 9 – SEAN McANNA
– THE PLOT THICKENS

Back on Koh Tao, things had taken a turn for Sean McAnna. I was first alerted to signs of trouble when he made a rather disturbing post on his Facebook page in the early hours of the morning.

Sean McAnna's post read, "Thai mafia are trying to kill me. Please help me. Sky news phone me". Sean had been speaking to Jonathan Samuels from Sky TV and was now, it seemed, trying to enlist his help. Sean then posted another post that read, "Owner of AC bar did it", and posted a photograph of Montriwat Toovichien with a good friend who also happened to be a policeman. A further post read, "Guy on the left is the leader". The guy on the left was Mon.

There would have been nothing Jonathan or any member of the press or public could have done at this stage as it was gone by 9 p.m. when the last boat left.

Sean went off the radar for a while; his sister was actively looking for him on social media and there was great concern as to his safety. When he finally did emerge, he left the island in front of a news camera that filmed him boarding the Lomprayah Boat to Samui where he gave this interview to the BBC:

"I went to a bar where a guy started asking me questions because he knew that I knew the guy who had died. I didn't tell him my name. Three of them sat me down and started asking me questions, and I was a bit drunk so I was

answering them, and then they just said to me *"it was you who killed them, you've got two people's deaths on your hands, we knew it was you, your'e gonna hang yourself tonight, you are going to hang yourself tonight, we are going to watch you hang, but you die tonight"*, so I just ran. The interviewer then asks Sean if he thinks they are connected to what happened, to which he replied – *"I think they needed a scapegoat, I think they might know who it was, they don't want it to be locals, they want it to be a westerner, so if I kill myself here, if I hang myself here, it is easy to say that's it, "It was him". I genuinely thought that was me dead, I was gone. I thought of my mum and of my sister and my sister managed to call me back and I basically wanted to say my goodbyes, like if anything I was so scared, so scared, I just did not want that to 'be it' you know"*. The interviewer asks Sean what he said to his mother, to which he replied, *"I told her I loved her and that I was trying to get home, I said that if this was going to be the last conversation I had then it was a sad one to have but she has been great and I love her. I needed to get off this island, get on a ferry [that was carrying nobody that knew me], get [myself to] another island [where nobody knows me], try to make my way to the airport, there is a big gap between the ferry and the airport and obviously [with] friends all over you know, something could still happen to me in the next 24 hours"*.

Nothing happened to Sean McAnna in the next 24 hours. He fled to Milan. Not, however, before some people noticed what they thought looked like blood splatters all over his guitar. In another interesting twist prior to his departure from Koh Tao, it was believed by some that a cut that looked like a stab wound on his left arm bore disturbingly close resemblance to the injuries that David sustained.

Sean McAnna always maintained he had not been out with David the night he was killed; however, photographs of

Sean out on a pub crawl from Facebook with dates suggest otherwise.

Sean may have escaped the island, but the media was not done with him. A few days later a BBC news report revealed he had a criminal past of his own. According to the *Scottish Record*, Sean pleaded guilty to possessing indecent images of children last year in his native Scotland. He was ordered to complete a community payback order of 170 hours following his guilty plea.

CHAPTER 10 – THE KOH TAO MAFIA, THE WARE BROTHERS, AND ANDY HALL

Once it became apparent that Mon and Nomsod were no longer in the frame for the murders of Hannah Witheridge and David Miller, the word on the street dried up. Police were now not speaking so openly about the murders. Rather than being happy to share information over a bottle of beer, the murder chat had become somewhat more clandestine. In ex-pat quarters, the chat had turned to who was going to be fitted up for committing such a crime and the opinion of most was that it would be some hapless Burmese migrants. However, attention first turned to the Ware brothers, the travel companions of David Miller.

On the 18th of September 2014, at 11:20 a.m. *The Gulf Times* reported, *"Police continued to hunt for clues on the small, normally laid-back diving island of Koh Tao as post-mortem examinations of the victims' bodies in Bangkok did not find any DNA links to 12 people they have questioned so far.*

Those include two of Miller's British friends who were asked to stay in Bangkok pending the forensic results - and several Myanmar migrant workers".

In fact, several days earlier, British brothers, Christopher and James Ware, who were both believed to have spent time with David Miller on Koh Tao, were questioned by the police investigating the Miller-Witheridge murders.

Christopher Ware, who it is believed shared a room with David Miller despite being cleared, and his brother were stopped at Bangkok International Airport as the pair were reportedly preparing to leave Thailand. Police Colonel Kissana, deputy police spokesman, said that none of the men who had been questioned, 2 Britons and 11 Burmese, had been taken into custody; however, the two Britons had been escorted and questioned by the police. He went on to say, "We cannot rule them out. They were close friends and knew all about the victims. We have got to do whatever it takes to obtain concrete evidence".

A few days earlier the Thai Military Junta announced to the world in a televised speech that female foreign tourists in bikinis may not be safe on his shores. He said, "There are always problems with tourist safety. They think our country is beautiful and safe so they can do whatever they want. They can wear bikinis and walk everywhere". He added, "Can they be safe in bikinis … unless they are not beautiful"? Prayut's comments echoed remarks he made previously in which he said the behavior of the victims should be looked into and warned that "it is not always safe everywhere".

After Chris Ware had been questioned for the second time, Police Col. Kissana said that strong evidence had now pushed the investigation into the direction of a number of Burmese suspects after blood stains were found on some of their clothes. He went on to say that DNA tests were being completed and the results would be available in one or two days. Investigators then released CCTV footage of a man, Asian in appearance, seen walking near the scene of the murders.

After the CCTV footage was made public, social media erupted with comments that one of the individuals looked like the son of one of the local headmen. Interestingly, no evidence of any blood on the Burmese clothes was ever presented to the press.

Another little-reported fact about the Hannah Witheridge murder is that she was clutching a blonde hair when she was found. However, there was one report that suggested that a blonde hair was found on David Millers telephone that had been missing but had later been found. A further report suggested that a blood-stained pair of pants had been found in the room where both David and Chris were staying.

A report on the 17th of September 2014, in the UK's *Daily Telegraph* said that

"Christopher Ware and his older brother, Jimmy, who were travelling around South East Asia with Mr. Miller, were detained in Bangkok and asked not to leave the country while DNA tests were carried out on the two victims. But Mr. Ware, a carpenter, who has known Mr. Miller since childhood and is one of his closest friends, has told sources at home in Jersey that he fears he is being "stitched up" by the police who are under immense pressure to solve the double murder. In a phone call to friends back home, he denied any involvement and said he feared he was being set up. The father of one of his close friends, who was also friends with Mr. Miller, said his son had spoken to Mr. Ware by telephone yesterday.

He said: "The Thai police are going to stitch Chris up. They will try and blame it on anyone they can". "My son and his girlfriend have spoken to Chris today".

"From what I've heard, the police said to Chris that they wanted him to stay not because he was in trouble but because he was so upset they didn't want him to travel".

Friends of Mr. Ware insisted he and Mr. Miller were incredibly close and suggestions that he might be responsible for his death were unbelievable.

Aaran Higgins, 24, who went to Haute Vallee state school in St Helier said: "I'm very good friends with Chris and Jimmy".

"Chris is a lovely bloke. He and Dave are best mates you see, they are brilliant friends and I don't know what has happened".

Siobhan Philippe, another friend of Mr. Ware added: "Chris is a very popular person on Jersey. They are all lovely people. He is a decent guy and would never ever do anything. Dave would never screw over a friend and the Wares are exactly the same".

"But Thai police insisted they were keeping an open mind in relation to the murder, with suggestions that the motive may have been connected to a love triangle which went tragically wrong".

As it turned out, neither of the Ware brothers were detained or accused of any involvement in the murders and flew home. As predicted on the 2nd of October, it was announced that two migrant workers had been arrested. At that moment, and long before I met the accused, Zaw Lin and Wai Phyo, a couple of things crossed my mind. Having lived on Koh Tao myself, I knew that it was impossible to be there for any significant amount of time and be unaware that the island was run by what the locals refer to as mafia. It is worth explaining that while the term mafia conjures up images of men running around with shotguns in violin cases or being involved with highly organized crime that is not what the term represents in Thailand. On the islands, mafia is more a group of influential families who inhabited the islands long before any kind of administrative bodies turned up with courts and police. Those who lived a rather tribal existence never really paid much heed to the inhabitants who arrived later, even if they wore police uniforms or any other attire that represents authority. Each village in Thailand has a *Poo yai Ban*, roughly translated as the head man of the village. The mentality is far more tribal than anything that ever originated in Sicily and has nothing to do with organized crime, as such. Having said that, the locals and even the police, do not deny the existence of mafia in Koh Tao. In an article by Richard C. Paddock and Muktita Suhartono, published in the *New York Times* on the 3rd of November 2018, police major general Surachate Hakparn, who investigated the rape of a British girl on Koh Tao that year, was quoted as saying "We admit that in the past, there was a mafia there that took advantage of tourists. Today, we have got rid of them."

Most of the so-called mafia, particularly on the islands, are not particularly well educated. However, that does not mean they do not have a great deal of power. Quite the contrary. Money talks in Thailand, and for those families who claimed the rights to the islands, money was not hard to come by. As the tourists started to flock to the virgin shores of islands such as Koh Tao, more and more boarding houses, resorts, dive schools, and restaurants and bars popped up along the beach. Later came the pharmacies, internet cafés, bike rental shops, and souvenir shops. Each set up home on a part of the beach owned, or rather squatted on, by one of the, in Koh Tao's case, five families. This meant that as every inch of the beach became covered in some money-making business, the pockets of the local families swelled. When the police did turn up on Koh Tao, they also played the game and supplemented their income with a percentage of the 'tea money' they collected on behalf of the families, and as that tea money was considerably more than their meager income from the government, it's not hard to see where their loyalty lies. 'Tea money' is a term that is commonly used in Thailand for money businesses give to the police on a regular basis to keep them sweet.

With this in mind, I found it unimaginable that anybody wishing to commit a murder on a beach owned, and run, by powerful local families would stick around to face the consequences. It had been three weeks between the deaths of Hannah Witheridge and David Miller and the arrests of the Burmese. And yet, assuming these two tiny men had committed the crimes, they had been dumb enough to stick around. Anybody who understands how things work in Thailand would immediately surmise how preposterous this scenario is. If it were me, I would be far less worried about being arrested than facing punishment 'Thai style'. It is not uncommon for residents of the islands to deal with problems in-house rather than involving the authorities. The second thing that struck me as rather odd was that, generally speaking, the Burmese are very slight in stature. I wondered how two small Asian men could manage to overcome a strapping six-foot three lad like David. Not to mention they had no motive.

Knowing, or rather having a very good idea, that the men who had been arrested could be scapegoats, despite the assurances from Pol. Lt. Gen. Panya Mamen that no scapegoats would take the fall in this case, I immediately set about trying to find some kind of representation for them, as no Burmese migrant would have the funds available to instruct a lawyer. I believed the public defender would be less than helpful. Burmese earn a pittance in Thailand and are generally only working in Thailand because they would earn an even smaller pittance back home. Far from having a gap year in paradise, as did the western tourists, the Burmese were brokered to the country in order to find work and send what money they could to their impoverished families. Bearing this in mind, it was obvious to me that the two boys' families would not be doing what western families do in these kinds of circumstances and wiring money over for lawyers via Western Union.

I called many organizations over the course of the next few days, such as Amnesty International and Prisoners Abroad. Word had got out and many of the organizations I spoke to knew of the case and the arrests but didn't offer much in the way of practical help. One of the organizations I contacted was Migrant Workers Rights Network that was fronted by an English man named Andy Hall and it was he who offered the most in terms of practical support. I had heard of Andy Hall from seeing him in the news. He had become newsworthy by having written a report for Finnwatch, a Finnish civil society organization focusing on corporate responsibility. The report focused on migrant workers working in Thailand's lucrative pineapple industry and specifically for a company called Natural Fruit. His findings were less than savory with regards to how the company treated its employees and now he was fighting a court battle for his part in the report issued by Finnwatch that had had a considerable impact on Natural Fruit who now wanted his backside in a sling on defamation charges.

At the time, I was simply grateful that anybody was going to be onboard and attempt to ensure true justice was done in this case. From what I had already witnessed in Thailand over the years, I knew these two men were going to need all the help they could get.

CHAPTER 11 - LESS THAN LEGITIMATE PROCEDURES IN THAILAND

I had not been in Thailand very long before I realized money can get you anything you need. My first inkling was when I tried to stay for longer than the 28 days you get stamped in your passport on arrival. I originally planned on staying on Koh Tao for six months and got what I thought was a visa that would allow me to do just that. In actual fact, the visa I had been issued was good for two months on arrival. After two months, the visa could be extended for one month by making my way to the immigration office in Koh Samui and parting with a few pounds. In order to be allowed to stay in Thailand for two further months after that, I had to leave the country and come back in again.

The process of getting down to the Malaysian border to walk out of the country and then simply walk back in again for a visa stamp is known as a visa run. Anybody who has spent more than a few weeks in Thailand will be aware of the visa run. Even those who are granted a one-year business visa are expected to leave the country for a few minutes, for no reason, before returning with a new stamp that again only lasts for three months. As Koh Tao is rather a long way from any border, a 'visa run' involves 12 sticky hours packed in like sardines on the smelly wooden night boat to Surat Thani before been hurtled at Formula 1 speeds for 8 hours in a mini van driven by a lunatic on speed to Malaysia, being herded in and out of Malaysia, to what looked like the annoyance of the Malaysian immigration team, and then the whole process would go in reverse.

If this trip does not sound very safe to you, then you are right. There have been many well-documented fatal visa run trips. If the risk to your life was not enough, the pit stops on the way down to use a hole in the ground for a toilet and eat some dirty fish head soup are enough to put anybody off. It stands to reason that nobody 'lit up' at the idea of doing a visa run and for those without a bona fide tourist visa, who just got 28 days on arrival, this dreadful journey raised its ugly head once a month; only it didn't have to.

On the top of the hill between Mae Haad and Sairee Beach was a wooden curiosity shop owned and run by a Chinese chap called Mr. J. who was one of the most memorable characters I ever met in Thailand. It was rumored that he was descendant from Triads but I doubt that is true. Mr. J. was into all sorts: money lending, secondhand books, hammocks, condoms, secondhand diving gear; anything you could possibly want on Koh Tao could be found at Mr. J.'s shop, including a way out of the dreaded visa run. For 1500 baht, around 30 quid at the time, Mr. J. would take your passport along with those of everybody else who needed a visa run and have them couriered down to the border where he would have them stamped for you. Like everybody else I trusted this scheme and went along with it. It was only years later, when Mr. J. got lazy and started making his own visa entry stamp that people started to get arrested. I narrowly missed arrest on a trip to Malaysia with my Thai husband a few years later. Thankfully, when my dodgy fake stamp was discovered, it was by my husband's cousin, who as luck would have it, happened to be working on the border control that day. After considering throwing me in jail, she took a backhander to drop a cup of coffee all over the offending page. I was advised a trip back to the UK was in order to get a new passport, which is exactly what I did.

Years later, my Thai husband got busted on Koh Tao for selling opium. I had no idea he was selling drugs and, thankfully, for me, it was a short-lived career. After I bailed him out of the police station on Koh Phangan, which neighbors Koh Tao, he was given a court date. His bail conditions required me to put a plot of land, rather than cash, in the hands of the police. Since I didn't have any land on Koh Phangan, the police organized for me to rent a plot, which I did.

In those days, the court was a less impressive building that the imposing one Samui has today. Back then, it was in Nathon, the port and commercial capital of Koh Samui. My husband's parents arrived from the mainland, all was going well as he only expected a small tap on the wrist and a fine. Then he noticed the amount he was being charged with was enough to have him convicted of drug trafficking that would, without a doubt, land him with a lengthy custodial sentence. The family went into some sort of controlled panic and frenzied phone calls were made. A little while later, a man arrived with an envelope full of cash. Shortly after that, I was made to follow my husband down a back alley where, to my utter astonishment, the judge was waiting for us, the money was handed over, the court document was amended, and he got a tap on the wrist and a small fine. This was the moment when Amazing Thailand took on a whole new meaning for me. There I stood with first-hand experience of paying off judges. This may have been a one-off incident involving my husband, who I divorced not long after, but it is far from a one-off incident in Samui. I know many people who also have paid off judges, and in drug cases, have bribed workers at the laboratory who test police-seized drugs to report them in a far lower quantity than when they were seized. This can make a huge difference when drug sentences in Thailand are generally one year in prison per gram. These practices are commonly known as 'paying under the table' in Thailand.

CHAPTER 12 – THE ARREST AND IMPRISONMENT OF ZAW LIN AND WAI PHYO

Only a few days after Zaw Lin and Wai Phyo were arrested, they were taken to Koh Samui Provincial Prison. At this stage, no one knew what had gone on during their arrest; the horrors of that all came to light at a later date. They were now commonly being referred to as the B2 (the Burmese two).

There are very few people who know what it is like to be processed into the Thai prison system. Most people would rightly imagine that conditions in Thai prisons are horrific. However, prison life on the island of Koh Samui, while far from pleasant, is less daunting than life in city prisons such as Bangkok's notorious Bangkwang Central Prison, nicknamed by westerners "The Bangkok Hilton", and "The Big Tiger" by Thai people for its ability to eat grown men alive.

When the B2 arrived at the Koh Samui Provincial Prison, it would have been in a clapped-out old police van. They would have been under the protection of several armed Royal Thai Police Officers. Once they arrived at the prison for the very first time, they would have been taken through the outer reinforced-steel door, and subsequently locked into a chamber inside made of solid steel. From this 5-meter square box, the prisoner can see nothing but the steel walls. It's very hard to imagine what would have been running through their minds at this point, but other prisoners have told me they had nothing but a paralyzing feeling of absolute dread.

When the door closed behind the B2, the guard would have made his way through a separate door, adjacent to the one the B2 would have been forced through. He would then have opened the second door to the box from inside the prison. To the left-hand side of this door is a long corridor that goes all the way down to the Prison Captain's desk. From here, the captain monitors all of the prisoners coming in and out of the prison, including new inmates and existing inmates who are let in and out to go to their court hearings.

At the end of the corridor is another steel door. The guard will then put his hand through that door and open it from the other side. Once through that door, the B2 would have seen a big open-roofed area on the ground floor. This area is used to count all of the prisoners going in and out. There is a desk on the left-hand side where the captain sits with fans blowing to keep him cool. More often than not he has prisoners massaging him for his own relaxation.

Once you reach the captain, he goes through a list of questions: your name, your charge, and are you carrying weapons or drugs. Once answered, all of the belongings you had with you at the time of your arrest are brought to you in a bag. The bag is then thoroughly searched; every item is methodically creased and crushed to make sure nothing is being concealed. If you had a backpack with you, every square inch of the material is examined, and almost ripped apart in the process. Once this process is complete, your watch, jewelry, valuables, and ID are taken from you, although in many instances this will be the last time you see them as it's not uncommon for prison trustees, prisoners who have risen through the ranks and are given some responsibility, to take their pick of your belongings. Anything that is not taken is put into a clear Ziplock bag. A list is then prepared of your personal items, credit cards, and cash for you to sign. Once this has been completed, the new inmates would have had to wait for the big boss to come. The big boss, who is the prison commander, eventually arrives and will sit down with his legs crossed and take time to stare at the new inmates with a look upon his face that instills a feeling of utter worthlessness in you. It is commonly believed inside the jail that the commander feeds information on the prisoners to the police. Once he has finished his reportedly sadistic stare, he will interrogate the new arrivals about what they did that landed them in his 'care'.

When the interrogation is over the new prisoner will be asked to strip naked in front of the commander and the prison trustees who wear white shirts and, of course, anyone else who happens to be milling about. Once naked and humiliated, the prisoner is instructed to hand his clothing to the trustees who put it into a bag. At this point, things get rather more intimate as the prisoner is asked to turn around with their back to the commander and spread his buttocks so the area can be checked for contraband. The next procedure is to squat and cough before, if they are uncircumcised, prisoners are asked to pull back their foreskin for inspection. Prisoner's heads are shaved at some point during this process.

Prisoners are then left to stand naked for a while as paperwork is prepared for their entry into the prison system. Once completed, the prisoner is reunited with his T-shirt and underpants before being instructed to follow the trustees out of that complex and along a path that leads through a beautiful garden full of pretty flowers and immaculate landscaping. The sight is delightful, but the smell is less appealing as the sprinklers on the lawn distribute sewage to keep the grass green.

The path meanders its way to two big steel doors that are about 7 feet high. Either door can be opened independently from the other or both at the same time to allow entry for large trucks, tools, and industrial vehicles for the construction work that often goes on inside the prison.

Once through one of the doors, the prisoner will find himself in a caged corridor that leads to the captain's office. The prisoner is instructed to sit in the cage closest to the captain's office. On the other side of this cage are 1,000 prisoners who are keen to jeer at the new arrival and are known to place bets on the new arrival's ability to take care of themself in prison and on whether they think the new prisoner can win a fight.

Prior to their entry into the actual prison population, Zaw Lin and Wai Phyo would have met Max. Max is a Thai prisoner who, at that time, would have been in there for about 12 years. He deals with all the new arrivals, so the captain does not have to bother. He is known as a good guy, who, as long as you do not annoy him, will be fair to you. The two frightened Burmese would then have to squat down in the cage watching the other prisoners jeer as more paperwork was prepared, a process that takes about half an hour, before they would have been sent headfirst into the main population of the prison. Not able to go to the yard, a sand pit of around 50 square meters, their incarceration would then start with a shower and perhaps a few scraps of food left over from the other prisoners. At 4 p.m., the B2 would have been taken to their cells, but unlike the other prisoners they did not get to leave. They were both shackled to a stake in the room, unable to mingle, or visit the prison shop, as they were considered a risk to other prisoners and themselves.

CHAPTER 13 - A DAY IN KOH SAMUI PROVINCIAL PRISON

If you are not shacked up in a stinking hot cell, the average prisoner's day starts at 6 a.m. when the bell in the yard is rung six times, one for every hour. Inmates then get about 5 or 10 minutes to wake up and get their head around the new day. Inmates shuffle around the overcrowded room and roll up their blankets; a ruler is brought out to make sure the blankets are the right size. Some prisoners stitch two blankets together to give them more space. This is not allowed. Each prisoner is allowed two and a half standard-size bathroom tiles on the floor to sleep on.

The cells are about 15 square meters with a shelf that runs along one side of the wall where some prisoners sleep, because there is not enough room for all of them on the floor. Inmates then have to sit until 6.30 a.m. when the TV comes on with Thailand's national prayers. During this time, they must sit with their heads bowed down with hands together in prayer called a *wai* in Thai. Both Thai and Burmese inmates have to learn by heart the chanted prayers; however, most of the western inmates never learn this. Prayers over, inmates get their bed rolls and line them up from the front door of the cell down as far as the solitary and very small, squat toilet. There is always a fight about who has to put their beds where. A friendly captain can often help a prisoner get a preferred spot for their bedding. Between 6.45 a.m. and 7 a.m. prisoners sit in five lines on the floor. Nobody must be on the shelf, not even those who slept on it. There is not enough room in the cell for everyone to sit in this manner and prisoners report it being an act of contortion. No matter where you come from, for this procedure, you are to be in the Asian squat position, which for many is not easy. The captain then arrives and, once he has surveyed the room, nods for the room leader to shout "Aow Nap" and then, one by one, each prisoner shouts his number. Fifty-plus prisoners call out, however, should an inmate get his number wrong or is not able to speak Thai, the whole procedure starts again until the task has been correctly completed. But only after the captain has walked off and run through the same procedure with every other cell, so this can go on for quite some time.

The room leader is an appointed prisoner. He only speaks Thai. When the count has been done and the paperwork has been done, the trustee opens the door. When the second the door is opened, the rumble starts as prisoners shove and push their way down towards the yard. The faster the prisoners get out, the better chance they have of taking a shower as there is not enough water for everyone and it only lasts about 30 seconds in 35-degree Celsius heat (95 degrees Fahrenheit).

The corridor down to the yard is crammed and heaving and noisy and unbearable. There are five flights of stairs to navigate along with the crowds. The stairwell is dark with no natural lights; it's a dank and dark part of the prison and it is chaos, as prisoners turn the few working lights on and off repeatedly. Once at the bottom of the stairwell, prisoners make their way to the other side of the prison to the water troughs. Prisoners will visit their lockers to get soap and towels if they are lucky enough to have any. Then everybody fights for water, 800 people, all wanting to rid themselves of the smell and dirt accumulated on their bodies during the night in a stinking hot room full of 50+ hot bodies. There is only enough room for about 100 people round the trough so it's pushing and fighting in a frenzy. Traditionally, only around half the population of the prison would find enough water for a shower. However, a few years ago this system was changed. Now a trustee stands with a whistle and the men at the trough have one scoop of water to throw over themselves at each blow of the whistle: one blow for water, one blow for shampoo and soap, two more bowls of water, and that is their lot.

Prisoners who take more than their allotted amount of water at the blow of the whistle are punished Thai-style with military exercises. Even with the new system, many of the prisoners left the troughs covered in shampoo and are forced to use their essential drinking water they or their relatives paid for to rinse the foam off. Once prisoners are done with showering or getting wet, if they are lucky, at 7.30 a.m. they stand in one long line that goes from one end of the prison to the other. Dining room tables are then set up and are adorned with ten big metal pots that are full of what one prisoner described as 'nasty shit'. Prisoners then go up one at a time for a scoop of rice and a scoop of a gloopy substance that looks like gruel that goes into what looks like a metal dog bowl. Prisoners then sit on the ground in circles while captains, lower in rank than the main prison captain, hover over them waving their arms around to make sure nobody talks or messes around.

Once the prisoners have finished eating, they disperse and chat until 8 a.m. when a bell is rung that signals that it's time to go to the recreation yard and form 12 – 15 lines. The king's prayers are then played over the prison PA system, and everyone has to sing and stand to attention. When the prayers are complete the captain takes his place in the cage where prisoners first arrive and he looks over the prisoners standing in, what by this time, is already baking sun. The prisoners who have been sentenced are wearing blue, the ones who await their fate wear brown.

A British man who had spent time in the jail told me that the main prison captain then gives a speech about something indecipherable, in Thai. It would be something along the lines of "last night I came here and a pair of sandals was not in the correct space, so whoever owns these sandals come forward"; if nobody comes forward then one of the other prisoners tells the captain who the shoes belong to. The prisoners know whose shoes belong to who as each pair has been customized by its owner. This daily routine is designed to make examples out of prisoners. He told me on one occasion that two prisoners were told to masturbate in front of the entire prison population for being caught masturbating in the cell. They were not allowed to stop until they both ejaculated. It is hard to imagine the degree of humiliation this caused or the distress it caused to other prisoners.

After the speech by the captain, Max reappears for the next prisoner head count. This time the count is 100. The prisoners who call out 1 to 99 then squat down and the prisoner who calls 100 remains standing. This process continues until all of the prisoners are in the squat position. The prisoners are observed for a while before being dismissed. Once dismissed, they all rush to a small window in the prison yard, behind which is the shop.

The prison shop, also known as the tuck shop, sells crisps, chocolate, water, soda, biscuits, and basic toiletries. All can be purchased with money that friends and relatives put into the prisoners' accounts. At the time the B2 were in prison, each prisoner was allowed to spend 300 baht a day, around £5. Occasionally prisoners are allowed to buy razors. Unfathomably, they are allowed to walk around the jail with them. Even more unfathomably there are very few razor related attacks, but that is possibly because the prisoners can make more effective weapons from other items found in the jail, such as spoons and bones from the prison meals.

Cigarettes could, back then, also be bought from the shop. They have since been banned from all Thai prisons. However, cigarette lighters were not available for purchase at the shop and could only be bought from the guards for a few packs of cigarettes. However, buying a lighter does not mean the prisoner gets to keep it. It would only be in his possession until there was a shakedown, when it would be confiscated and would need to be purchased again.

After purchases have been made at the shop, the working day begins for Thai and Burmese prisoners who go to work in a factory making fishing nets. The remaining prisoners, of any other nationality, are left to their own devices, and occupy their time sunbathing, chatting, working out; or perhaps reading.

At 11 a.m. a whistle blows to signal lunch. Prisoners once again line up to wait for a spoon of slop to be put on a plate. Dinner over, prisoners then either go back to work or hang around until 1 p.m. when a bell rings. They are once again lined up to be counted in the now unbearable heat of the day. Once a prisoner has called his number, he sweats in the heat, in the squat position, for 20 to 30 minutes. Once counting is done the inmates are dismissed until 2 p.m. when it is time for afternoon shower. The afternoon shower is even more chaotic than the one in the morning. Almost a thousand sweaty prisoners, who are hot and bothered, and utterly hacked off, wish to cool down. It is very common for fights to break out at this time. By 3 p.m. the tables have been removed from the dining area and a bell rings to signal that it is time to return to the cells. Before going to the cells, the prisoners have to line up by room number. The captain goes around inspecting the lines. Counting then starts again. Each prisoner has to put their hand in the air and say their number. If the number is announced incorrectly the prisoner is smacked around the head with a stick that is held by the captain.

At about 3 p.m. when all the rooms have been counted, the captain acts as doorman and the prisoners go back up the stairs to their cells. Each prisoner is searched. The only item allowed in the cells is one bottle of water per prisoner. If food or cigarettes are found on a prisoner, he is beaten with sticks, steel toe cap boots, or punched in the face or ribs.

Everybody goes back up to the room in the same formation as when they came down. This process takes up to 45 minutes. As the prisoners filter back into their cells, they grab their blanket and settle in the position where they will later sleep. Nobody is able to move around in these cramped conditions until the following day, when the entire routine starts over again. The heat, I have been told, is unbearable.

The prison routine at the weekend is slightly different. Nobody works, so the daytime area is just a chaotic playground. Some of the Thai people gamble on games of marbles. Most of the day is spent betting on everything you can imagine: ants, cockroaches racing, and other things to get rid of the tedium.

CHAPTER 14 - COURT DAYS

Although court days are always something to worry about, with rampant corruption in the Thai justice system they are a break from the tedious routine. After the morning shower, anyone who is going to court, must listen out for their name to be called over the prison public address system. Those going to court are sent to the tiny 3 x 3 meter shackle room. Here there are chains hanging all over the walls, most of them old and very rusty. A few of the chains are bright and shiny. The shiny chains are the result of being worn by prisoners who have been forced to wear them as a punishment for months. There is nothing else to do but polish and clean them all day. Due to the humidity in Thailand, shiny chains do not stay shiny for long.

Prisoners on their way to court are lined up and wait to be called in to be shackled. The shackle machine is like a huge pair of scissors with an iron bar on the outside and a half pipe where you put your ankle. There is a pin halfway down and the half pipe is used, with a machine, to bend the bar around your ankle. This is a terrifying experience for the prisoners who fear their ankles will be crushed or broken in the process. Once both ankles are shackled, a rusty bit of chain is attached to each one. The prisoner must then find a piece of string strong enough to hold up the weight of the chain between their legs in order to walk. The newly shackled prisoners then head over to a 1970s Mig welder that has wires exposed. Sitting on the wet floor, electric shocks at this stage of the process are commonplace. A bit of cardboard is put under the shackle to offer the prisoner some protection as it is welded into place. When the metal gets too hot for the prisoner to handle, water is poured over it. While this offers some relief, the risk of electric shock is increased considerably. One prisoner described this process to me as "utterly barbaric".

At the 8 a.m. head count, those heading to the court stand in a separate line before being escorted out of the prison by two or three guards. They then head to the area where they first entered the prison and stand by the commander's desk. The prisoners' names are read out and each prisoner shouts their name as it's called. Prisoners are then loaded into secure vans under the watchful eye of armed guards. The van has a small cell in the back that contains a wooden bench. The van has an extractor fan in the middle that is useful for prisoners who wish to have a cigarette before they go into the court. However, this involves smuggling cigarettes out of the prison by concealing them in an orifice. Prisoners leave lighters in the air vents for the next lot going to court. Occasionally the captains give the prisoners a cigarette as they get into the van. The vans are surrounded by a mesh cage. Unlike the prison, there is little in the way of bad smells here, but they are as hot as a sauna.

Prisoners arrive at the court at 8.30 a.m. and are left sitting in a small room until 3 p.m. Prisoners are given some of the prison food that has been hanging around all day in the heat. The containers the food comes in are then used to splash water over the rear end of any prisoners who need to use the toilets. The day is long and hot and tiring. On the return to the prison, the same system is employed as the first time you arrived. One prisoner told me, "It's always a very, very long day, with no redeeming features other than a break in the normal routine". There is one other day when prisoners spend a day outside the jail and that is to reconstruct their crimes.

CHAPTER 15 – THE RECONSTRUCTION

It is usual in Thailand, once somebody has been accused of a crime, to be taken back to the scene to re-enact it. This is normally a fairly frenzied affair in high profile cases. I was familiar with the reconstruction process as I had seen it years earlier, in the case of Mr. Ban. The butcher who shot him was made to reconstruct his crime. I didn't go to Koh Tao for this reconstruction; however, I did watch the whole thing on TV. The TV crews push and shove their way to the front, trying to get the best possible footage, for their respective news group. Thousands of onlookers crowd around to get a look at the suspect and see how he committed his crime. However, when the B2 arrived on Sairee Beach to reconstruct their crime, it was startlingly different to the one I had seen in the Mr. Ban assassination case. During the Mr. Ban assassination reconstruction, the butcher knew exactly what he was doing and had very little difficulty re-enacting the crime. He clearly remembered it very vividly. This was in stark contrast to the Koh Tao murders reconstruction. Zaw Lin and Wai Phyo visibly had no clue what they were meant to be doing. They had to be physically prompted, at every turn, by the police, who very obviously choreographed the entire thing.

The two tiny men looked like puppets on a string. Dressed in bulletproof vests and motorbike helmets, for their own safety, they would point in one direction before being instructed by police to point in the opposite direction.

The police often manhandled the B2 into the position they wanted to see them in. This all played out in front of hundreds if not thousands of people who, perhaps unwittingly, were crowding around stamping all over the very spot Hannah Witheridge's body was found. It was a macabre sight on the one hand, and heart wrenching on the other. Both Zaw Lin and Wai Phyo, who looked terrified, tried to comply with the Thai police officers' orders when they understood very little Thai. It was a pantomime. The police became demonstrably agitated with the two slight figures of Wai Phyo, and Zaw Lin, and were heard shouting at them as well as pushing them around.

While watching this mockery, I focused on the man who had acted as translator for the boys during their interrogation. He was clearly not part of the police; he was Burmese but to me looked Rohingya. This struck me as odd as the boys are from what is known as Arakine State but is now referred to as the Rakhine State. The Arakine State has been at serious odds with the Rohingya for decades. This situation is commonly referred to as the Rohingya conflict.

The Rohingya conflict is an ongoing conflict in the northern Arakine State in Myanmar previously named Burma. The conflict is characterized by sectarian violence between the Rohingya Muslim and Rakhine (Arakine) Buddhist communities, and a military crackdown on Rohingya civilians and Myanmar's security forces and militant attacks by Rohingya insurgents in Buthidauang, Maungdaw; and Ratheducant Townships which borders Bangladesh. The conflict arises chiefly from the religious and social differentiation between the Rakhine Buddhists and Rohingya Muslims.

During WW2, Burmese Rohingya Muslims, who were allied with the British, were promised a Muslim state in return for fighting against local Rakhine Buddhists, who were allied with the Japanese.

Following independence in 1948, the newly formed union government of the predominantly Buddhist country denied citizenship to the Rohingyas, subjecting them to extensive systematic discrimination in the country. Rohingyas have a deep-seated hatred for Rakhine Buddhists such as Zaw Lin and Wai Phyo so it seemed odd, to me, they would want one translating for them on a capital murder charge that could result in their execution.

After the B2 were arrested, the police force, consisting of 60 officers who had been drafted in to investigate the crimes, left. Over half of them returned to help with the so-called reconstruction.

The once open chat about the murders had gone strangely quiet around the Soi Reggae bars. The police were no longer really talking to ex-pats and didn't seem to need any of us to buy them beers or whiskey anymore. In fact, they were not talking at all, and seemed to immediately shut down at the very mention of the Koh Tao murders. With no new information forthcoming I decided to change track.

A Thai friend of mine owned a bar with her English husband on the north shore of the island in an area called Bangrak. This area was also mainly frequented by ex-pats along with the odd tourist who happened upon a bar when taking a ferry to Koh Phangan or Koh Tao. One of her best friends was a policeman. He kept pretty much to himself when it came to socializing with the other police. Although he, like some other local officers, played in a pool team. He happened to be in the bar when I arrived, one evening, to try to find some inside information.

My Thai friend, a lady who originated from Udon Thani in the north, was far more sympathetic to the plight of the Burmese boys than most Thai people I had spoken to. There is a north-south divide in Thailand. When visited Chiang Mai, in the north of Thailand, a taxi driver told me that southern Thailand was run by people with black hearts. He said it was a common perception of people who lived in the north part of the Kingdom where corruption is far rarer.

My friend knew that I was very concerned about the plight of the Burmese. I often spoke to her about them. On this occasion she told me that the two men would not be executed. I asked her to have a word with her police friend, who spoke only one or two words of English. He confirmed that the men would only spend between two and three years in jail, and then would be released. This struck me as rather odd, given the magnitude of the crime they were both charged with. Her police friend seemed not to want to elaborate on this subject any further but was quite clearly convinced that I had nothing to worry about. He said the B2 were very aware they would not spend long in jail. I found this hard to swallow.

CHAPTER 16 - CSI LA

The Koh Tao murders had grabbed the attention of hundreds of thousands of people around the globe, who seemed as hungry for information as I was. One Facebook page that got a lot of traffic around this time is called CSI LA. The CSI LA Facebook page was set up by a US-based Thai man named Pramuk Anantasin, AKA David, who is known to people online as simply CSI LA. The CSI LA Facebook page quickly became the go-to platform for information on the murders. It was a place where super-sleuths from around the world met to discuss the case in an attempt to solve it. It seemed nobody on that group thought the Thai police had the right men either, although they somehow had access to a lot of relevant information about the case.

After the B2 were arrested, 700,000 CSI LA followers actively delved into the murders, picking each part of the crime apart bit by bit. The dedication of CSL LA, and his online team, was admirable. The site was updated and commented on 24 hours a day. It had become an invaluable source of information and resources.

CSI LA made an interesting observation on his page on the 2nd of October 2014. The CCTV footage of Wai Phyo, Zaw Lin, and Mau Mau, on a motorbike, clearly showed them wearing dark-coloured trousers on the night of the murders. The person of interest, the running man, captured on CCTV running to and from the beach where the murders took place, was wearing light colored shorts without a belt.

David's shorts, however, found at the crime scene, did have a belt on them.

One image of the CCTV footage depicted Hannah walking with friends. She wore a pink top and a short skirt. David was captured wearing a T-shirt that was grey and black with light-colored shorts. Another image from the CCTV showed Zaw Lin, Wai Phyo, and their friend Mau Mau all riding on the same moped past the beach. Mau Mau, who worked for the Toovichien clan, was arrested in connection with the murders but refused to confess and was later released.

More footage was released to the press that showed David and Hannah walking together at around 2 a.m. on the footpath close to the beach. However, it was clearly not them. The man in the footage was white, not as tall as David, and was wearing a vest top and had a much stockier frame. The woman in the image was very obviously Asian.

The running man footage showed an Asian man running to and from the crime scene with a rather odd gait. He threw his rather thin arms about in a way that was unusual. He was wearing light-colored shorts in the shots of him going to and from the beach. Many who saw the footage, including the police, believed the shorts were similar to the ones David had worn prior to being found naked in the ocean. In the still version of the footage, the running man did bear a slight resemblance to Wai Phyo. However, many who saw the moving version of the footage noted that the odd gait was similar to the odd gait of Nomsod.

On the 4th of October 2014 CSI LA put out a message to the international community via his page, however, it was mainly aimed at anyone in Thailand, and specifically Koh Tao, who had information. It read:

"I have reason to believe that Sean McAnna saw what happened and was there when David was murdered by a push knife. You can clearly see that Sean suffered the same type of stab wound as David. Please pressure Scotland Yard and Interpol to search for Sean McAnna. He is a key witness in this case. Sincerely CSI LA Community".

CSI LA also made an interesting post about David's height and that of the B2. He did this in order to question how they could have attacked him. With the post was a photograph that showed the B2 during the reconstruction along with David's image, to scale, superimposed onto the image. It was striking.

CSI LA posted, "David is huge. He is about 190cm (6 ft 2) tall. How could it be possible that 2 tiny Burmese could punch him in the face, temple and back of his head"?

On the 3rd of October 2014, CSI LA started to question what had happened to Hannah's mobile phone. On the 1st of October 2014, Police General Somyot, who had taken over the investigation from Pol. Lt. Gen. Panya Mamen, claimed that investigators found Hannah Witheridge's mobile phone and suggested the B2 had stolen it. On Thursday, the 2nd of October 2014, it was announced it had been found near the room of Wai Phyo.

However, this could not have been true. CSI LA published a photo from a few hours prior to the murders that clearly showed Hannah and her friends sitting around a table at a bar. Hannah had her pink phone with her. He also published a still image from a video that was taken when Hannah's travel companions were talking to the police after her murder. The image clearly shows Hannah's phone on the policeman's desk after one of her travel companions had handed it over.

On another post on that day, CSI LA asked, "Why is nobody talking about fingerprints on the hoe? The hoe is key evidence. How come it has been contaminated and was not left at its initial spot? I don't believe the rapists and killers are the same people".

CSI LA was quite right about this. It came out at the trial that the man who owned the hoe had taken it back to his garden after the murders. When the police discovered it, they gave the owner of the presumed murder weapon a rubber glove and told him to put it back where he had found it. Later reports suggest it was Mon, not the police, who made this request.

By the 5th of October 2014, the conversation on CSI LA had turned to why David had been found with no clothing (other than one black sock) on. CSI LA speculated, "This is because the killer and those assisting may have had some knowledge about forensics. They put his naked body into the water so that the DNA of the killer(s) would be washed away and be next to impossible to find".

CSI LA surmised that the reason there was no blood stain found on David's shorts was because he was likely struck on the head before falling onto sandy ground. CSI LA theorized that the perpetrator(s) would likely be 178 cm in height (not less than 5ft 10 to 5ft 11) to have been able to reach and strike the head of a person of David's height, 190 cm (about 6ft 2). He suggested that the assailants may have been bouncers at the bar who came to see off those committing a sexual assault on Hannah. He also discussed why two very small men, such as the B2, would waste their time trying to drag David's body out into the water. It would be difficult, if not impossible, considering that an unconscious or deceased human body is very difficult to carry and feels much heavier than normal. He said, "How could these two very small guys do all of this without Hannah getting away or struggling and fighting against her attackers. Can two attackers the size of dwarfs realistically fight two victims who are much taller and weigh much more"?

Around this time, the press was full of speculation about Nomsod's involvement in the murders. In order to prove he was not on the island at the time the murders' stills, taken from CCTV footage, were made public. Nomsod's lawyer maintained that the image was taken from CCTV footage at the university Nomsod attended in Bangkok. This proved, he said, that Nomsod had not been on Koh Tao at the time of the murders but was in fact in the country's capital. However, CSI LA established that, in fact, the images were not taken from the CCTV at the university, but from the Pon Amon Apartment next door. CSI LA put out a public request for the original video file from the owner of this apartment.

CSI LA had managed to get hold of a copy of Nomsod's university schedule and noted that classes started at 8.40 a.m. He also noted that the photo of Nomsod used to prove he was in Bangkok was taken at 9.16 a.m. He had no satchel, backpack, or books with him. CSI LA mused "This guy must have a photographic memory, but his GPA is 2.01". Inferring it was odd that a man with a very low grade point average did not need his books or his satchel.

By the 10th of October 2014, the public on the social media platform were pressuring Nomsod to prove his innocence. CSI LA posted, "It's very strange that Nomsod has claimed he is innocent, he's never provided any solid evidence. He still refuses to take a DNA test. On the other hand the Burmese suspects never tried to make an escape from the island, and have been DNA profiled two times already. (The first time their DNA did not match the killers DNA)".

Speculation that the murders were something to do with the Toovichien family had reached a fever pitch. CSI LA decided it was time to put pressure on the family and called for Nomsod to take action.

His post on the 11th of October 2014 read, "Admin and fans of CSI LA are giving Nomsod and his lawyer 24 hours to bring forward proof of the following.
- Video footage of CCTV from Nomsod's dormitory/ apartment
- Video footage of CCTV from the convenience store
- Video footage of CCTV from Bangkok University showing he was there on the date he claims.
- Nomsods exam results".

He said, "If they fail to comply with these demands, our fan page will go to crowd-sourced reviews page and give a bad review on his dad's business".

Pressure on the Toovichien family online was heating up.

CSI LA had been continually trying to track down Sean McAnna and finally succeeded via Sean's SoundCloud account. He told CSI LA:

"I don't know if Nom's son was on the island (Nom is short for Nomsod) Genuinely, But I've spoken to a journalist today to give all the information I have to them, including the fact that Burmese guys were always expected to be blamed. It's not much. I think you expect I know more than I do, but it's everything I have. Also, information has come forward about the guy who fell to his death on [Koh] Tao last year, so I expect the newspapers in the UK won't let this rest. I hope it's enough to save the two guys from Myanmar. I can't do any more".

Sean was talking about Nick Pearson but if he ever did give any information on that death to the police it certainly never came into the public domain.

By the 12th of October 2014, Nomsod and the Toovichien family had made no response to CSI LA's demands, so, CSI LA put into place his plan to attack the Trip Advisor pages of AC2 Resort, In Touch Resort and Restaurant, and AC Bar and AC Resort. Global times were given so the attack could be coordinated and come in fast. Bad reviews flooded in from all locations from people who had never stepped foot in Thailand, let alone any of the targeted venues.

On the 12th of October 2014, CSI LA started to try to track down a man who had been photographed in the bar with Hannah and had been seen with her on CCTV footage just prior to her death. His name was Tom.

On the 13th of October 2014 Sean once again spoke to CSI LA on his SoundCloud. CSI LA had been concerned about an apparent stab mark on Sean's arm that bore a striking resemblance to the ones David had sustained. He had been asking Sean about this as well as other questions.

This time the message read:

"CSI LA I don't have any means of contacting you directly. I deleted Facebook and I am not giving out my email address or phone number. The cut was from my bike, so was the burn on my leg. I don't know why that is hard to understand. I have said it enough times. In any case if it needs to be proven I can use video evidence from a bar I went to on the 10th and 11th. But they don't want the attention of plastic detectives or bad custom ruining their bar. Main thing is, it's provable. And the police took the blood from my guitar and my bag which matched my DNA (I had everything on when I came off the bike, hence why they all have blood on them) After the crash I went straight to the dive shop I was going to be working with and they seen it too (they had to sort my accommodation as part of the course. I spoke to the *Sunday Mail*. They haven't put anything up yet but the full conversation was about what happened the night I got chased to the shop, and why the accusations are being thrown my way. I've also mentioned that no one believes it was the 2 Burmese guys and anyone would be stupid to even consider it".

However, in the Channel 4 documentary Montriwat told the reporter that he chased Sean McAnna into the shop to find out why he was covered in blood on the night of the murders, not on the 10th or 11th.

CSI LA was not the only one trying to get to the bottom of what happened that fateful night. A man named Chris Hawkins was also on the case. He had decided to go on Change.org and try to get enough signatures to petition the UK government into taking action, also believing the story about the B2 committing the murders to be ludicrous.

His petition read:

Change.org appeal Christopher Hawkins

On 15th September, 2 innocent British citizens - David Miller, 24, and Hannah Witheridge, 23 were found raped and murdered in the most horrific manner possible whilst on holiday in Thailand on the island of Koh Tao. The Thai police's flawed handling of this crime has been a grave cause of concern from both the local and international community from the very start of the investigation. The Thai authorities insensitive obsession with tourist figures and the police's notoriously corrupt reputation around the world, has been in the forefront of these concerns.

From a completely destroyed crime scene, racial slurs and finger pointing against foreigners, victim blaming from the General turned Prime Minister, police posting pictures of the dead victims' bodies on their FB accounts (with no regard for the victims friends and families), countless releases of unnecessary and highly conflicting pieces of information/evidence to the media, reports of investigators beating and offering bribes to false witnesses (and then still being allowed to work on the case), reports of torturing of suspects, suspicious and insensitive re-enactments of the crime, and the well known fact that citizens of Myanmar are the usual choice of scapegoats in Thailand.

The International and local community are now not able to trust that the two Myanmar nationals, Zaw Lin and Win Zaw Htun [AKA Wai Phyo], have not had their confessions forced out of them or that evidence against them has not been tampered with. As such we cannot also trust that they are responsible. This being said, we demand a full independent investigation to be conducted by the government of the United Kingdom into these deaths. This is in the hope that the families of these victims may know justice has been served, and that the deaths of two more possible innocents might be avoided.

By the 17th of October it had 100,000 signatures. It was also the day Nomsod sent a message to CSI LA. It simply read "5555," the Thai way of saying " hahahaha" as the Thai word for 5 is 'ha' in English.

CHAPTER 17 - ANDY HALL

Andy Hall first started corresponding with me on Facebook instant messenger on the 16th of October 2014. I wrote to him that I was the owner and editor of the *Samui Times*. I explained that, through a friend, I had access to the overseas prisoners abroad support group who regularly visited foreign prisoners in Samui and provided them with funds, food, and other essential provisions. Andy told me he had taken up the case and he and his legal team had met with the B2. Together they had attended court with the B2 for their first hearing on the 14th of October 2014. He said his legal team was prepared to offer pro-bono legal representation for the pair. Despite the team being happy to work free of charge defending the B2, they would require funds for expenses. I offered to help raise some. This came as good news to Andy, but, interestingly, he made it clear that any fundraising I did should under no circumstances be made public. I asked Andy if the prisoner support group could help the B2. He replied that the only visits the men would be allowed was from lawyers, embassy (politicians), and their families who were not yet in Thailand.

I offered to buy food and water for the men as Andy confirmed that as far as he was aware nobody was providing anything for them in the prison and it would be impossible for them to survive without outside help. During our conversations, Andy made it very clear that it would be difficult for him to do anything for the B2 without substantial financial help. As luck would have it, a friend of mine with a hotel in the same village as my house offered to let Andy and his team stay there. She was happy to help, at least until her hotel would fill up for high season in December. Her hotel was off the beaten track, and she did not share the same concerns as others. Many people were reluctant to get involved or help the B2 in any way or form. *Thai PBS* had reported that a local man had been arrested. Pol. Col. Gen Panya Mamen named that man as "Mon", the brother of the village headman. The article said he was arrested after evidence the police collected were examined and proved he was involved. The article went on to say that the son of the village headman was another suspect, but he had gone to Bangkok. Many locals told me there were scared to do anything that might risk upsetting powerful local families.

The following day I told Andy I had arranged a visit to the prison to buy food and water for the B2 and gave him the news about the hotel rooms, expecting him to be over the moon. However, rather than thanking me, he simply said that he would require accommodation on occasion for up to 15 lawyers and a translator. Andy told me that he had already spent 150,000 baht on flights for his team for the B2's first hearing on the 14th of October 2014. After I suggested that some of the team could stay at my house, or with friends of mine, he said it was highly important the whole team stayed at one hotel. He suggested I could find other hoteliers with more rooms, free of charge, or at a heavily discounted price if my friend was unable to accommodate them all.

I felt a little put out that Andy would expect me to call on my friend to offer so many free rooms. She clearly had a business to run and a limited number of rooms at her hotel. I assured him I would do my best. Obviously, there would be no guarantee how many rooms I could get at short notice as paying guests would need to take priority. Andy mentioned that on a previous visit to the island he had been very disappointed with the breakfast in his hotel. He asked what sort of food would be provided if my friend put them up and what sort of Wi-fi and other facilities would be on offer. I was taken aback he was so picky when the offer of free accommodation seemed so generous. I felt asking for free food was rather cheeky, but my friend agreed to lay on more rooms and free breakfast.

Andy was pleased. He told me, "I am trying to set up donation website, but my team won't allow it as they don't want to be seen asking for money. If people can donate privately it would be great, so far I got 90,000 baht" (around £2000). I was happy that he was trying to raise funds.

I told Andy that I knew a few people who would be happy to donate, but, obviously, they would need to know where to send the money. He told me any donations could go directly into his bank account.

I was taken aback by several aspects of this conversation. For one, I felt very uncomfortable asking my friends to donate to his private bank account rather than that of his organization's or charity. I thought a crowd funding site would be far more appropriate. I quashed these nagging doubts with the fact that I had no real reason to distrust this man who was willing to help the hapless and incarcerated Burmese. My second concern was how unprofessional he appeared to be in his manner. Thirdly the pidgin English he used in our correspondence was less than I would have expected from a man who professed to have a first-class honors law degree and would be representing the B2 in a capital murder case.

I put my misgivings aside in favor of being happy there was hope for the B2. I realize now with hindsight that this was a huge mistake.

Andy's next question was to ask for my phone number and if I had any contacts at Bangkok Airways. I gave him my number and told him that while I did have a contact at Bangkok Airways—I knew the owner of Bangkok Airways was a business associate, as well as a great friend of the head guy on Koh Tao—so I thought it unlikely they would help. It may have been very dangerous to even ask. His response to that confused me. "Yes, I already asked and assumed like that but I don't care to ask them".

He then gave me his email address and said, "So if coming down, even last minute, I can ring or email you and you can help organize hotel rooms for the legal team and translator? Even hire car? Although we used a car last week 1000 baht a day it was, I think"?

I was starting to think this arrangement could turn out to be rather problematic for me. So far, I only had one friend with a small hotel who was willing to offer rooms but could not guarantee free rooms at the very last minute. As for a free hire car, I had no idea where to turn for that. I put my worries to Andy but reassured him that I had a car he could use to get to and from the prison. The offer to use my spare bedrooms was still on the table if I was unable to get him free accommodation at a moment's notice. Again, his response surprised me. "It's best we are seen as WALK IN, if you know what I mean". To be honest, I didn't really know what he meant, but assumed perhaps it was to avoid the press. He said, "We just happen to walk into your friend's hotel, happen to ring and get a car. It shouldn't be seen as planned for your own safety".

I told Andy I had been on the islands for a long time and knew the drill, even though I was rather perplexed by what he seemed to see as an undercover clandestine mission. He said, "Great stuff. We need people like that, Anyway is great you can subtly pass round my bank details and the hotel/breakfast/car can assist. My heart really opens so full of joy for hearing people like this. I struggle a lot now on my own legal case, this helps too much and help like this really helps".

At this point, I was not sure why he wanted to keep everything so much under the radar. I found his sentence structure and choice of vocabulary a little different from any other lawyers I have ever known, or members of any other profession for that matter. He then told me that he was just waiting on arrival dates to coordinate with the legal team and translators and prosecution decision and court date. I told him to just get in touch when he needed help and he said, "For now the promise of attempt for funding support and hotel/food promise enough". I told Andy that I was sure some friends of mine would help out 'under the radar'.

His response, "Exactly, all under the radar. People like me have to be out there in front, in the media, and as risk, but without you guys we cannot do anything". I didn't realize at this point how much he wanted the limelight and wanted everybody else to be hidden, providing for his every need and wish free of charge, with no thanks or even acknowledgment, but I was starting to suspect it might be the case.

On the 18th of October 2014, *Fox News* reported that UK detectives would be travelling to Thailand to observe the Thai investigations. On the same day, Andy informed me that he and a translator would be arriving on the island the following day to speak to the B2.

Our conversation then turned to the fact that I had read reports in the *BBC* and *AFP* suggesting it would be possible for the UK to investigate the murders of the two British backpackers, Hannah Witheridge and David Miller. Andy confirmed that if it had been reported by the *BBC* and *AFP* then it would be true. He told me the military Junta Prayuth and UK Prime Minister David Cameron had discussed this on a recent visit to Italy. He went on to say, "Hope they don't shoot the messenger, between you and me, especially if one of them is a British guy". So the *Fox News* report had been true.

Our conversation that day ended with Andy making enquiries into my private life and asked if I was married to a Thai man. I had been married to a Thai man and told Andy that my ex-husband and I had divorced. I was slightly surprised when he asked me if I could still call on him if required. I answered honestly; it had not been an amicable split with the man from Surat Thani. He signed off by saying, "Your kindness will be rewarded through happy life and mind". However, it didn't really turn out that way!

CHAPTER 18 - ANDY'S CONTINUED INVOLVEMENT IN THE KOH TAO MURDER CASE

On the 19th of October 2014, CSI LA reported two Instagram posts from Nomsod's girlfriend on the 15th and 16th of September 2014 (the night of the murders) saying he was 'missing'.

On the same day, I got a message from Andy informing me he had arrived at Koh Samui airport. We arranged to have dinner at my friend's hotel. He seemed friendly enough. He spoke pidgin English to me for the entire evening, but that didn't surprise me because of all our written communication. Many *falang* get into the habit of speaking pidgin English to fellow Brits even when it is completely unnecessary to do so. He seemed to me to be far more of an activist than a lawyer. He was a rather bohemian chap who had arrived with a large, smiling Burmese lady named Sar, who was to act as a translator for the accused.

Andy and Sar explained that both were part of an organization called The Migrant Workers Rights Network that operates out of both Burma and Thailand. The organization helps Burmese migrant workers as well as investigating labor abuses and fighting for the rights of the truly downtrodden.

Despite my misgivings about the nature of Andy's vocabulary and his rather unprofessional appearance, I have to say he seemed incredibly committed to the B2's plight. What concerned me was his apparent naivety when it came to the both the law and the ways of Southern Thailand and the islands. His blind faith in the justice system disturbed me. I tried to put my fears aside and gently reiterate to him that I knew a great deal more about what happened on Thailand's southern islands than he did. This information seemed to go straight over his head.

I very quickly realized that my normal sledgehammer approach with people would not work in Andy's case. He was a very sensitive guy who really only responded well when his ego was being stroked. Andy spent a great deal of time looking at himself in photos from press coverage of his various cases. He was always asking which photos of him we thought were the most flattering.

After days of deliberation, Andy Hall decided that in order to defend the B2 he would bring in his own lawyer, Nakhon Chompuchat. I was not sure how useful this would be as he was a civil lawyer and not a criminal one and therefore had never defended, or had any experience with, a capital murder case.

Andy and I discussed endlessly whether or not the B2 should plead guilty or not guilty. To anybody outside of Thailand that probably seems like an odd thing to discuss. The B2 had pled guilty but told Andy they were entirely innocent of the crimes and had only given the guilty plea after days of torture. If they were telling the truth, it would probably seem ridiculous that any guilty plea would be up for debate. In Thailand, if you plead guilty your sentence will be halved and the possibility of being executed will be taken off the table. There was also amnesty to be taken into consideration. The king and queen often heavily reduced or halved prisoners' sentences on auspicious occasions such as their birthdays. This meant a guilty plea could see a possible death sentence reduced to life, then reduced to 50 or possibly even 25 years and then that sentence would be halved each year seeing the men free after 5 to 10 years.

The only problem with this scenario was that amnesty is not given for rape and both men had been charged with raping Hannah Witheridge. Wai Phyo had been charged with stealing David's mobile phone and both had been charged with illegal entry to the country. Wai Phyo had certainly been guilty of that, but Zaw Lin had a legitimate passport. Like every other Burmese working in Thailand, both paid the police every month to be able to stay in the country. The going rate was between 500 and 2000 baht. Every Burmese worker was given a piece of paper and a number. This was nothing whatsoever to do with national immigration. It was a private deal struck between the police and the workers. At this stage Koh Tao had far more Burmese workers than Thais who had long since left their menial jobs and menial salaries and the island. It's hard to say how many Burmese migrant workers were actually the working cogs behind the big wheel that was Koh Tao, but it certainly ran into the thousands.

The trouble with a not-guilty plea would be threefold. If the men were found guilty, they would most certainly be sentenced to death. We had no witnesses at this stage either for or against them. If the judges had been paid off, as we suspected, both men were in a no-win situation.

Having lived in Thailand for almost twenty years at this stage I had no faith in the justice system whatsoever. Tossing a coin would have been a more reliable method of establishing the guilt or innocence of anybody who passed through the Koh Samui Provincial Court. It stood to reason that simply pleading not guilty to a crime you did not commit was not the obvious choice in Thailand, and certainly not on the islands.

I advised Andy that a guilty plea was less of a risk. I had concerns that the judges could be paid off. In an article in the *Independent* a local man was quoted as saying he didn't think anybody local would commit such a crime. Jonathan Head's article for the BBC on the 19th of September 2014 quoted the "senior police officer the island assured us the culprit could not have been a Thai person. No Thai could possibly commit such a crime, he said, forgetting the equally ghastly murder of Welsh tourist Katherine Horton in 2006, by, it turned out, two Thai fishermen". An article on Channel4.com stated that the police were focusing their investigations on the Burmese community. If Burmese men were found guilty it would certainly protect the image of Thailand and its people.

There would be no jury. Trials in Thailand are heard by three judges. It was unlikely journalists would be allowed access to the court and basically it would be a whitewash. Andy did not buy this. For some reason, he was under the somewhat naïve conclusion that the men would be given a fair trial. I thought Andy understood Thailand and how it worked, but then he had never lived on the islands. Andy did not have my experience of a society that relied solely on how much money was on the table. As a lawyer, or so he said, he clearly had high regard for the law, which is fine, until you find yourself on islands that are entirely lawless.

It was at this stage that Andy and I started to fall out. Over the coming days Andy started to tell me less and less about the legal case he and his lawyer were building for the defendants. He was less than impressed I had no faith in his lawyer, who had no criminal law experience and was also defending Andy in his civil cases.

Andy seemed to enjoy being in the press. It was also of my experience that trial by media is the worst way forward in Asia. Asians hate losing face as I have already mentioned. In the case of the Bali 9 it proved fatal when two Australian men were executed ten years after their arrest for drug trafficking in Indonesia.

My idea was to keep this case as far from the press as possible. While it is great to have the weight of public opinion on your side, it does nothing for the actual case. The public's opinion in this case would not have any influence on Thai judges when even the British police and British Embassy have no jurisdiction in Thailand let alone the courtroom.

In order to allow the Thais to save face and get the boys out of jail, in my mind, it was essential to keep the press out of it. A situation I explained over and over again to journalists around the world who were contacting me through the *Samui Times* from the second the news of the murders escaped Koh Tao. My experience of Thai psychology had taught me that Thai people backed into corners often act in the exact same way animals do in similar circumstances and come out fighting which could be scary. I conveyed my fears to Andy who responded, "Not scary if you think about it, fear sometimes makes no sense, I try to avoid thinking about bad things that may never happen, sister".

I had to agree with that as I believe there is little point living in fear as that is often what gives those forcing you to do so their power. Andy suggested that it would be a good idea for me to cover my back in regard to helping him with accommodation and said, "We are walk in, nothing planned. And we pay for each night, even if we didn't in reality". At the time I thought he had genuine concerns for my safety by getting involved in the case. He simply wanted me to stay in the shadows and not put my head above the trenches. Looking back now it is easy to see that Andy wanted all of the limelight, something he was not at all willing to share. More worryingly, he wanted to make sure it looked as if he were paying for the rooms.

However, despite all of my misgivings, I was relieved that somebody was fighting for the B2 and that they had received much needed visits by Andy and the translator as nobody else could visit them to give them any kind of hope and reassurance.

After a visit to the B2, Andy told me he and Sar had had an unrestricted visit and funds had been put into the prison accounts of the B2. However, the B2 had not been told how to access it. Andy told me he had complained to the officials who had assured him the system would be explained to the B2 and Andy had assured them he would make sure that was the case. He finished our conversation that day by saying, "Saw computer money is there waiting for them. Was going to donate more but office for money closed for lunch and had to leave".

What Andy meant by "Saw computer money" was that if you leant over the booth where one deposits funds for prisoners, you can see if it has been logged on the computer.

The money he had successfully deposited was made up from funds I had given him from my friend who owned the hotel and some of her friends. Andy assured me that the B2 looked well and mentioned that he had tweeted about the money he had deposited. I checked my twitter account and discovered that he had indeed made it public that he had donated funds but made no mention of the fact that he had raised none of the funds himself.

Andy and Sar reported the B2 were very pleased to see them, were very scared, and had said they were tortured into a confession.

Keen to find out more about the B2, I asked Andy what the B2 had said about the night in question and what they knew about the crimes. He said, "I didn't ask them that question, Suzanne, was great visit though I felt really happy with it. And surely after my polite reminded to officials we no need worry about the issue of them getting food".

Through my friends on the prisoner support team, I found out later that Andy's reminder was anything but polite. He had already upset the prison officials who, if you wanted to ensure the men were looked after and visits could take place, were the last people on earth you wanted to upset. This mild-mannered man could be very condescending in the face of authority. This did not go down at all well at the prison. His attitude was concerning for the prison support team whose vital work for foreign prisoners could be badly affected if a westerner was seen as being highly disrespectful to those in charge of the Samui Provincial Prison.

I was keen to find out if Andy had gleaned any information about the allegations of torture the men had said they confessed under. He said it was a subject he had not brought up despite saying earlier the B2 had reported the abuse.

He wrote, "I didn't focus on the past abuse allegations as there were forensics and NHRC (National Human Rights Commission) with the guys last week when I was at the prison, so don't want to step on anyone's feet as those guys expert on torture issues".

I found it a bit odd that in the capacity of the B2's lawyer, Andy did not ask the B2 if they had alibis for that night, if they saw anything, and what their allegations of torture were. I wondered what in fact they did actually talk about, If Andy and his team were prepared to represent these men surely they would find these sorts of significant issues, well, significant!

As Andy seemed to have received no information from the B2 on this occasion, I told him I would not publish anything in my paper about the visit, as I had nothing to report. He told me, "Yes the real issues for us are trying to document the torture as part of the investigation process on Koh Tao, and also speaking to those workers or migrants on Samui, Phangan or Koh Tao who have experienced similar abuse, extortion or beatings involving the police in the past. Any help welcome".

I told Andy I knew of a German guy who had been in prison where he was beaten, but I was not sure if he would be any help. Andy said, "I think beatings of a foreigner and Thai people is a general issue, but if we can get media interest it's through the migrants given these two, sis".

I told Andy I would ask around, but I was dubious about making this case public. Andy did not heed my advice and pushed for me to find evidence of Burmese being beaten in prison. He reassured me that if we successfully found a Burmese person who was willing to go public it was in his power to get them off the islands and back home to Myanmar safely. He said if anybody wanted to speak of mistreatment by the Thai people confidentially, he could ensure that the victim's identity was never revealed, and they would be able to continue with their daily lives.

Once again, he got off the subject and asked me if I knew of a good masseur. Andy told me he had a problem with his back and arms that causes migraine and poor sight. He said his body was badly broken by heavy work and no rest. He was looking for somebody who could put things back in place.

I told him I knew of a Turkish guy who was a sports masseur, but he was expensive. He said this was no problem as his back problem affected his stomach and his sight. He impressed upon me that he would need the services of this guy every day as well as a lot of rest. All I ever saw of Andy other than the rare occasion when he went to the jail was him swimming for up to four hours at a time, having two-hour massages, sleeping, resting, or having a gin and tonic on the beach.

CHAPTER 19 - INVESTIGATIONS CONTINUE

CSI LA continued to look into the CCTV images that put Nomsod in Bangkok at the time of the murders. He believed the images were fakes and asked if anyone knew if the furniture had been rearranged at the Phon Amon Apartment, reaching out to anyone who may live there. He also had discovered that the main CCTV provider on Koh Tao was a good friend of Nomsod's family.

On the 21st of October 2014, CSI LA released a photograph of the 'forced confession document in Thai for the Burmese to sign.' He also released a photograph of CCTV systems commonly found on Koh Tao and pointed out that most beachside restaurants on the island had CCTV cameras that faced the beach. He questioned why images from the cameras at AC1 bar, AC2 bar and Maya bar were not taken by the police and used in the investigation. CSI LA speculated that those three bars were all owned by one family. In fact, they were. The Toovichien family owned all three of those bars.

Andy got in touch a couple of days later to say the B2 were in shackles and needed sweat bands for their ankles, which were sore and missing skin due to the heavy weights. They were still shackled in their cell all day, still deemed a threat to themselves and the general prison population.

I reflected back on my first impression of the tiny B2 from the images in the press and found it difficult to imagine they could be a threat to a fly. I wondered how they would be coping being left in one of the cells in heavy shackles every day with no access to the showers or the tuck shop. I wondered how they could be getting access to their prison accounts. I worried about how they must be wondering if their families knew of their predicament and how much they must want to see them. I didn't have to wait long to find out. I told Andy I would go and buy some sports socks for them.

A few days later the accused were to appear in court, as they would have to every 12 days until they were officially charged in order for them to continue to be legally detained.. At this point, the public prosecutor had not yet agreed to officially charge them and was continually asking the police for more evidence as he deliberated as to whether or not he would even take the case. Andy invited me to join him at the court hearing.

Andy, Sar, and I drove down to the court. The Koh Samui Provincial Court is a rather impressive-looking building perched on top of a rocky outcrop with panoramic views of the ocean a five-star hotel would envy. We walked up the steep flights of steps to the front entrance where we were met by a rather stern-looking court security guard.

We had to swap our passports at the entrance for our passes that we pinned to our chests. Our bags were then searched before we made our way into the foyer of the building via a metal detector that did not appear to be working. There are seating areas to the right and left of the court's foyer then a series of offices on either side of a long corridor that leads to another seating area on the left with a set of stairs leading to the courtrooms directly in front. The stairs lead up to a long balcony on the left from where the courtrooms are accessed. The courtroom itself is wooden paneled with church pew-style benches to the left and the right. Towards the back of the room there is a place on the left for the prosecutor and the court recorder. On the right, there are two benches perpendicular to the public benches for the defense team and a box in the middle where the witnesses sit. The far end of the court has a raised area where three judges sit on chairs that look like they might have been thrones in the Tudor period. Of course, there are no seats for a jury because in Thailand there is no jury. I started to wonder if any or all of the three judges who would oversee the case had taken a bribe.

CHAPTER 20 – MY FIRST ENCOUNTER OF WAI PHYO AND ZAW LIN

Andy, Sar, and I sat in the silent courtroom for what seemed like hours. It was very cold in there thanks to some efficient air-conditioning. The air felt very sterile as did the court. It was an imposing room and felt very formal. I was strangely nervous to see the accused men in person. I knew they were small, but nothing could have prepared me for the two tiny beings who appeared through the door on the right in dirty, salmon-colored cotton tops and shorts. The most disconcerting thing about the first time I set eyes on them was the fact I could hear the chains that had been welded onto the shackles on their ankles shuffling up the corridor long before they got into the courtroom. It is a sound that will haunt me for the rest of my life.

Wai Phyo, who was known as Win at that time, waddled into the court first, his tiny legs almost buckling under the weight of the shackles he was doing his best to hold up with a piece of string that was attached to the chain that stopped his legs from being more than a foot apart. He saw me and smiled. He looked miniscule, utterly helpless, completely harmless, and as innocent as a babe. He also looked petrified. I had never seen an Asian look pale. His face looked like what the Thai people describe as "chicken in hot water". He was followed by Zaw Lin, who also struggled to hold open the heavy courtroom door while holding up his shackles and not to fall over. I was aghast at how tiny these two men, who looked no older than twelve years old, were.

I am not prone to tears but even I have to admit to holding them back by biting hard on my lower lip so as not to upset them. Andy spoke to Sar and she spoke to the B2 as they took their place on the bench in front of me. I reached out to touch the shoulder of Win. He turned around and smiled his little boy smile that will haunt me for the rest of my days. Win has feminine features and I defy any mother not to want to pick him up and hold him in her arms. Zaw, on the other hand, has a far more masculine look about him. He is not as slight in stature as Win but nonetheless is a very small man. I was not as drawn to him. However, as time went on, a bond would form between he and I that I have never experienced with another human being and defies any emotion I felt prior to knowing him or since.

We all sat there patiently waiting for I didn't know what. Sar was amazing with the B2. She was kind and I could tell she had a genuine affection for them. Asians are not known for being tactile, certainly not in public, but she touched the B2 to reassure them, and they looked pleased by her friendly gestures. Eventually, a door to the left of the raised area opened and three judges walked in. They all looked very stern and very young. Proceedings began. As I am not fluent in Thai and only know one word in Burmese, I understood little of what was going on other than the fact the men were remanded for another 12 days and were reassured by Andy and Sar that we would take care of them.

We met the B2 again in the prison a few days later where I put several thousand baht in the B2's prison accounts so they could buy food and water in the Koh Samui Provincial Prison where you might die of starvation if you were left to live on prison-issued cuisines. The area in the prison where visits take place is not really ideal for communication. Each prisoner has a booth that separates them from their visitor by thick Perspex. Each side of the Perspex, at about waist height, is a small shelf that is home to a rather old-fashioned, badly maintained, telephone that looks like it came out of the 1970s.

Win spoke very limited English in those days so for the few minutes I got to speak to him out of the 15 minutes we spent at the Perspex barrier between us, he simply made it clear he was happy and thankful we were there. Zaw Lin spoke slightly better English. Above the din of all the other prisoners trying to hold a conversation with up to five visitors at a time, he managed to get his message across. Despite the language barrier he conveyed to me that he did not commit the crime he was in prison for and asked after his mother.

Up until then, it had not crossed my mind how their mothers would take the news. I found out from Andy that Zaw Lin's father had died many years ago. Zaw Lin and his brother had left Myanmar to find better paying work in Thailand that would allow them to send money back to take care of their mother and grandparents. Zaw Lin found work in a bar in Koh Tao. His brother found work within the fishing industry, a common place for immigrants to find poorly paid work, but more lucrative than earning money in their own country. Zaw Lin's relatives are subsistence farmers in a village with no electricity or running water in some far-flung area of Burma, a country now known as Myanmar. Zaw Lin's mother had never been formally educated and did not even speak Burmese, only her local language. Zaw Lin could speak limited national Burmese and enough English to serve the customers in Brother Bar where he worked in Koh Tao prior to being arrested. Wai Phyo's dad was alive; he was from the Burmese capital of Yangon and spoke the national language as did May Thein, Wai Phyo's mother. However, they were equally as poor and also lived without electricity and running water. So remote were these two families' villages that it took Andy and his team three days to get a phone call through to them. The villagers shared one or two mobile phones between them that were charged on tractor batteries, so the fact that the right sets of parents were tracked down was something of an achievement.

I am not sure that the B2's families could really comprehend what was going on, but we set to work raising funds to bring them to Samui to see their young sons whose future was looking incredibly uncertain. Any income the B2 provided for their families was well and truly cut off. The second time I saw Zaw Lin in court, I told him I had put six thousand baht into his prison account, (about £115). It was the most we were allowed to deposit at that time. I told him he must buy himself a pillow or at least a blanket that could be used as a pillow and other things to make his stay in jail at least bearable. Rather than being pleased, he looked utterly dismayed. I don't think it had ever dawned on him he would be spending more than a few days in jail. He thought it would be sorted out very quickly and he would simply go back to work. When I persuaded him that this was not the case, he asked me to take the money back and send it to his mother who surely needed it more than he did. I reassured him we had other money for his mum, but it took a lot of persuading. I remember thinking these were not the words of a man who had raped and bludgeoned a woman to death and stabbed and drowned a man.

CHAPTER 21 - ANDY AND THE ONGOING INVESTIGATION

On the 22nd of October 2014, the police on Koh Tao put on a big show by printing out banners in 3 languages offering a reward for any tip off that would lead to the killers' convictions. Nobody came forward.

On the same day Andy told me that he had arranged for the B2's parents to Thailand to see them. I knew he had visited them as I saw his picture with them in the Burmese and Thai newspapers. B2 had their first family visit and on the 23rd of October 2014.

I knew how emotional this trip would be for both the B2 and their families. The families had never been on a plane before; as far as I was aware they had never left their village, although I knew the father of Wai Phyo was from the capital of Yangon. Photographs in the press showed Wai Phyo's mother May Thein and father Tun Tun Htike arriving with the mother of Zaw Lin. They looked very small, very Burmese, very bewildered, and very scared. The presence of the paparazzi, albeit small, must have only made it more bewildering for them. Tun Tun Htike arrived carrying a picture of the Thai king, this respectful gesture touched me. It made him look very unworldly with a blind faith in the monarchy and justice.

While Andy had been busy with the press and the B2's families, I had been busy raising more funds for the defense team and funds to top up the B2's prison accounts. I had a good following on my own Facebook page, my *Samui Times* Facebook page, and a lot of friends on the island, so getting funds was not impossible to achieve. It was just very time consuming. I told Andy I would give him the funds I had raised at dinner that night. It had become a routine that we would meet up and discuss the case over dinner; however, on this occasion, he told me he may be sleeping as he had not slept for a week. He asked me to shove the cash into an envelope and put it under his hotel room door. He went on to say that he had some interviews to do that afternoon and was then off for another massage. I was finding Andy's endless massages and whining rather irritating.

With many people on the islands being afraid to have anything to do with the case, or at least being seen to be helping the B2, raising funds 'online' was not as easy as doing it in person behind closed doors. The fundraising site that Andy had organized seemed to be going nowhere. On the 23rd of October 2014, I approached a friend of mine in PR to see if she would help getting Andy's fundraising page made more visible to the public. To ensure we did not double up on our requests for help I asked Andy whom he had approached for help. He told me that he was happy that I had enlisted help and anything anyone could do would be welcomed. He told me he personally had not approached anyone and had simply put out a request for funds to be donated via his own Facebook page and Twitter account. He cut the conversation short before I had the chance to ask him why he was not using his national celebrity and contact with international press organizations to raise awareness of the fact we were desperate for funds.

On the 22nd of October 2014, it was reported that the B2 were making steps to sue their translator, the Rohingya man who, it turned out, was also a pancake vendor on Koh Tao.

On the 23rd of October 2014, CSI LA got another reply from Sean McAnna having discovered a photograph that appeared to show Sean out drinking on the evening after the bodies of Hannah and David were discovered. He wanted to know why Sean appeared to be out having fun having only just learned of his friend's brutal death.

Sean said "Yes, I just checked the dates. It's from the 15th of September 2014. And being in Choppers [Bar] that would have been around 7 or 8 p.m. about 13 hours after the murders, would be a bit strange to be out partying after witnessing something like that would it not"?

CSI LA asked Sean for his side of the story to which Sean replied, "I don't have a side of the story for that night because I wasn't out that night. Ask THEM for evidence that I was out. Don't ask me for evidence that WASN'T out. That would be absurd. Search the meaning of burden of proof if you don't understand why. If you look carefully you'll see that everybody in that photograph is wearing a Koh Tao Pub Crawl T-shirt. So think that is the day after the murder. And it's definitely Choppers [Bar] at this point. Yes I was scared of Mon. You can see that he's vicious. The more lies I hear he is spreading about me, the more I believe he knows something or had something to do with it. What happened with the CCTV footage (of what is obviously) him walking up and down Sairee with no shirt on just after the time of the murder"?

On the 24th of October 2014, CSI LA reported that he had heard that Nomsod was planning on leaving Thailand and believed that his country of destination was an English speaking country but not the UK.

By the 24th of October 2014, Andy had posted some photos of the B2's parents visiting them in jail. They were stirring photos. I asked Andy if he would give me permission to publish them in my paper. He had no objections, and once again complained about how tired he was. Andy was still making use of the rental car I had organized for him at a reduced rate and was being very vague about how long he was going to be using it or when he planned to give it back. This was frustrating the car rental guy who was good enough to offer to let him have it. The reduced price that I had negotiated had only been for two days. Andy eventually told me he needed it for another week, after which he would be flying to Bangkok with Bangkok Airways to fight his own legal case with Natural Fruit.

Prior to his departure, Andy informed me that he would need someone to take care of finances and put money into the B2's prison account. With no hesitation, I offered to take care of this. He said I could use funds from the campaign, but, as it turned out, over the next few months that I kept to my part of the bargain, he never sent any funds for food, water, fruit, bedding, clothing, or toiletries. This meant it was down to me to raise funds and dig into my own finances. Despite this Andy, via the Migrant Workers Rights Network, made a public statement that he would be talking care of the B2's welfare in jail.

At this point, the public prosecutor had still not taken the case against the B2. I asked Andy if he thought the case would go to trial. He said he thought it would, but then, "Who knows". He said, "Thailand is full of surprises". I asked him what he thought the outcome would be if it got to court. Andy said the B2 would get off as "We always win" and went off for yet another swim.

On the 25th of October 2014, the six British police officers, sent out to investigate the Koh Tao case, made a surprise visit to Koh Tao to inspect the location of the murders. They arrived on the island by helicopter from Bangkok, accompanied by Jarumporn Suramanee, an adviser to the national police chief, and Suwat Jaengyodsuk, acting deputy commander of the Metropolitan Police Bureau. Police Major General Suwat was now the chief investigator having been assigned earlier by National Police Chief Somyot Poompanmoung to take over from the local officers. Pol. Gen. Jurumpron is a forensic expert who went to the crime scene some days after the murders occurred. The visit by the UK Metropolitan police had been kept a secret. None of the Thai police officers in Surat Thani province or Provincial Police Region 8 had been informed of their visit. Local police based in Koh Tao and neighboring Koh Phangan had been prevented from attending the meeting or taking pictures of the UK officers. However, one member of the Volunteer Koh Tao rescue group had been invited to attend and provide information about the events of 15th of September 2014, when Hannah Witheridge and David Miller had been murdered. The UK police officers were taken to Sairee Beach and the AC bar where both victims had been seen prior to being murdered. The police also visited the location near the clock tower where local police said they had found David's mobile phone.

The Met took pictures and asked for information before holding 'behind closed door' talks in the meeting room of the Koh Tao municipality before returning to the nation's capital, Bangkok. One of the British police officers was a homicide detective while another was an experienced crime scene expert. The UK police had arrived in Thailand on Wednesday 22nd of October 2014. The Koh Tao mayor at the time, Chaiyant Turaskakul, told the press he was not aware of the visit and was only ordered to arrange local officials to facilitate it.

The visit of the British officers was a response to widespread concern about the Thai Police investigation into the killings.

The Military Dictator Prayut Chan-Ocha had agreed to a request by British Premier David Cameron to allow British police to observe the work of Thai Police when the two met at the Asia-Europe Meeting in Milan on 17 October 2014.

On the 25th of October 2014, I messaged Andy requesting a meeting for an update and to discuss strategy. His response did not surprise me. He had no time to meet up as he needed to have a swim and had meetings planned for the evening, but he was going to go and visit the B2 on Monday the 27th of October 2014. The next part of our conversation didn't exactly surprise me either, but I found it quite disturbing. He said he would like to put some money into the B2's prison account during his visit and asked if I had any funds from anyone who wished to donate. He explained that he could use the money from the fundraiser, but he would rather use money from people who did not feel comfortable donating online so now was their chance.

The following day, the 26th of October 2014, Andy called me to say that he would like me to accompany him on a visit to a temple on the main beach in Koh Samui, Chaweng. This was not your average Thai Buddhist temple; this one was for the Burmese community. He was very insistent that it would be a very important trip during which I could make a solid connection to the Burmese community. As most of them did not speak English and I spoke no Burmese, I was less than enthusiastic and was not sure what it was going to achieve. I went along and despite the language barrier I had a marvelous time. The Burmese people were so welcoming and seemed to have a very high regard for anybody from the UK. They made a huge feast for us and could not do enough for us and treated Andy like some sort of demigod. Despite my own personal misgivings about Andy, I could understand why they did this. His organization was there to help the Burmese migrant workers and protect them against labour law abuses in Thailand, a problem that was rife nationwide. These people had little defense over such abuses. The police and authorities did not care in the slightest about migrants so, for them, having an organization, especially run by a westerner, was quite something.

As much as I had enjoyed my visit to these kind and welcoming people, I was still not sure what the purpose of the visit was. However, later when Andy messaged me, his motives became apparent. It read, "I need people like you, as too much for my two shoulders right now, but these guys crucial for the case, if they want they can find all the evidence without anyone knowing as the Thais have weakness they cannot speak Myanmar language and these guys can run circles around the Thais, but they really need our help to strengthen their community".

I had no idea if these rather poor-looking Burmese in their little temple could solve the case and save the B2 or not, but it seemed unlikely. They were obviously having a rough time in Thailand, had little or nothing in the way of personal possessions, and looked as if they would have trouble talking their way out of a brown paper bag. But stranger things happen and if they could find intelligence that could help the B2, I was all for it. My main impression of the Burmese community was that they could use all of the help they could get. I had no way to raise more funds to help their obviously dire financial situation. It was taking me all my time to find enough funding to keep the B2 in food and water, but I did want to help this friendly little community who had made such a huge impression on me.

Andy was really happy that I had made a connection with the Burmese and told me the community had been very happy to meet me and had said they had felt very hopeful now they had connected with Andy and me. He gave me the phone numbers of two of the community elders one of whom spoke excellent English. His name was Koh Zaw Tuu.

Andy's next message perplexed me: "If you anything significant to them need to check their banking and finance system first check it's strong and reliable". I knew what this garbled message meant. He wanted me to ensure any funds I gave them was spent on what it was intended and did not simply disappear into the mist. I assured Andy that this would not be an issue as I had no intention of giving them money as all of the funds I raised would be used to help the B2. I did, however, tell him that I would send them a gift to thank them for being such excellent hosts. His reply was, "It's a great idea, they were eagerly asking me it's really true you will help them or not. They really look up to foreigners to help them, we need to use our experience to empower them to fight themselves however. But they so scared, we can start by educating them and helping them cover the cost of funerals". I discovered that funeral costs are a huge issue for the Burmese. Many died in industrial accidents with alarming regularity and often did not enjoy good health. Most Burmese also earned far too little to ever consider having any savings so a funeral could be a huge problem. For them not respecting their dead was out of the question.

With no funds to give to the Burmese community, I pondered how I could help them and discussed the matter with another Brit who also happened to be an English teacher. We decided to offer the Burmese community free English lessons, something Andy later took full credit for even though he had absolutely nothing to do with it. My English teaching friend had been working at an international school that had just shut down. As luck would have it, the owner agreed to let us donate all of the educational materials to the Burmese community. I messaged Andy on the 26th of October 2014, at 11 a.m. to tell him. He told me he had just got in after swimming for hours and hours in the ocean. Not for the first time I felt my eyes going north in their sockets.

CHAPTER 22 - CSI LA STILL HARD AT WORK

CSI LA was still hard at work and clearly, from his posts on his FB platform, had some contacts in Thailand and possibly Koh Tao. He posted that he had some more intelligence from the islands.

Convinced the perpetrators of the Witheridge and Miller murders were a group that included Montriwat and Nomsod Toovichien he posted "The gangs on Koh Toa move in 2 groups. The first group fled to Chumpon (A town on the mainland almost directly west of Koh Tao). Nomsod hired a speedboat. The boat has a short name and is red and white. It is thought Nomsod took the privately hired boat to either Nakhon Si Thamartat or Surat Thani (both south of Chumphon)". He also said that another trusted source suggested that one group made their escape via Phangan the next island to Koh Tao and then onto Kanom, a coastal town on the mainland. He later found out that the name of the speedboat Nomsod hired was called Little Duck. He suggested that Nomsod disembarked at Konom and headed to Nakorn Si Thammarat airport, a small, quiet airport where he would attract very little, if any, attention. I had no idea if this information was correct. However, I had seen photographs of men on Koh Tao posing with guns on social media. In his article on the 6th December 2014, Scottish journalist Andrew Drummond shared those images in an article on his online news publication.

On the 27th of October 2014, Andy told me the socks and sweat bands I brought for the boys had yet to reach them. More of a worry was that the prison officials had told him that the Myanmar embassy had requested a ban on any further visits by Andy and his team or any other outsiders.

Andy was back off to Bangkok, so for a while would not need the room at my friend's hotel. He asked me if I could buy a gift for my friend to say thank you while he was away as he and Sar had forgotten. He then gave me the contact details for his lawyer in case he ended up in jail.

Andy's problems with Natural Fruit started in early 2013. The Natural Fruit Company, also called 'Natfruit' is a privately owned Thai fruit wholesaler who specialized in the production of pineapples. It was established on 17th of March 2001, to manufacture canned pineapple and pineapple juice concentrate. The company has a factory that has a production capacity of 400 tons of raw material per day and employs a workforce of between 500–800, many of them Burmese migrant workers. Concerned that the Burmese workforce was being exploited, Andy was employed by Finnwatch, a Finnish civic organization focused on global corporate responsibility. It seeks to promote ecologically, socially, or economically responsible business by engaging companies in economic regulation and public discussion.

Andy produced a report called "Cheap Has a High Price". In the report Andy said that some of the workers, who were undocumented migrants, had reported poor working conditions, unlawfully low wages, confiscation of official documents, use of child labor, and excessive overtime. This report promoted Natural Fruit to bring four cases against Andy for defamation and computer crimes. However, many international human rights organizations and trade unions as well as UN agencies and the European Parliament and the European Trade Commissioner have condemned Natural Fruit's actions as judicial harassment and an attempt to silence Andy and called for the cases to be dropped. Andy was off to Bangkok to attend two court appointments. The first appointment was at the Prakanong Provincial Court on the 29th of October 2014, when the judgment in his first criminal defamation trial was handed down. Andy was acquitted on a technicality, avoiding a possible jail sentence.

The second appointment, on the 30th of October 2014, was at the Nakhon Pathom Provincial Court. This also happened to be his birthday. This was the larger of the two civil actions against him. It was called a 'meditation conference' or 'conciliation conference' and is part of the pretrial process in Thai civil courts. The Natural Fruit Company was claiming damages of approximately US$10,000,000.00 for submitting his report to Finnwatch who published a report based on Andy's findings on their website. This case could also result in a 7-year prison sentence.

As Andy was heading off to Bangkok, the press was now reporting that the police were looking into footprints found next to Hannah's body. CSI LA published crime scene photos that showed there were no footprints next to her body. It is curious how there could have been as the crime scene photos of her body showed very clearly that the tide had been in and had subsequently gone out again.

On the 29th of October 2014, CSI LA published copies of both Nomsod and Montriwat's ID cards. He also made it public that Police General Somyot, now in charge of the investigation and his wife had purchased 7.5 million and 2.5 million shares from a company called WAT worth 270 million Thai baht and 2.5 million Thai baht respectively. In Britain it was worth over seven million pounds.

The headline news in the *Thai Rath* on this day was that Worapan Toovichien, the father of Nomsod was to sue CSI LA.

On that same day, CSI LA had surmised that Wai Phyo was too short to be the running man on the police released CCTV. It was a busy day for Nomsod, too. In an effort to clear his name, Nomsod took a DNA test that was televised on national TV. The test came back negative a day later. However, there were many questions about the "test" including where it was tested and how it came back so quickly. According to dna-worldwide.com the results of DNA tests in Bangkok take 3-5 business days to come back. The police never revealed where the sample was tested, nor did they ever show journalists the paperwork ascertaining to the results.

CSI LA had hoped that Scotland Yard would conduct the test. He also hoped that CCTV footage from the AC Bar would be released, and that Scotland Yard would ask Nomsod to take a lie detector test.

On the 1st of November 2014, CSI LA had noticed that both Wai Phyo and Zaw Lin wore a lot of wrist bands that could be clearly seen on the photos on the day they got arrested and on the day they were forced to do the macabre reconstruction on Sairee Beach. The running man shown on CCTV running away from the crime scene, had nothing on his wrists.

Andy contacted me to tell me he was heading back to Samui on the 5th of November 2014. He had asked me to appeal for help from the Rotary on Samui. Andy was not interested in giving them the formal presentation I had suggested because they thought his highly publicized issues with Natural Fruit would put them off.

On the 4th of November 2014, CSI LA posted some observations sent to him by a follower of his page. The contributor suggested that the Thai people deserved better governance and a more 'just' system and went on state that he found the media coverage of Nomsod taking a DNA test baffling. He pointed out that Worapan had made a public statement that the DNA test had cleared his son, but no mention had been made about how the test had cleared him or who else, other than Worapan, had access to the results.

He pointed out that the physical evidence the police had was taken from an unsecured crime scene that hung around for two days before any forensic investigation team arrived. The police had publicly stated that Nomsod's DNA would not be part of the investigation. If Nomsod's DNA did not match that at the crime scene this would suggest that the Toovichien family had access to the DNA from the crime scene and this was highly irregular, and could suggest the family had conducted private DNA testing.

Early on in the investigations, the Thai police had confirmed they did not have labs certified to conduct criminal DNA analysis; only to conduct paternity tests. This left a huge gap in the legitimacy of the labs clearing his son of the Koh Tao murders. The press reported that four hospitals were involved in clearing Nomsod's name but made no mention of the chain of custody of the samples tested. The man who had posted on the CSI LA Facebook page said, "I am hoping for Mr. Toovichien to publicly release the documented testing results which explain the procedures used and how it is determined that there is no DNA match. All I am hoping for is that his son will be properly cleared if he is in fact innocent of involvement. I am sure that he also wants to remove any remaining doubts. That is surely why he had these very public tests conducted in the first place"

On the 5th of November 2014, protests took place around Australia proclaiming the innocence of the B2 and protestors demanded a fair trial.

CSI LA asked his followers to brainstorm some points about the investigation such as where the blonde hair Hanna had in her hand had come from as neither of the B2 had blonde hair, why a pancake seller was used as a translator, and if he was either qualified or trustworthy enough to be given that task. Another point pertained to why the B2 had not been questioned sooner when they admitted they had been playing guitar and singing on the beach on the night of the murders and it had been weeks before they were considered prime suspects; they had no blood on their clothes that had not been DNA tested. The point about the pancake seller being used as a translator interested me so I decided to investigate. I knew exactly where I could go to get some information.

CHAPTER 23 – THE PANCAKE MAFIA

The Burmese lessons we promised to give were now taking place once or twice a week at the tiny Burmese temple that was overshadowed by the large gleaming Thai Buddhist temple next to it. During our visits, I had got to know the Burmese students pretty well and found them to be quite friendly. Ko Zaw Tuu, who Andy had got me to exchange numbers with on our first visit, became a good friend of mine. He was a leader in his community and spoke excellent English. We had quite a lot in common. Although we both came from different corners of the globe, both of our respective communities often felt marginalized by the Thai people. Koh Zaw Tuu was a keen political thinker and gave me a great insight into the problems in Myanmar and how most of the citizens had been happy under British occupation.

I had developed some good relationships and a good degree of trust within the Burmese community. On one visit, I took a photo of a Rohingya translator for the B2 during their arrests to see what I could find out about him. My students recognized him immediately. They told me his name was Kamal and informed me that I must be very careful of him. The students told me that he was a very dangerous man and the head of the pancake mafia. Pancake mafia? At first, I thought I had misheard, but no, he really was head of what locals refer to as the pancake mafia. It turned out that this man had a small food truck propelled by a motorbike in Koh Tao from which he sold roti, as well as pancakes. I never discovered any kind of mafia connections for this man, but I did discover that there are many hundreds of these pancake trucks on the island who sell sweet and savory pancakes as street vendors.

Karmal was in charge of all of them and took 2,000 baht a month (about £40) from each of them on Koh Tao, Koh Phangan, and Koh Samui. I was pretty shocked. I started to look into this and spent many evenings driving around Koh Samui accosting any pancake vendor I could find and quizzing them about this guy. It turned out that, without exception, he was known to all of them. I unwittingly discovered the man did not speak fluent Thai, a fact I heavily disputed until I saw him testify in court months later only with the aid of a translator. How on earth was this man who did not speak Thai with a century-old grudge against Arakine state citizens end up being the translator for the B2 when they were arrested and interrogated, without, I might add, any legal representation.

On my next prison visit to Zaw Lin and Wai Phyo, I asked Zaw Lin what the police had told him on his arrest and subsequent torture. He said they had told him to plead guilty and that if he did, he would only serve two or three years in prison. I asked him if he had been offered any money to plead guilty, but he seemed to not understand and told me what had happened to him when he refused to admit he even knew Hannah and David, let alone brutally murder them. Zaw Lin told me that he had been kept in an air-conditioned room naked for three days. This may not seem like much in the way of torture to anybody who has not grown up in a country that barely drops below 38 degrees Celsius and has on average a 100% humidity rate. Believe me; I spent many a night shivering during rainy season when it dropped below 25 degrees Celsius. You really get used to intense heat and feel it when, in rainy season, it gets cold. He went on to tell me they had put plastic bags over his head which prevented him from breathing. They told him they would tie him onto a burning car tire and threatened to cut off his arms and legs and throw him into the ocean. He also told him they hit him in a way he was amazed did not result in bruises. He told me they had done the same to Wai Phyo as well as spending a great deal of time pinging his testicles. He confirmed he had no legal representation during his police interrogation and was relying on a translator who did not speak Thai or the B2's dialect of Burmese. It is interesting to note that, during the interrogation, no formal arrests had been made and the B2 were, at that time, simply helping the police with their enquiries.

I asked Zaw Lin if he had ever met Hannah and David. He told me no. The first time he set eyes on them was when he saw them in the news and in the newspapers and he felt very sorry for what had happened to them. I asked him if he had any idea who had killed them. He said no, but had been told on Koh Tao, by both Thai and Burmese nationals, that it was the mafia. He went on to tell me that he wanted to go home and did not want to stay in prison. However, he said he would have been more than happy to stay there if he had indeed committed the crime.

Prison visits were long affairs. It took me around an hour to drive to the prison from my house. Once at the prison I would have to hang about waiting for the office to open along with about 100 other visitors. We waited in a hot and stuffy room that had a few fans, a TV, and a cupboard housing a rather smelly example of the 'food' that was being served to the prisoners that day. Once the office opened, we would have to queue up for about half an hour to get a form to fill in stating who we were, our passport numbers, and who we wanted to visit. Once filled in, this form was handed in and then we spent up to 90 minutes waiting for it to be processed and then we were given a number on a colored card. We then had to wait for up to 2 hours for visits to take place 20 prisoners at a time until our number and color were called. The visits themselves were 15 minutes long. During our visits, the B2 told me what they needed from the tuck shop. Water was high on the list as it could be traded for other goods. I always brought them a lot of fruit it would have been impossible for them to consume before it went bad to ensure they had to share with other inmates who would in turn take care of them and also share food.

CHAPTER 24 - AND ON IT GOES

The B2's next hearing was on the 7th of November 2014. At this stage, the public prosecutor had still not taken the case. Even though logic told me there was no way the B2 would walk free, I still hoped in the back of my mind that there could be some miracle about to happen, or, perhaps, the public prosecutor would see that the evidence in the case was not sufficient to secure a verdict. I asked Andy if he thought it was possible. He said no.

Andy visited the B2 the day prior to the hearing with six members of his legal team. He thought the visit had been very successful. The team had spent six hours in the prison. Three legal representatives went through the case with each of the B2. Andy relayed that the B2 felt happy and confident. I was completely baffled as to why they felt confident and could only assume they had no idea how corrupt the islands were, let alone the police and the courts. I started to make enquiries of my own as to why the B2 were still being detained when the prosecutor had yet to decide if he would take the prosecution's case.

Predictably the B2 were not released on the 7th of November, and were once again remanded for another 12 days. I decided to go to the next hearing so I could be close to the B2 and try to offer them some sort of emotional support. Being in court gave me the opportunity to give them a hug before the judges arrived in the courtroom. I knew how scared and upset the B2 were and how much they missed their mothers, who are about my age, so I felt some sort of physical contact was vitally important. I was becoming more and more attached to the tiny B2 with their scared but hopeful eyes and utter naivety of the charges they were facing. I started to feel responsible for them as well as outraged at the utterly corrupt system.

I started to think ahead, wondering if it was time to think of alternative methods of securing the B2's freedom. Anything is available for a price in Thailand; I asked Andy if he would be willing to save the B2 by less than legitimate means and, he refused to discuss it.

On the 8th of November 2014, Andy told me he was looking for witnesses on Koh Tao among the Burmese community there, but none seemed to want to come forward. He asked me if I had any ideas of how this could be accomplished. He seemed incredulous that nobody on Koh Tao was willing to talk. I did not find it hard to understand at all. By now it was fairly obvious to anybody who had anything to do with Koh Tao that it was highly unlikely the B2 had committed these crimes. Suspicion had never got too far from the influential and powerful local family that nobody in their right mind would testify against, let alone other hapless Burmese migrant workers watching their fellow countrymen have their lives destroyed. I tried to explain this concept to Andy who told me that he was happy to find the means to relocate anybody who did want to come forward, as they would certainly have to leave Koh Tao and Thailand if they had even a modicum of sense. This did not seem to me to be a very tempting prospect for a potential witness, as their entire motivation for being exploited on low wages in Thailand was to provide an income for their families back in Burma where wages were even lower and jobs harder to come by. Should they agree to testify that income would be lost, and that is if they even got out alive once they had been seen in court testifying. Andy could not understand why local Burmese would not take this kind of risk. I couldn't understand how anyone with a reasonable amount of intelligence or any understanding of the islands whatsoever could fail to see why nobody was going to take him up on his offer.

CHAPTER 25 – MORE QUESTIONS THAN ANSWERS

While Andy was seemingly getting nowhere with his investigations, CSI LA David was still hard at work. I mentioned the CSI LA investigations to Andy who said he was aware of the Facebook page and had sent a lot of the information from it to the B2's lawyers. Rather than solely spending his time focusing on the B2's case, Andy had been taking time out to organize a protest on behalf of abused migrant workers in Thailand, a project that now appeared to be his main focus. He asked me to raise some money for this enterprise as he was too busy to fundraise as well as rallying around for people to join him on his mission. I had made progress tracking down the interpreter, Kamal, and gave Andy his number. I also made progress with the Rotary, who, although unable to donate cash for the Burmese community, kindly offered to donate goods for a 'bring and buy sale'. They suggested the Burmese community organize this event themselves. I relayed this information to Andy expecting him to be pleased but instead he asked me if the Rotary would be interested in funding transport for his upcoming protest. He asked me to inform them that it was simply a solidarity walk and nothing illegal. Although Andy was requesting funds for transport, he was unable to provide any information about who he would be transporting. His reason for this was that he didn't want anyone to know who was going to march. I declined to help.

On the 11th of November 2014 Andy told me he had been busy sending emails to the mainstream media in the UK requesting assistance to contact the victims' relatives and asking for any witnesses to come forward. I thought it was highly unlikely that the relatives of Hannah Witheridge and David Miller would want to speak to the press. I decided to track down the police liaison officers dealing with the victims' families. I managed to contact the officer dealing with the Witheridge family but not the Millers. I mentioned this to Andy who asked me to tell the officer that he wanted to speak to her, but only, he said, to give her information about the situation and not to suggest the guilt or innocence of the B2. He said he understood if the liaison officers did not want to help him but asked me to pass his name on and do my best for the B2. He reiterated to me that he did not want to say who was right or wrong and his motivation for speaking to the families of Hannah and David was to ensure a fair trial. Andy said he would be more than happy to fly to the UK to facilitate a meeting with the victims' families because he was prepared to do anything to save the B2 from the death penalty. Andy said that as the B2 had retracted their confessions and were pleading not guilty they would face a harsh penalty if found guilty and he did not trust the Embassy or Honorary Consuls as their main concern was diplomatic relations and trade. Worryingly, Andy said that he was sorry fewer people were coming forward to help the B2, but he was sure there were angels out there and he prayed for them to arrive every day. I wondered how many other lawyers relied on angels for the outcome of high-profile capital murder trials.

While Andy felt it irrational of the families of the victims not to wish to talk to him, I felt it was Andy who was being irrational. Not everyone was impressed by Andy as he surmised.

I reached out to Jill Smith, the 'significant other' of one of the Metropolitan police officers who had come to

Thailand to investigate, or rather observe, as all they had been given was observational status. She was also one of the liaison officers in the UK. I had a long conversation with her on the phone during which she seemed genuinely concerned about the plight of the B2. She told me that she was interested in the B2 getting a fair trial and would stay in touch. We decided, as my involvement in the case in any capacity other than raising funds could be dangerous for me, we would communicate in code by email. I had previously worked part-time as a wedding coordinator so we set up the emails to look as if we were old friends and I was organizing a wedding on the island that I had hoped she and her friends could attend. In one email she said that she hoped her friends, "Would be made welcome".

I asked Andy if he had asked his lawyer to find a criminal psychologist as I knew this would be pivotal to the boys' defense. The kind of person who would be capable of committing a crime so foul was not, to my mind, the two men who I had met in the court and continued to visit in jail. Andy said he would try. I cannot say whether he bothered to try or not but to the best of my knowledge nobody of that ilk was ever consulted. Criminal profiling is pivotal in cases like these, but not, so it seems, in Thailand. One thing that had struck me throughout this entire process is that nobody ever seemed to come up with any reason why anyone would commit crimes of this magnitude on a paradise holiday island, let alone the hapless B2, who had no prior convictions or criminal history.

Later that day, Andy reiterated he needed witnesses, he said the crux of the matter was not who knew what, but who was prepared to come forward and stand up during the trial. I offered to do an interview with Andy in the *Samui Times*, asking for witnesses to come forward.

Andy continued to impress upon me how important it was for him to be in touch with the families of Hannah Witheridge and David Miller. As he had made no headway into achieving that, I spent a lot of time trying to track them down via Facebook. I found the Facebook page of Sue Witheridge, the mother of Hannah, but after sending the link to Andy, he told me it had been disabled. I wondered just how many people would be contacting the family now, for both good and bad reasons. Andy pressured me to find contact information for the victims' families via the honorary consul on Samui at the time, who was a friend of mine. I found this rather odd. Andy said he was a lawyer, so surely, he must have known that while it is pretty easy to get any information out of a Thai in a position of authority if you had the right connections, getting it out of a British Honorary Consul would represent somewhat more of a challenge.

After several rounds of correspondence with Jill Smith from the Norfolk Constabulary, I decided to stop playing the wedding planning game with her and sent her this email.

Hi Jill,

How are you? Hope all is good your end.

Jill, I have been working closely with Andy Hall. You may have seen him in the news recently. He is a human rights activist who has done a great job in raising money and getting legal representation for the two Burmese boys who stand accused of the murders in Koh Tao.

Andy has asked me to help him get a message to the parents of the victims and I wondered if there was any way you could help.

Andy strongly believes that the parents of the victims should know the situation of the accused. He does not wish to proclaim their innocence or their guilt, only to ensure that the victims' parents are aware of the situation. He fully understands if they do not wish to know but he feels that it is important that there is transparency for them. We are under the impression that the Embassy have possibly told them not to get involved, and we are not sure if they are aware that by law in Thailand they can be joint plaintiffs in the case and have some input into the outcome. I know in the UK that criminal cases are tried by the CPS and not relatives, it's a little different here.

Andy, and our team here really want to ensure that justice is done for Hannah and David and we want to ensure that their parents are getting the correct information with regards to the case here.

Would it be possible for him to talk to the family liaison officer perhaps? He could then explain why he feels this is so important.

Warm regards, hope your friends had a useful and meaningful holiday!

Su

xx

In the meantime, the friend who had helped me teach English to the Burmese community at their temple in Chaweng was researching the case. She called round to my house to tell me that she had found a friend on Koh Tao who said she had some information. However, like everybody on Koh Tao, she feared for her life if she came forward. I told Andy who asked me to press this girl as a possible witness. I asked Andy what sort of information he would like us to get from the girl in Koh Tao. He said, "We want to know if Hannah was verbally or sexually abused in the bars that night". There was a lot of talk about Hannah having an altercation in the AC bar on the night she died, on the islands and in the press. Passages in an article published on the 21st of September 2014, in the *Daily Mail*, written by Jennifer Smith for *Mail Online* and Ben Ellery in Koh Tao, Thailand for the *Mail* on Sunday read "British backpackers Hannah Witheridge and David Miller may have been arguing with a local gangster when they were brutally murdered in Thailand last week, it has been suggested". And "Police revealed they were investigating rumours the pair had argued with a man in a bar before they were killed". Interestingly the article touched on the darker side of Koh Tao. "But residents today said they were hesitant to speak out against local suspects as the island has an 'underbelly' of violent crime and no one is talking. People are afraid".

We had not got any concrete evidence about the altercation. I passed this information back to my English teaching friend and she asked the girl on Koh Tao who told her that Hannah's drink had been spiked with rohypnol and she was all over the place and people thought she was "pissed out of her mind". Andy asked me how the girl could know this. I wondered too. I had to assume she had been there and seen what went on and got to chatting with others about it.

On the 12th of November 2014, Andy went to visit the B2 in prison. On the same day we got a response from the girl on Koh Tao with regards to whether or not she was prepared to speak to Andy. The response read, "I really don't know why you think I have any information that will help. I guess it would depend on the questions he asked as to whether I can add to what he's got. I'm frightened but I trust you that it would be confidential. I was at bar with Hannah and David for 5 mins then I left….. it's only what I know about AC Bar staff that could help. OK I'll do it, but ONLY if it means I am not involved ANY MORE".

Although this was not the most encouraging lead it was the only one we had so I got Andy to call the girl. After he had spoken to her, he sent me this message, "Suzanne I quite confused. You mentioned about Hannah being drunk or date rape drug from this girl we spoke tonight, but this girl said she never saw Hannah and didn't know anything about Hannah, Am I confused".

My English teacher friend asked the girl why she had clammed up. It turned out the girl said she did have this information but was not prepared to share this information with Andy. I wondered if he had told her he could relocate her, as he had suggested he could do with Burmese migrant workers if they decided to testify. I wished he had got more information out of her but whatever went on during his conversation with her no more information was forthcoming.

We started to try to piece a bit more together about the B2. We discovered that Zaw Lin had been working at Brother Bar on Sairee Beach prior to his arrest and that Wai Phyo had been working at the Safety Stop Bar in the main town of Mae Haad. Neither were owned or run by the island's influential families. The *BBC* ran a story saying that on the 6th of January 2015 there would be a full inquest into Hannah's death. By this stage, a vigil had been held for Hannah and David on Koh Tao. Andy was totally unaware of the news about the inquest. After I told him, he said he had sent a request to the embassy for more information.

One of the main pieces of prosecution evidence was a cigarette butt found on the beach. I asked Andy if the boys smoked, as this was rather key to the investigation. Andy's response once again surprised me, "I'm not sure, I didn't ask, but I heard the DNA matches from cigarettes so I guess lawyers will investigate".

I was having serious conversations with myself as to what sort of lawyer/investigator Andy was; I told Andy it was vital to find out if the boys smoked and if so, what brand of cigarettes. He replied, "I am under lots of pressure now with my other work and case on Monday, sometimes too much pressure".

What kind of pressure would prevent you from asking the B2 if they smoked when a cigarette butt that could contain the DNA of the killers was pivotal and could be the difference between life and death for the B2?

As any hopes of the B2 getting bail were fading, the need to keep raising funds for them continued to be a priority. Most of my friends and contacts knew of my involvement in the Koh Tao case, and with many contacts locally and around the world on my own personal Facebook page, I decided it was a good platform from which to reach out and ask for donations. I got word from a staff member at my friend's hotel where Andy stayed that he was not at all happy about me using my own social media platform to raise money. My relationship with Andy had long been on rocky ground but as he was my only connection to the legal team and the case, I decided to keep him happy and take the posts down.

Andy contacted me to ask me why I had removed the posts, so I told him. He said that it was not a case of him being not happy, he was concerned for my safety as I lived on the island. He said people stayed away from him, so he did not have to be so careful. He went on to say that my posts had succeeded in raising more funds.

I told him that he need not worry about my safety as all I was doing was raising funds to assure a fair trial and not publishing any of my own personal thoughts about what went on that night. Before making the appeal in my own name I had already approached locals who were in with the mafia and local police and asked them if raising funds would land me in hot water and had been assured it would not. Looking back this could have been because the outcome of the trial had already been decided.

On the 14th of November 2014, I contacted the owner of the CSI LA Facebook page, who told me that he was working hard with the legal team and told me that in his opinion the police did not have enough evidence to convict the B2. Andy said, "I am not so sure what he said. If they didn't have enough evidence they would release the guys, so obviously if they didn't have evidence they must be trying to find more".

The CSI LA Facebook page had produced plenty of evidence to suggest the B2 were not guilty. I hoped the lawyers were taking it all in and documenting it. I put the question to Andy who told me he understood from the lawyers that CSI LA David had not been in contact with the lawyers. I found it hard to believe CSI LA David would be telling me he was in contact with lawyers if he was not. He had certainly invested a huge amount of time and energy into investigating the crimes. I decided a more likely scenario was that Andy had either not bothered to ask the question or the legal team were not telling him as much as he liked to think they were.

Jill Smith from the Norfolk Constabulary got back to me by email. I told Andy the response from them had not been great and they had basically told me to sod off. In her response, she thanked me for my email and said that she was aware that human rights groups were involved with the accused. However, this was not something the police could get involved with at all. She told me the family were fully aware of what their rights are in Thai law and would make their own decision in respect of that.

She went on to say that due to the suspicion raised about accusations made and the detainment of the two Burmese men, the British Police were tasked with attending Thailand and reviewing the processes and action taken by the Thai authorities and how they came to focus their investigation on the two men in question. She said this review had been done thoroughly over a period of three weeks and the Thai police co-operated fully throughout. She said the full report compiled by the reviewing team would be made available to the British authorities and the families themselves in the first instance and that whether the report, or its conclusions only, would be promulgated further after that, would be a decision made at HM Government ministerial level. She ended by saying she hoped I understood that the police were unable to facilitate or pass on any information other than organizations unconnected and independent of the police in this matter to the family.

I was saddened but not surprised by the response.

When I visited Zaw Lin and Wai Phyo they often talked about their families. I told Andy I found it very moving to hear Zaw Lin tell me how his father had died, and he was desperate to be released from prison to care for and send money to his mother. Andy informed me that Zaw Lin's father had died a long time ago and his mother relied on the money he sent to her from his job in Koh Tao. Andy told me he wanted to give the letter I had received from the police in the UK to the media. I told him this was not possible as it was a private conversation between me and the UK police. Andy said it was interesting that the correspondence I got had gone into a lot more detail than the official response. Andy told me he was very confused that I was getting more information than he and his legal team.

I asked Andy if the B2 had entered Thailand with their own passports. He said the police had told him neither of the B2 had a passport.

I had been feverishly contacting people I used to know in Koh Tao. One friend, who I had not spoken to in years, told me that he remembered that at the time Mr. Ban was shot it was widely believed Mon from Buddha View had ordered the hit. He said he would happily testify to this. He had no proof that Mon from Buddha View was involved in the crime, so his testimony would have been useless. All I know for sure was that Mon from Buddha View left the island shortly after the killing and. According to my friends on Koh Tao, to this day has never returned.

An interesting article appeared in *The Nation* about the fact that one policeman, Maj General Paween Pongsirin, had been removed from the Koh Tao investigation due to public complaints about the bungling of the case. However, he had been brought back on the case by General Somyot Poompanmoung. Paween complained to the press about public criticism and warned that anyone posting false information online would be prosecuted in the criminal courts. This comment came about due to Nomod's public DNA test, having not been subjected to one by the police who initially said he was a prime suspect. Nomsod had claimed he was not on the island at the time of the murders but there was still a lot of speculation online about his actual whereabouts. Paween felt that Nomsod had subjected himself to a test due to public pressure and the public had no right to put pressure on anyone to do anything. Interestingly, the article also made mention of a British tourist who had taken a photograph of two men pestering Hannah shortly before her rape and murder, and one of the men had been identified as the bar manager, none other than Nomsod. The British tourist had later sought protection from the British Embassy after receiving death threats over the internet. The article pointed out that:

"The public has every right to point out lapses by the police in the investigation of homicide. A trained crime investigator takes nothing for granted. Since the bar manager, a close relative of the bar owner, was, (allegedly) groping and annoying the victim before her rape and murder, police could rightfully scrutinize him and other male relatives of his who were, or could have been, in the vicinity at the time of the murders. If the manager of the bar took a DNA test that ruled him out as a suspect in the rape, then the press failed to report it and the public is right in demanding he take the test".

Did police ever look into the death threats made against the British witness to trace their source? That might lead to the rapists and murderers. The press did not consider the possibility. They must not overlook it. The public must not be intimidated by an inept policeman who has no business in this matter. Somyot cannot provide a reasonable explanation for bringing back Paween to the case, especially to oversee it.

Piyapong Mahakan
Bangkok".

My own investigations turned up that a guy named Brian was the manager of Planet Scuba Diving and the owner of the Safety Stop pub where Wai Phyo worked. I had also got hold of the manager of Big Blue who said that he knew one person who could verify that the day after the murders Wai Phyo turned up to work as normal and was not displaying any signs of distress or acting out of character in anyway. I wondered how that would be possible if he had raped and brutally murdered a girl, and a man, the previous evening. I had also got hold of Chris Rayner at the BBC who said he would help us get an article out there to ask the travel companions of both Hannah and David to come forward. I also spoke to a friend of mine who lived for many years in Jersey who said he would be able to put me in touch with Chris Ware, one of David's travel companions.

While all of this was going on, there were rumblings that Koh Tao was getting very sick of being in the press over the murders of Hannah and David. It was common knowledge that the many of the locals wanted the B2 tried and convicted as soon as possible in the hope that the whole thing would die down and be forgotten and business would go back to normal.

Their prayers for the future of Koh Tao went unanswered and the island once again went under intense scrutiny when Swiss-born Hans Peter Suter went missing not long after the horrific murders of Hannah Witheridge and David Miller.

CHAPTER 26 - HANS PETER SUTER

Hans Peter Suter went missing from Koh Tao on the 8th of November 2014. He was last seen on Sairee Beach near Maya Bar. Unlike other missing tourists in the years to come, the news of his disappearance quickly made the press. I was very interested in the story of his disappearance for my publication and started to investigate.

Mr. Suter, it was reported, had gone snorkeling and never returned. The 44-year-old had just completed a Divemaster SCUBA Course. As an experienced scuba diving instructor myself, who has trained many divers to become Divemasters, the first professional diving qualification on the PADI ladder, I knew exactly what his training would have entailed. To qualify to take the Divemaster course a candidate must first complete a Rescue Diver course. To qualify to be a Rescue Diver, you must be able to rescue divers in trouble, get them out of the water, remove them from strong currents while giving them mouth to mouth, identify areas of danger in the water, and instruct divers accordingly. There are many rigorous physical scenarios that are played out in front of instructors and anyone who has got as far as being a Divemaster is very competent in the water and a very strong swimmer; so strong in fact they can get themselves through horrendous currents with an unconscious diver.

With this in mind, I found it highly unlikely that a man who had successfully completed his Divemaster course would run into any kind of trouble snorkeling off the shallow coast of Koh Tao on the side of the island that seldom has currents.

The *Bangkok Post* report said that "three days before he went missing, he was told by a doctor he should not swim because it could lead to blindness". As an experienced diver and a qualified Master Scuba Diver Trainer, it was hard for me to imagine what sort of condition this man had. It seemed rather more likely to me that he had a condition of the ear that would prevent him from diving. The report in the *Bangkok Post* went on to say that at the time the man went missing he was also suffering from stress and did not have any money.

You have to ask yourself where the *Bangkok Post* got this information. If they had access to tourists' and divers' bank accounts, I had never been made aware of it, but then, let's face it, anything is possible in Thailand AKA The Land of Smiles, the country expats sometimes referred to as The Land of Smiling Assassins.

According to the same report, the man had hired snorkel gear from a shop on the beach and left his passport and personal items there; however, he did not take a life jacket. This snippet of information I found very confusing. There is not a single diver in the entire world I have come across who does not own their own set of fins and mask, and I have never once seen any diver wearing a life jacket so it's hardly newsworthy that somebody who was proficient enough in the water to pass a Divemaster course did not think to bother with a life jacket. Every competent, qualified diver I have ever met would not be seen dead in one.

On the 11th of November 2014, a report in the *Bangkok Post* said a body had been found between Koh Tao and Koh Phangan. It would have been an obvious assumption to make that this body was that of the missing snorkeler, but no, it was later reported that it was not him. This really grabbed my interest; not only because we still had no idea where Hans Peter was, but who did the body that had been found belong to? In order for the press to consider that it might be Hans Peter it would, quite obviously, have to be Caucasian and approximately Hans Peter's size and age.

I made several calls to the marine police, the local police, and PADI, but no information as to who the dead body belonged to was ever released. The grisly discovery of the dead body was never mentioned again.

I thought perhaps the mystery of the whereabouts of Hans Peter was solved when a second body was found a few days later floating off the coast of the mainland at Kanom. These remains also belonged to a Caucasian but disturbingly also did not belong to Hans Peter either. I never did find out who the second set of human remains belonged to despite more phone calls to the authorities to try to establish its identity. Like the first set of remains nothing was ever mentioned about them again by the press or the authorities.

On the 18th of November 2014, a third body washed up, this time it was off the coast of Chumpon, in the Lang Suan district north of Surat Thani on the mainland. This time it was Hans Peter Suter. Reports said that he drowned. The Lamare police station said that villagers had found his body on Lamare Beach. All identifications on the dead body matched those being given earlier to the police in Koh Phangan. According to a report in the *Chaing Ria Times*, those identifications included a tattoo on his back, a gold tooth on his upper jaw, orange shorts, and black shoes. His body was sent to Surat Thani hospital for forensic examination. His friend Michael Phillip Klissing was sent to identify his body. No further news was ever released. Later it was speculated that from where Hans Peter was located on Koh Tao he could well have witnessed Nomsod leaving the island on the boat, Little Duck, on the morning of the Hannah and David murders, and he was not the only person who had a vantage point who ended up dead.

CHAPTER 27 - THE SEARCH FOR EVIDENCE CONTINUES

As the case, and our search for evidence, continued so did rumors that I was going to be bumped off or was at least in grave danger. Andy told me there was no way he, or I, could be bumped off for helping the Burmese. "They don't just bump people off these days. Even a Swiss snorkeler goes missing it's headline news". But the other bodies were never named in the news or even spoken of. His apparent words of reassurance did nothing to quell my fears of what might happen to anyone helping the Burmese. As time went on, my fears hit fever pitch as dead tourists and Koh Tao made headline news around the world with alarming regularity and in 2021, at the time of writing this book, it is still happening.

By the 13th of November 2014 CSI LA had made a lot of progress analyzing the wounds David had sustained. He had theorized that in all likelihood they would have been caused by a punch knife. CSI LA posted a lot of photographic evidence of knives, wounds, and David's wounds that seemed to support this theory.

By the 16th of November 2014, there was still no sign of Wai Phyo and Zaw Lin being released. This was the fifth time they had been to court only to be sent back to the Samui Provincial Prison. At this stage in the game, by Thai law, they could only be held for a further 35 days if they found sufficient evidence and the public prosecutor decided to take the case. In the meantime, human rights lawyers from human rights groups including Amnesty International were requesting the men be released as they believed them to be innocent.

On the 20th of November 2014, it was reported by *The Guardian* in the UK, a paper that I knew Andy Hall was working closely with, that the B2 had appealed to the families of both Hannah and David. It read:

"Two Burmese men detained in Thailand for allegedly killing the British backpackers Hannah Witheridge and David Miller have told the Guardian they are innocent and have appealed to the victims' families and the UK government to help them clear their names.

In their first media interview since being arrested almost eight weeks ago Zaw Lin and Wai Phyo, both 21, stressed their sorrow over the deaths of the Britons, whose battered bodies were found on the beach on the holiday island of Koh Tao on 15th September. But they said they were not involved and asked UK authorities to share with their lawyers the results of the Metropolitan police review of Thai investigation.

The pair described their shock at being accused, and their concerns for their parents in Burma, who were reliant on the men's earnings from bar work on Koh Tao.

The pair, who were arrested a fortnight after the double murder and face possible death penalty, passed The Guardian *an open letter addressed to the victims' parents.*

Handwritten in Burmese, and with their names signed in English, it reads "We are really distraught about the loss of your children, and we share your grief. But we want to stress to you that we didn't do anything wrong and this crime has nothing to do with us.

In order that the truth can be revealed, we want to ask for help from all of you to ensure that we get access to information that the British government has. We would like this information to be shared with our lawyers so the truth can come out. We really want to express our thanks for your help".

On the 21st of November 2014, CSI LA posted "A Thai judge on Thursday extended remand for the two Burmese men suspected of murdering two British tourists, but indicated that they may each apply for bail at a bond of 500,000 baht (US $1,500.00) I think it's time for us to act. However, let me talk to their lawyers first".

On the 23rd of November 2014, a picture was released to the press of a Thai police officer searching the ocean off of Koh Tao for clues. CSI LA asked, "If the hoe was the only murder weapon [as police had stated in a press release] why did this police diver have to search for other clues". He had a valid point.

On the 25th of November 2014, the following post appeared on the CSI LA Facebook page.

"Today I have talked to the Burmese translator and Thai lawyers. The lawyer told me that they are working together with the Burmese Consulate to bail these two boys out. According to the Thai lawyers, we can bail them out but it is up to the judge. He has to see the behavior of the boys and the nature of the crime. The bail amount will be higher than usual since they are foreigners. They need a bail bond man who can guarantee with money that those boys won't run away. The money will be give back to bail bond man if the boys don't run away. The Burmese translator told me that Mr. Khin Ang Mint, the Burmese Upper House Speaker, will bail these boys out. He has money which is donated from Burmese politicians".

I asked Andy if this was true. He didn't know. He said he would check.

The following day he told me, "Suzanne, the senior lawyer told me they authorized a very junior lawyer (24 years old) to liaise with CSI LA as they tried to engage lawyers a while now. That young girl is not authorized to say anything and apparently CSI LA has been asking for more information than been giving. It is confidential information for you, please don't share but as you asked, I investigated for you".

By the 25th of November 2014, Andy was in Yangon visiting the B2's families.

Absent from the island, Andy asked me to go to the court hearing on the 26th of November, the day we thought the B2 could get bail. I asked him who had the two-million-baht bail money we were told was required. Andy said he thought perhaps the Myanmar official had it. I found this a little vague as if they were my clients, I would make damn sure I knew who had the money. In the end, though, it didn't really matter who had it as bail was refused on the grounds that it was a maximum-security case. I asked Andy how he felt about bail being refused. He told me he did not feel anything; he didn't have any expectations, which was better in such a case. He went on to tell me that Myanmar did not really care about the two boys and never sent anyone to visit them or taken care of them. I pointed out that they did turn up to court with 2 million Thai baht. He said it was nothing to them, just bail money security that they would get back. Andy was due back to the island on the 27th of November 2014. My friend's hotel was booked up with no rooms available for him so I told him he and Sar could stay with me. Andy told me he didn't mind where he stayed, as long as it was free. He asked me to talk to my friend at the hotel. He said he was so busy in a meeting all day he had not had time to do anything. He said "I am OK as long as I don't have to think a lot". He went on to say "I am grateful for any support for this, sorry for inconvenient my disorganized mind, I almost at the end of my tether, too much pressure for me actually but I try to let it flow by and stay calm every day, my hair fall out surely soon". My faith in his competence continued to dwindle.

I went to visit the B2 on the 26th of November 2014. Wai Phyo had his prison uniform top embroidered with the words "Don't forget me" which I found endearing.

I found out later that day that Sar had not been to Myanmar with Andy, but rather had stayed at the hotel and by the 26th, of November 2014 had taken herself off to Koh Tao to talk to other Burmese migrant workers to see if she could unearth any information that might help the B2.

The owner of the hotel Andy had been staying at had confided in me that she was having money troubles. As much as she wanted to help Andy, as well as wanting to help the plight of the B2, it was going to be hard for her to continue to give him free accommodation. Especially on the run up to Christmas which, being high season, was a lucrative time of year.

Despite my previous misgivings, I suggested to Andy it might be an idea to contact the families of the victims and impress upon them how unlikely it was that the B2 would get a fair trial. We discussed the possibility of contacting a newspaper in Jersey to see if we could send out a direct public appeal to the parents of David Miller. Andy thought this was a good idea, but at that time seemed to be more interested in where I lived and whether it was a "public area with lots of people". Andy told me he would stay until the 1st or 2nd of December 2014.

Andy was due to arrive on Samui on the 27th of November 2014. He sent me several messages suggesting, or rather making excuses about why he would need to pop over to the hotel first. I was getting rather concerned that he would push his way back into a room and deny my friend income. He did just that. I asked him why he had done this when I had told him of my friend's financial problems. He simply said when he arrived many rooms had been available.

Sar was due back from Koh Tao the following day. Andy said he would pick her up and take her directly to the prison to visit with the B2. Sar had not visited Koh Tao alone. She had taken my English teacher friend with her. My English teacher friend had contacted me from Koh Tao to tell me that she and Sar had found a man who was a witness to the dreadful events of that night. They would be bringing him back to Koh Samui with them the following day. He would accompany them to the prison before the preparation of his witness statement which would begin back at the hotel.

This witness had been promised to be relocated in Thailand with a new identity and a new job. I was pretty hopeful that Sar and Andy had the sense to keep him very much undercover. However, I was slightly concerned that my English friend, who had gone along, was involved in hooking a witness off the island and hoped they would all disembark the ferry separately and ensure they were not followed. Andy clearly had the same concerns. His solution was that I should go to the pier and pick up Sar and the witness and take them directly to the prison that was located on the opposite end of the island. I should then drive back to the pier and pick up my English teaching friend and take her home, then go back to pick up Andy and some Burmese elders and take them to the prison. I was not sure what Andy was playing at, but he said that he was praying they all got off the island of Koh Tao safely. I asked Andy if he had any real reason to think they would not be OK. He said he was sure they would be fine. I decided that being seen ferrying all of these people around the island in my car was a mad idea, as well as being time consuming. I told Andy it would be better if they all got cabs.

Later that day, Andy sent me a message to say that the witness had visited the B2 in prison but the B2 had told Andy that everything the witness has said was untrue. From what little information I could glean from Andy it seemed that the witness had said he was on the beach with the B2 on the night in question and had been left alone there when they left. The B2 denied this. I asked Andy what he was going to do now. Unbelievably, he told me he had sent the hapless witness back to Koh Tao. Andy told me the guy was a bit of a 'Lady boy' and the boys did not like him. I asked Andy why the only star witness would lie, he said, "He said, he wanted to go to prison with them and he don't understand what happened why they ignore him, he want to tell the police he was there, who knows, rumors from beginning that the three guys arrested made some bond or deal involving money".

There were indeed rumors floating around the Burmese community that the B2 were taking the rap for money, so perhaps this 'witness' wanted to cash in on the act. Regardless of what sort of stupid idea that was, I thought it was even more stupid that he returned to Koh Tao.

While this was going on, a British witness came forward to say that her friend was with Hannah on Koh Tao. She also told us that the sister of Hannah, Laura Witheridge, had been in the hospital having brain surgery at the time of Hannah's death and any chance of us trying to speak to the Witheridge family with regards to ensuring the boys got a fair trial would fall on deaf ears as they wanted to be left alone to mourn. I could see that getting any kind of support from the families or the British public was going to be problematic as most people in the UK don't have much clue that the idea of a fair trial in Thailand was rather like the ideas of pigs flying. In fact, on my own Facebook page, several of my friends in the UK questioned why I was getting involved and asked why I did not simply let the police and the judges do their job.

The police in Thailand were about the most corrupt bunch of people I had ever met. One friend of mine had bought a moped from a policeman that still had its police badges on it. Later, this bike was stolen. With the badges, it was not really very hard to find once it had been reported to the police who, surprisingly, actually bothered to investigate and track it down. What was even more surprising was that once they had found the bike, already partly stripped down in readiness for resale, the police came back and said that in order to return the bike they would need to pay the thief around 100 pounds in order to compensate him for the time he had spent on it. While I know there are corrupt police in the UK, I am certain they don't pull tricks like this and would therefore find the bike incident utterly unbelievable. Getting the British public to believe what a joke the trial would be was not going to be easy. I assumed that most of the British public wouldn't even know there is no such thing as a jury in Thailand and all cases are decided by three, often corrupt, or bribed, judges.

At this stage, knowing what to do for the best was a complete conundrum. We needed the public on our side to put pressure on the Thai government to offer a fair trial. However, keeping the press out of this trial would ensure that they, the Thai people, could make the right decision behind closed doors without loss of face. It was impossible to find a way of putting pressure on Thailand without putting pressure on them in public.

As the editor of the *Samui Times*, I got calls from every news agency in the world just about and told all of them it was vital not to get too involved. I also refused to be quoted as my situation was very precarious. It was a delicate business getting the idea out there that the B2 were not guilty but in a way that did not annoy the Thai authorities, who in my opinion would be perfectly happy to execute them without a trial just to make a point.

CHAPTER 28 - PUBLIC PROSECUTOR TAKES THE CASE AND THE B2 WILL STAND TRIAL FOR RAPE AND MURDER

The CSI LA Facebook page was picking up speed. Administrator David was picking apart every bit of evidence that was making its way into the mainstream press and dissecting it within an inch of its life. The number of followers on that page reached over 700,000 and almost all of whom were in support of the fact that the Thai people had the wrong men. We knew there was a great deal of support out there.

I got disturbing news about the event that took place the day my English teaching friend and Sar arrived in Koh Samui with the witness who Andy sent back to Koh Tao. It seemed that when the boat docked, there were mafia and police on the pier, who had not only seen them disembark but had followed Andy to the prison. This worried me for many reasons, but not least that they would have had the license plate number of the hire car Andy was using that had been provided by my friend.

I relayed my fears to Andy. He told me he had managed to secure some kind of deal with my friend at her hotel at a reasonable rate. He was happy to return the car if I did not think it was safe for the owner to have it involved in a case. The case was now starting to grab the attention of not only the media, but the attention of the local corrupt police and mafia, who were clearly not impressed that the B2 had a team on the case and a few hundred thousand people calling them liars on Facebook.

I asked Andy if he really thought it had been a good, and safe, idea to send the witness back to Tao. He simply asked me not to mention it again and that the lawyers had passed a message on to him that none of this should be made public. Unsurprisingly, the witness was never heard from again.

Andy sent me the iconic picture of Mon and Pi Ched on the 28th of November 2014, and asked me which one was Montriwat and which one was the policeman. I was pretty astounded that as the head of the legal team he had not managed to figure that out for himself, especially at that stage in the game.

About this time, we discovered that the night before the murders of Hannah and David, a pair of British women were mugged by a Thai motorbike gang on Sairee Beach. I asked Andy if he or his lawyers were aware of this and if they had looked into it. They had not. I advised Andy to get the police reports that related to this attack.

On the 1st of December 2014, Andy told me he was going to the court hearing the following day then was flying to Malaysia. He told me Sar was going to Bangkok so neither would be able to visit the B2. He asked me to visit them. Oddly, he said, "If you could visit them during our absence it's great, but please just ask about their happiness and situation and not about the case or evidence or facts".

He told me he had put a lot of money into their accounts so they could buy bedding, food, and fruit. I wondered how he could possibly think the two accused had any happiness and asking about their situation seemed rather futile as it was hopeless. Andy messaged, "It's really great the boys can see people every day. For me, I felt sorry and sad cannot visit them every time but I had to do some other work also my life at this time. I told them I will think of them every day always and miss them, I would never forget them even

I am not there". I continued to wonder what Andy was actually doing for the case. He had not grasped many of the facts. He did not know who all the players were and had no information on the case being prepared by the legal team.

The following day was to be the sixth detention of the B2. Andy then confused me by telling me that he did not know if the B2 would remain detained in custody. The prosecutor still had not taken the case, but Andy had advised the B2 to plead guilty. I questioned his motive for this, he said, "Not guilty sorry". I remember thinking that I hoped he did not make that sort of mistake during the trial!

He went on, "Sorry a lot on right now, actually this is legal team issue, I cannot involve too much with them, now I just found the bail money two million was never submitted, its false news".

I suggested to Andy that as we were reaching a pivotal part of the B2's future (i.e., would they continue to be detained and if so on what grounds), I did not think it was a good time for Sar to be leaving as she was the only one who could translate for the B2. He said, "Lawyers team have to manage they will find a way. If they need they will surely call her back, please trust the lawyers, I give them space, if some error I am watching always".

I told Andy the last thing I would ever do in Thailand was trust lawyers and asked him if this team, the ones I was meant to trust but had never met, had ever tried a capital murder case before. He simply said, "We will manage, trust us please". I had never at this point trusted anybody less. With the possibility of the trial starting any day, I once again impressed upon Andy that Sar, the only translator, leaving would be stupid. He told me he could not speak and was off to a meeting. The following day I asked him again, as the trial could be held in the next week, if I should organize a new translator for the boys, he said no, the lawyers would take care of everything.

Before Andy left, I questioned him as to who would cover fuel costs for my visits to the B2 in his absence and who would fund the money going into their account as I had exhausted my donations. He said not to worry; he would cover fuels costs for me to go to the prison three times a week. He also said, "Please just be their friend, ask they happy or sad, what they want, I never discuss the case or witness or anything as want it to be relax and happy time, lawyers can deal with case". I was starting to wonder if Andy was seriously out of his mind. He had been visiting the B2 all this time and had never discussed the case with them? The lawyers, or rather Andy's lawyer had only visited the B2 once. We were under the impression the trial could start any day now and he had never asked them about the case? What could possibly be more important than asking them about the case, as in fact their lives depended on us knowing every last detail there was to know about the case. If my jaw had actually hit the floor, it would have shattered.

On the 1st of December 2014, Samui Public Prosecutors said they had enough evidence to prosecute the B2.

CSI LA reported, "Based on my observations of the wounds on Hannah's face, along with the results of my experiments, I believe Hannah was hit by a garden hoe at least three times. It took me at least 3 times to reproduce similar wounds on a whole chicken with the dull side of a small axe. So why didn't Hannah fight back or at least try to protect her face. The only logical explanation is that she must have been unconscious while she was being attacked. This is why I don't believe the B2 are the killers".

On the 2nd of December 2014, Andy sent me a link to a BBC article asking for the friends of Hannah and David to come forward as witnesses.

It read:

"The bodies of Hannah Witheridge and David Miller were found on a Thai beach on 15 September. Friends of

two British tourists killed in Thailand earlier this year are being urged to come forward as witnesses.

Nakhon Chompuchat, who is representing two Burmese men accused of the murder, said the victims' friends "Should know many things" about what happened.

Suspects Zaw Lin and Win Zaw Htun, both 21, are awaiting trial for the killings amid criticism of the police case.

The migrant workers from Myanmar - sometimes known as Burma – could face the death penalty if found guilty.

BBC south-east Asia correspondent Jonathan Head said prosecutors were ready to put the men on trial, two months after their arrest.

Under Thai law, suspects can be held for a maximum of 91 days before facing formal charges.

Our correspondent said: "Despite the claim by the Thai police that they have built a perfect case against the two Burmese defendants, the prosecutor has rejected the police dossier several times, saying it needed improving".

Officers in the country have been accused of poor collection of evidence, reluctance to investigate influential families on Koh Tao, and allegations they tortured the suspects to get confessions.

Mr. Chompuchat said he was appealing to any friends of Miss Witheridge, 23, from Hemsby or Mr. Miller, 24, from Jersey, who may have information to come forward.

"Their friends should know many things about this to prove the true situation", he said.

But the lawyer claimed witnesses were scared to come forward, adding that he had also requested information from a British police team which travelled to Thailand to observe the investigation, and from the British pathologists who examined the bodies after they were repatriated.

'Scapegoats'

Post-mortem examinations found Mr. Miller died from drowning and a blow to the head, while Miss Witheridge died from head wounds.

The two men accused of the killing are also charged with conspiracy to murder, conspiracy to rape and robbery.

Failure to seal off the crime scene after the killings and early claims by the police that no Thai person could have committed such a crime have attracted criticism.

Mr. Zaw's mother has said her son is being made a 'Scapegoat' by police and the case has been fixed".

In this article, the name Win Zaw Htun is used for Wai Phyo who goes by more than one name.

My English teaching friend, who had been to Koh Tao, was getting creepy messages from a guy who was friends with Andy on Facebook. I asked Andy repeatedly who this guy was. My requests for clarity fell on deaf ears. Andy and I had started to fall out and according to Andy this fact had not gone unnoticed by the B2. He told my English teaching friend that the B2 were distressed about this. How the B2 could possibly know what was going on beyond the walls of the Koh Samui Provincial Prison was beyond me.

The information I was getting from Wai Phyo was negligible. He had nothing to say about that night. He seemed incredibly reluctant to talk about what happened and who he was with and was very unwilling to give me any information that might help me investigate on his behalf.

By this time, I had decided to no longer heed any of Andy's advice about only asking the B2 if they were happy. I had lost all faith that the so-called 'defense team' were actually investigating or doing anything at all. I started to panic. Andy clearly had no clue what was going on and if he had indeed assembled a legal team who did not speak Burmese, it seemed to me the boys' lives were in great peril, and somebody had to do something.

With Wai Phyo speaking virtually no English, our conversations during prison visits were going nowhere beyond what he wanted me to get him from the tuck shop, how his football team was doing, and if he was coping. Zaw Lin had a rather better command of the English language, but it was still very sketchy. I managed to ask him what he was doing that night and persuade him to give me a thorough account of his movements so I could try to help him. During our conversations I asked him again whether or not he had ever met Hannah Witheridge or David Miller. He told me point blank he had never laid eyes on either of them.

Zaw Lin told me that he had been on the beach that night playing guitar with Wai Phyo but had not seen anything. It was in December that he told me he was told by the police that if he pleaded guilty then he would only spend two to three years in jail. He was happy when Andy came along and told him to plead not guilty because that would mean he would not have to spend two or three years in jail during which time he would not be able to provide for his mother. His only aim in life seemed to be providing for his mother and he asked me on more than one occasion to take the funds out of his prison account and send them to her.

Zaw Lin gave me the distinct impression that he did not expect in a million years to be found guilty and often asked me how he could find me again if he was released from jail before my next visit. I assumed he was basing his optimism on the fact that he was not guilty and at some point, somebody would realize that and simply set him free. I felt a chill run up my spine when it became clear to me that he was under the impression that the deal to plead guilty and go home after a couple of years was still on the table despite the fact he had changed his plea.

With my faith in the defense team at an all-time low I began to think that pleading guilty would have been a better option for him, despite being totally convinced he played no part in the rape or the murders. I felt sorry he did not seem to grasp the fact that pleading not guilty took the deal the police offered him off the table and he was now playing a very dangerous game with his own life. He was hedging his bets but blindly so. I started to get even more annoyed with Andy and his team.

Zaw Lin grew up in a village with no electricity, no TV, and no access to books. He had no knowledge of what a plea bargain entailed. To understand Zaw Lin you need to understand that the only experience he has is from his life which has consisted of subsistence farming and working in a bar on a tiny island. Zaw Lin could not possibly be aware of the dangers of putting his ball in two courts with regards to getting only a couple of years if he pleads guilty and getting off completely if he pleads not guilty and if he is found guilty the two-year deal is still available to him. I don't think Andy or his team ever made this clear to him in a way that he could understand therefore he never had or made an informed choice.

It is hard to describe how unworldly the B2 are, or how they think. The best words I can use to describe their uneducated mentality are simple, gullible, green as grass and as innocent as the day is long. Zaw Lin had no clue that he was even playing a game let alone what the rules were. He just sat quietly and patiently waiting for someone to set him free. During my prison visits, Zaw Lin told me what he did that night many times. Years later when he sent me a long letter describing his movements not a single detail had changed. He either has an absolutely photographic memory for lies or he is telling the truth.

Despite the fact that Andy and I were no longer on what was considered 'the best' terms, I continued to investigate the case and pass on information. As time went on, it was clear that nobody on Koh Tao had seen or heard anything or at least if they had, they were certainly not willing to pass any information on to me or Andy or the police or anyone else for that matter. That being said it was widely understood that people on all three islands knew what had really happened and who was involved.

There was very little in the way of CCTV footage, and what there had been had predictably gone missing. At the time on Koh Tao most of the CCTV cameras were privately owned so its child's play to have them taped over or misplaced should you want to and lucrative for the owners of the footage.

There were no witnesses to the actual crimes for either the defense or the prosecution. If these accused men, who in the grand scheme of things, were worth very little to anybody and had no power of influence whatsoever, why was it that nobody was coming forward?

I found it incredible that a crime of this magnitude could have gone undetected and un-witnessed.

To my mind, somebody must have seen something, and fear would be the only thing stopping them coming forward. I am very certain nobody would have had anything to fear from the B2 who had no power to influence anybody or cover up anything, let alone put witnesses in danger.

CHAPTER 29 – MY OWN INVESTIGATION CONTINUES

During my investigation I discovered that the person in charge of taking care of the beach was a Burmese man who was partially sighted. On Koh Tao each morning the beach would be covered with litter. There would be the debris from endless fires and fire dancers to clean up, bottles both broken and unbroken, and cigarette butts littered the beach on a daily basis. It was the job of the man in charge of the beach to ensure it was cleared, swept, and in pristine condition before dawn when the tourists started to filter down for a day's sunshine.

Interestingly enough, the police had let slip that they learned of the crime after receiving a phone call from a young woman, but it never occurred to them to ask who she was. They didn't even get a name. We cannot be sure who actually arrived at the crime scene first, but we do know that Montriwat Toovichien was there very early on because there were photographs of him at the scene before the bodies were put into body bags. He told the press that he had taken a phone call telling him of the crime and quickly dressed and went to investigate. As previously mentioned, he told the Channel 4 documentary crew, when they arrived on the islands to investigate, that a member of his staff banged on the door to his room. Regardless of which version of events is true there is no doubt he was one of the first on the scene. Mon told the CH4 crew that he was the first Thai person to see the bodies in his interview with them for their documentary. There is a press photograph of him very close to the bodies, and one of him stepping over the rope the police had used to cordon the area off. What he was doing there we will never know but we do know that he trampled all over the crime scene and, due to this, his DNA would have been present. Whether he felt he needed to find a legitimate reason why his DNA might be present or whether he felt his position as the brother of the local headman gave him the right to show total disregard for the authority of the police, only he can know.

As I continued to investigate and analyze the photos in the press, the ones released by the police and the ones that were popping up with disturbing regularity on social media sites, I noticed that some of the crime scene photos show David's clothes strewn all over the beach. Others showed them neatly folded up on the rock along with Hannah's. This was also before the bodies were wrapped in blue plastic bags. To an impartial observer it would seem the crime scene was contaminated almost as soon as it was discovered. Footage from the CH4 documentary shows people other than medical personnel and police at the scene.

The time of the deaths of Hannah and David was never confirmed by the Thai autopsy or coroner, but by the doctor who attended the crime scene when the bodies were first found. The coroner said he was unable to ascertain the time of death as the bodies had been frozen when they came into his care. He estimated that the time of death would have been around 5.30 a.m.

We attempted to find the Burmese girl who had been the first to find the bodies to no avail. Rumor had it she was found dead on a rubbish dump on Koh Tao, but it has never been proven, like so many other happenings on Koh Tao. Andy told us that she had left Thailand and was alive and well in Burma. All I can say is that all of our attempts to find her that continued into 2019 failed to locate her.

It was established fairly early on that the murder weapon was a garden hoe. This was recovered from a nearby garden, but only after it had once again been used as a hoe, until the owner of the tool was told by the police to put it back where he found it.

By the 8th of December 2014, Andy and I had a total breakdown in communication. He was refusing to give me straight answers to any questions about any aspect of the case. It seemed that anyone other than him who had an interest in helping the B2 was simply there to raise funds and praise him for his work. I think Andy saw all those who wanted to help as disposable humanitarians who would step in for him and take over visits to the prison whenever he was jet-setting around using funds he simply never accounted for. I asked Andy several times to explain to me the funding of the case as I was still going to and from the prison under my own steam and using my own funds and those I raised to pay into the B2's' prison accounts so they could use the tuck shop and to buy them food, fruit, and toiletries. Andy was not only evasive he was starting to become obstructive.. Andy continued to tell me that the B2 would be unhappy if it turned out we were all fighting and asked me to stop sending him messages suggesting he was doing anything other than a spectacular job. Andy certainly saw himself as in charge of the entire case and sent me a message:

"I am very grateful what you did for assist me in my work to assist them (car, hotel), and also respect your hard effort to help the boys. But I don't need negative energy as I am getting abusive and strange emails from people all day and it's really cause me distraction, I want positive stuff. I want hugs, happiness, laughter through all this hard work Suzanne".

Every time I got a message from Andy he sounded less and less like a lawyer and legal representative to the boys and more and more like a kid on a gap year trying to make out that he was very important in a case he seemed to know little to nothing about. He tried to get me back on his side by telling me that he and Sar both cared for me and always wanted to be my friend. I had no motivation to have friends such as he and Sar. I only wanted to see that there was a fair trial for the boys. He went on, "I just want to work with you, I want to be your friend, I don't want to be your enemy". He continued "The reason I set up the fund was to assist the case and I am doing all I know how to do to assist it, Maybe it is not all correct but I try my best, of course but please don't attack me as it weakens me, it weakens the team, we gave attack many people!"

Andy clearly had no idea who he was dealing with in Koh Tao. I responded, "When I sense danger, you do not, that is normal. You did not spend the years I did dealing with this level of corruption. I was on Koh Tao before the police ever were. I know how they think. I know how they operate. It is hard to be told you are crazy when you know the situation better than the person who is accusing you of being crazy".

Andy said he knew we were in danger, but he and I thought differently. It was the only thing he said that I had agreed with for quite a while. Andy went on to say he was insulted that I had suggested he was not accounting for funds and that I thought he was lazy. He asked me to go and meet with him to have some fun and share happiness. "I know in your heart you want to be like my big sister too. And I need big sisters, I also argue a lot my big sister. My happiness I only had my heart to give and my good intention". My faith in Andy was completely gone. It seemed to me that Andy was at the least incompetent, and at most was dishonest.

Despite deciding I wanted nothing else to do with Andy, I did eventually go and see him and try to explain that his overall attitude, his lack of transparency with the funds and his utter lack of communication was less than conducive to any kind of respect for him on my part. It didn't go down too well. I didn't hear from Andy again until Christmas Day when he sent me a Happy Christmas letter. The next court hearing was on Boxing Day. He told me the parents and family had arrived. He told me that nobody was really being allowed into the court, so I decided not to go. I was just happy the B2 would see their parents.

On the 23rd of December 2014, Nomsod was back in the press. This time because he was going to enter the monastery. His monkhood ceremony was being paid for by the governor of Surat Thani province. This did nothing but throw more suspicion on the young Thai man who appeared to the masses to be doing this to make some kind of peace with his crime, a common practice in Thailand.

On the 27th of December 2014, I asked Andy to put out a plea in international newspaper for anybody who stayed at the same bungalow as Hannah and David to contact us. He said he would discuss it with the lawyer. Andy said he was planning a visit to the prison with some community leaders who would help to support the boys over the next nine months. The prison was closed on the following Wednesday and Friday for the New Year.

Through my publication *Samui Times,* and the Hon British Consul on Koh Samui, I had formed a good relationship with the British Embassy. Having spent so long on the island, I often helped Brits out who had run into trouble. I published press releases for the British Embassy and they had been in touch to say they were going to visit the island and wanted to meet up to discuss the problems British holiday makers and ex-pats faced on the island.

On the 28th of December 2014, I told Andy about the visit and asked him if there was anything specific he wanted me to ask them about. He said, "Ask about the general situation, crimes on the beach in the location of the murders, situation of migrants, police officer practices". He then told me he had just met with "all the police including responsible ones for Koh Tao at the police station". I asked if it had gone well. He simply said, "Well head of region

8 was there, I think success and I am new enemy no1 of Samui police, nah I am sure it is OK".

The head of region 8 at the time was a policeman called Danchai, although Andy was very convinced it was Decha. On the 3rd of January 2015 we got news that a French guy, Dimitrie Povse, was found hanged with his hands tied behind his back on Koh Tao. It was at this point some people started to think that Tao was playing host to a serial killer.

CHAPTER 30 - DIMITRI POVSE

Dimitri Povse was a 28-year-old French man who had been living on Koh Tao. At around 3 p.m. on New Year's Day, 2015, police were called to his bungalow where he was found hanging from his balcony of his Thai-style hut. The hut overlooked the bay where it was rumored the Little Duck speedboat left on the morning of the murders carrying Nomsod, the headman's son.

Dimtri had left a suicide note that read, "Iris, I love you, suicide seems easy but it is actually difficult"! No handwriting expert was ever called in to make sure the note was a match. It was reported that he had taken his life on New Year's Day 2015, after partying with his friends on New Year's Eve. He had been dead for around two hours when the body was found. It did not take me very long at all to get the crime scene photos and several things struck me as rather odd. For one, there was nothing on the balcony that Dimitri could have jumped off if he was to have hanged himself from the rafter where his body had been found. He appeared to have hung himself in a boot lace with a knot so far above his head he would have simply fallen out of it in his death throes. There were no marks around his neck at all. He had a clothes iron shaped red wound on his left arm and, most interestingly, his hands were tied behind his back.

It was reported in the national press that it is normal for those who hang themselves to tie their hands behind their back so they cannot get out of the noose once they have jumped. In this instance, even if that was true, there was nothing he could have jumped off once he got his head in the shoelace and tied his hands behind his back. I also thought it rather odd that this young man had partied all night and had fun till mid-morning and then suddenly decided to take his own life.

I was not the only one who thought this case of suicide was highly suspicious. In a news article, Associate Professor Charnkanit Krittiay Suriyamanee, a criminologist and lecturer at the faculty of social science and humanities of Mahidol University, said he doubted the suicide theory. He told reporters that if Dimitri had been as drunk as some people had suggested he would not have been able to tie himself up so tightly he could die of suffocation. He pointed out that bruises would have appeared on his neck and noted that the several pieces of rope that were used appeared to be different and that might suggest it was not suicide. He noted that the wound on the elbow could have been inflicted by somebody else.

A long-term expat resident of Koh Tao confirmed that he saw a speedboat fleeing the island early on the morning of the 15th of September 2014, and he had the same view from his balcony as Dimtri would have had from his. Mr. Posve's friends claimed they had gone out with him to a bar called Next Door on New Year's Eve where they stayed until 5 a.m. on New Year's Day before moving on to an Experience Party. They stayed there until 11 a.m. before going home leaving him to drink alone.

I didn't have a lot of communication with Andy for the first 2 weeks of January. I was still visiting the B2 and was under the impression he was too, so was quite surprised that a plea for visits and money for the Burmese boys appeared on the CSI LA website. I asked Andy if he had been visiting and providing for the B2. Surprisingly, he told me he was going three times a week. I found this hard to believe as prisoners are only allowed one visit per day three days a week in either the morning or the afternoon. I had never been refused any of my afternoon visits because someone had been in the morning. I had also never seen Andy at the prison. Andy then let it slip that he was in Myanmar, and he had asked a Burmese girl to visit the B2 and he would check if she had been doing that. He reiterated once again that anyone who did visit the men should never ask them anything about the case and only have general chit chat and reiterated that he himself had never discussed the case with them. Andy then told me that the B2 were able to have both visits in the morning and the afternoon. This was not true.

CSI LA had turned his attention to David's phone that the police were now saying that they had found behind the residence of Wai Phyo, having previously said, and been proved wrong, that the phone that had been found had belonged to Hannah.

CSI LA posted, along with a photo of the phone, "Do you think David's iPhone was opened on purpose. Maybe someone wanted to destroy the Flash Memory in order to hide some important images. The police reported that Mr. Wai Phyo destroyed the phone by smashing it and mentioned that the iPhone screen and back cover cannot be opened unless you use the right tool".

The post read, "This is David's iPhone. According to the police, Mr. Wai Phyo stole it, smashed it, and threw it in the jungle behind the room of Mao Mao's residence. If you observe the iPhone carefully, it looks like someone tried to open the screen rather than smashing it. It also looks like somebody put this phone under the water or [it has suffered from] water damage".

The following day CSI LA noted that the police claimed that Wai Phyo had stolen David's phone and threw it away in the forest behind the residence of Mao Mao who worked for AC2 and lived in one of their workers' dormitories. Of course, the AC2 Bar and its accommodation was owned and run by the Toovichien family.

On the 1st of January 2015, CSI LA was concentrating on the DNA evidence and the fact it was widely rumored that no proper procedures had been employed in its collection. He posted, "DNA evidence is key to convictions of suspects. However, there is the possibility that DNA evidence can be switched and [is] not reliable at all, if the DNA collection process is handled wrongly".

On the 20th of January 2015, CSI LA turned his attention back to Sean McAnna and posted a picture of him holding an AK-55. He said, "Is it possible that this picture was taken on Koh Tao? By observing the length of Sean's beard and hair I can tell it is identical to the pictures he took at the bar in Koh Tao. If this is true, it means somebody has access to military style weapons. Who are these people"?

However, on the 21st of January 2015, the focus of our investigations made a dramatic U-turn after another British tourist was found dead on Koh Tao. This time it was Christina Annesley. On the 22nd of January 2015, I asked Andy if he was aware that Christina Annesley had been found dead at the In Touch resort. He told me he did not know, and he had been "overwhelmed with many issues". He asked me to keep him informed of any developments as he was "too busy right now to follow anything". I found it amazing he didn't want to follow up on yet another suspicious death on Koh Tao.

CHAPTER 31 – CHRISTINA ANNESLEY

Christina was born on the 3rd of January 1992, in Lower, Hut New Zealand. After moving to the UK at 3 months old, Christina grew up in Orpington in Kent where she attended the Darrick Wood Secondary School. The youngest child and only daughter of Boyne Senior and only child of Margaret, (known to her friends as Maggie) she graduated from Leeds University (the same university David Miller attended), in 2013 with a 2:1 honors-degree in History. At the time of her death, on the now notorious island of Koh Tao, she was working for the financial news firm, Dow Jones.

Christina Annesley was a bright and vibrant young lady, sister to the late Boyne Junior and Aaron and aunt to a nephew and niece. Christina, a keen political activist, was known for her loving, caring, and compassionate nature around senior citizens. She was passionate about animals, especially cats, and had spent many years devoted to her cat, Scamp. Holding both a UK and New Zealand passport, Christina was known for her love of travel. Hating the cold, she tried to escape the UK as often as possible. Her parents say she was unaware of the dangers of travelling to Thailand.

The pretty, young, 23-year-old flew to Thailand on the 7th of January 2015. The island of Koh Tao was part of her four-month vacation itinerary prior to returning to the UK to start a master's degree in English Literature in September. While her boyfriend, Olly, was studying for his law exams,

Christina intended to travel to Thailand and Cambodia before going to Australia. This would not be her first trip to the Far East; she had previously enjoyed adventures in Vietnam and Laos as well as Thailand. On this trip, it was her intention to enjoy the natural beauty of Thailand, meet a school friend in Australia, and catch up with an uncle and other friends and relations of her parents she had met previously but didn't know so well. Before Christina left for her trip, she had a combined birthday and farewell party, at the time her wide circle of friends who attended had no idea this would be the last time they saw her alive.

During her vacation on Koh Tao, Christina developed a chest infection. Interestingly enough, Christina was staying at the In Touch bungalows on Sairee Beach owned by Montriwat Toovichien. It is believed that she called into one of the many pharmacies on the island where she was given antibiotics for her condition, as well as the powerful painkiller, Tramadol. In Thailand, prescriptions are not necessary for any kind of pharmaceutical drugs. If you are unsure of what you need you only need ask the advice of the pharmacy staff. Whether or not they are qualified to give you sound advice is debatable.. Both of her parents became concerned after Christina told them she was suffering from a chest infection and had pains in her chest. They became more concerned when 36 hours after she had told them she was unwell they had been unable to get hold of her.

At around 6 a.m. on the 21st of January 2105, she was found dead in her room. Reports suggested there was blood leaking from her nose. Local police said that her body showed no signs of being involved in a fight, and no wounds were discovered. Local police officer Lieutenant Colonel Napa Senathait told the *AFP* by phone that her body would be sent to Surat Thani on the mainland for an autopsy. However, on Friday, the 23rd of January 2015, he went on to say that there was no boat to Surat Thani until the night of Saturday the 24th, so her body would not arrive at the hospital until Sunday morning. In her first post on her social media site, Christina's mother, Maggie, who had all but collapsed when she opened the door to the UK police, wrote that her daughter had died of natural causes, having been told her death was due to mixing pharmaceutical drugs with alcohol. However, she very quickly realized that in light of the murders the previous September, things were not always as they appeared on the tiny island in the Gulf of Thailand. Her father Boyne told me, "Initially we did think she died of natural causes or accidental overdose of painkillers, but the more we found out about the place, we became very, very suspicious, as we still are with the Coroners open verdict".

A report in the *London Evening Standard* said that her mother demanded that her body be returned to the UK for examination as she feared a 'cover up' by the police. Mrs. Margaret Annesley and her husband, Boyne, said that they could not face flying out to Thailand. She said "I do not want to fly out there, I don't think I can face the trip. We want the autopsy to be done in the UK and not Thailand. We are worried they could cover something up, especially with the murders last year". She went on to say that her daughter did not have a pre-existing medical condition but had been given antibiotics for a chest infection and suggested it was possible she could have died due to a blood clot.

Christina's body was sent to the Police General Hospital's Institute of Forensic Medicine in Bangkok rather than the local hospital in Surat Thani. The autopsy revealed no trace of semen or signs of foul play. Her blood was sent off for analysis. Social media sites were rife with speculation that she had been murdered. Koh Tao was now dubbed as 'Death Island'. The similarity in looks of Christina Annesley and Hannah Witheridge were startling.

Despite the Koh Tao police claiming they had done a full investigation into Christina's death; they had failed to interview or even locate the last person to see her alive. Christina's family were left to hold their own investigation, a fact they shared during an inquest at Croydon Coroner's Court. Margaret and Boyne Annesley tracked down the man, who had left the island on the morning of their daughter's death, in Sweden. Boyne says that this man had left Thailand six hours after he last saw Christina; thirty hours before she was found dead. They spoke to him on the phone and said they found speaking to him very helpful. They went on to say that they were very disappointed that the local police had not done it themselves and had to get this person to write a statement for the UK coroner, which he did. The coroner said that her office had already received a raft of documentary evidence, including reports from pathologists in the UK, Thai officials, and Mrs. Annesley's general practitioner all of which had been shared with the family. However, in a report in the *Daily Mail* she added, "I've seen some emails regarding the effect of medication and so on and so forth and it troubles me that some of the information is not correct".

The coroner warned the family she could not force witnesses from abroad to come to Britain and explain in the witness box. She added "It's not only difficult for me, but it's difficult for the family. You are casting around for answers and I fully understand that. I would hope that the new witness could write a report or statement about it". The family simply wanted answers as to how and why their young daughter had died. To this day, they remain deeply suspicious about the nature of her death. In a statement by the Thai police, Christina's parents were told that she was seen with the man who last saw her alive on CCTV walking back to her room away from the bars and he was seen leaving her room alone. Her parents requested to see this footage as it was the last recorded sighting of their daughter. They even offered to pay, but were told that it had been deleted and was no longer in existence.

Like many other families of the victims of Koh Tao, Boyne and his wife did not have an easy experience with

Thai or British officials. While the Foreign Office did make phone contact with the family, an expected call back never came. After calling the Foreign Office three or four times, the family were given a list of lawyers in Thailand. Boyne recalls that in a state of grief, shock, and numbness, he was amazed he was left to organize everything himself. He said when he tried contacting the Foreign Office for assistance the phone just rang and rang. The repatriation of Christina's body was handled solely by her parents who also had great difficulty with blood samples. Initially they were told they couldn't have them but then were told they would be made available for a price. At the time, Christina's parents were unaware that the Thai embalming process would make toxicology blood tests impossible in the UK. The Thai authorities eventually provided the blood samples they took from Christina, free of charge; however, they were of little use due to the elapsed time of them being taken and her death. She had already been dead for thirty-six hours before her body was discovered and then had lain in the temple for two to three days. The Foreign Office offered no assistance whatsoever in this part of the case.

Was Christina a victim of what is widely believed to be a serial killer on Koh Tao? If so, why was she picked? Like Hannah Witheridge, she was young and pretty. Was that all it took? Did she turn down the advances of a local and influential man as it was rumored that Hannah had done? Did she let on she was an activist and a journalist? If so, did the killer think she was investigating the other deaths and wanted to stop her? Boyne said he had heard that Christina had been asking about other deaths on the island, and possibly about Hannah and David, but he is not sure how true this is. He does know she was taking a lot of photographs and that friends she had made there asked her not to. Was it indeed a medical reason or a combination of alcohol and pharmaceutical drugs? At her age it seems unlikely. All we know is she was staying in the bungalows owned by Montriwat Toovichien, possibly registered in his wife's name, and he had previously been announced as involved in the deaths of Hannah and David by Pol. Lt. Gen. Panya Mamen. Perhaps if the families of the victims were given answers, they would have more confidence; but Christina's parents were left with far more questions than answers.

CHAPTER 32 - MORE ANDY
HALL AND A MAFIA HIT

On the 16th of February 2015, I informed Andy that I was going to a press conference to meet with Mark Kent who was the British ambassador at the time. I wanted to ask him why a statement had been released by the embassy on behalf of the families of both Hannah Witheridge and David Miller in which it was stated that the evidence against the B2 was damning. I did not know how the families could have got hold of this evidence, or, why they were issuing a statement prior to the trial, a move that would have called for a mistrial in the UK.

Their statement read:

"There is a great deal of detail and vast areas of investigative work which has been shared with us. We respect the need for such detail not to be shared publicly before Royal Thai Police start their trial process.

We would like to stress that as a family we are confident in the work that has been carried out into these atrocious crimes.

Our thoughts, as always, are with the Miller family. Together we stand united and focused on seeing a fair and transparent trial process to bring about justice for our beautiful children."

David's family, Ian, Sue, and Michael Miller said: "We would like to express our relief that progress is being made in Thailand and this case is finally coming to court.

The support for the Myanmar suspects has been strong and vocal, but please do not jump to conclusions until you have considered the evidence from both sides in full. From what we have seen, the suspects have a difficult case to answer. The evidence against them appears to be powerful and convincing".

When I questioned British Ambassador Mark Kent, he told me that the British Embassy had not written that press statement but rather had assisted the families of the victims in releasing the statement at their request.

By this time the organization Reprieve had got involved. Reprieve is an organization of courageous and committed human rights defenders. Founded in 1999 by British human rights lawyer Clive Stafford Smith, the organization provided free legal and investigative support to some of the world's most vulnerable people, those facing execution, and those victimized by abusive counter-terror policies, rendition, torture, extrajudicial imprisonment, and extrajudicial killing.

On the 2nd of March 2015, Reprieve released this statement:

"Questions have been raised over British police support for a Thai investigation into the murders of two young Britons, which could lead to death sentences for the accused.

British police have refused to allow two young Burmese migrant workers, charged with the murders of Hannah Witheridge and David Miller, to access information about themselves that was gathered during investigations into the crime. The information on defendants Zaw Lin and Wai Phyo, which they are entitled to under the Data Protection

Act, has been shared with the Thai prosecution but not with the defense.

In correspondence with the police, legal charity Reprieve and law firm Leigh Day have outlined concerns that UK police assistance to the prosecution will reduce the chance of a fair trial and could lead to death sentences for the men, whose local defense team is significantly hampered by a lack of resources. The decision not to allow the men to see the information on them could, the letter says, lead to a miscarriage of justice; it could also put the police in contravention of UK policy against the provision of support for the death penalty overseas.

Accusations that the men were tortured by police into making forced 'confessions' were raised immediately after the Thai prosecution investigation, supported by British police, began. A forensics expert has also expressed doubt about the forensic evidence against the men.

The Burmese migrant community is routinely discriminated against in Thailand, and other Burmese workers on Koh Tao have described serious mistreatment by police, including scalding with boiling water and suffocation."

Maya Foa, head of the death penalty team at Reprieve, said: "Our sympathies are of course with the families at such a difficult time, and we understand their desire to see those responsible held to account. It is therefore essential to make sure that we see a fair trial, but this can only happen if there is a level playing field.

"That's why the one-sided assistance provided to the Thai prosecutors by the UK police is so worrying, especially when they are aware that two young men could face the death penalty following torture, and a deeply flawed trial. It is essential for all concerned that the UK is transparent about their role in the Thai investigations, and that they ensure that they do not do anything to jeopardize a fair trial where the death penalty could result".

The Bophut Fisherman's Village is one of the most popular areas of Koh Samui. It used to be a very quaint village with only a couple of shops and restaurants before it flourished into a thriving beachside town. Over the years, it became rather overdeveloped and lost a lot of its charm, if not its popularity. On Friday nights, the village plays host to what is called Walking Street. Hundreds of market stalls are set up selling cocktails made of cheap alcohol, street vendor food, arts, crafts, clothes, trinkets, and souvenirs. Local bands set up and the atmosphere is fun and vibrant. Thousands of people pack the streets and most of the time, a good night is had by all. On the 6th of March 2015, terror flooded the streets when 49-year-old Panas Kaoauthai, known as Tek, a local businessman with mafia connections was assassinated in broad daylight in front of tourists and children. The 'hit' took place in a café called Kama Sutra. After the mafia-style hit, it was reported that police had arrested a Mr. Chanai Soksom, a 50-year- old former Samui City Council candidate, after being accused of hiring somebody to murder Mr. Panas. Police also arrested Mr. Chayut Kaewaram, 35, for shooting him. The police said the motive for the murder was conflict of business interests. They were also hunting a second gunman. I knew Tek personally. He was a friend of my Thai ex-husband. He ran Bophut for many years, the location of his lucrative speed boat snorkel tour company, Popeye Tours, before disappearing to the mainland.

I told Andy that I was very shaken by the shooting, especially after going to the funeral where over 200 people from the mainland had attended, many looking more than just a little bit pissed off. At this time, it had emerged that two Burmese migrants had also been murdered on Koh Samui. Andy said, "Many shootings, indeed, be careful".

For most of February and March 2015, I was not able to see the B2. Wan, a Burmese lady Andy hired, had taken over all of the visits with an American Andy had picked up with whose name was Heidi Anna. I told Andy I was unhappy about this. I snatched a few seconds to chat with the B2 while I was visiting another prisoner with the Samui Prison Support team who take care of foreign prisoners in the jail. The B2 had asked me why I had not been to see them and told me they had missed me. I lied to them and told them I had been away, rather than admit that Wan, on the orders of Andy, had totally monopolized the visits.

Andy said, "It's great you got in the same visit, they had nice T-shirts? They look well kept and looked after so hope our money is used well and not just cigarettes which I tried unsuccessfully to forbid them from smoking". This statement confused me. While it is not beyond the realm of my comprehensions that a non-smoker would encourage a smoker to quit, I find it curious that Andy would expect two men, in jail for crimes they did not commit, and facing the death penalty, to give up smoking. It was about the last thing they had in their lives to enjoy even if it was bad for their health.

Andy continued, "You should liaise with Wan and go with her sometimes? Sometimes some other persons contacted me and I also told them to liaise with Wan. We sponsor Wan to go three times a week as monitor for the case, lawyers and other things, but unless some specific or confidential issues, usually another could go with her". This statement was confusing to me. For starters I was the one who asked Andy to come and see the B2, so quite how anything was now confidential from me was rather strange. I also found it odd that he was paying Wan to go and visit. This new arrangement of his not only prevented people who wanted to visit free of charge going, but Andy was the one who refused to help me out with fuel money or funds for the B2.

I asked Andy how things were going in terms of bail, and he said that it was the responsibility of the Myanmar embassy; he told me that he was taking a break and was in a temple. "The lawyers have assigned this issue to the Myanmar Embassy and Myanmar investigation team". I also confided in him that I had grave concerns about Zaw Lin as his mouth was dropping on one side and that his spirit seemed to be breaking. Andy told me he was monitoring things too and he would visit with the B2 soon. Zaw Lin, and no doubt every other prisoner, was suffering with the heat in the cramped and overcrowded prison. March 2015, in Thailand, was exceptionally hot and there was little ventilation in the prison and worryingly very little water. There were 28 people in Zaw Lin's cell, and he was sleeping right next to the toilet. He told me he was being woken up constantly by his cell mates wanting to use the only squat toilet in the cell.

Wai Phyo had told me there was a shortage of drinking water in the prison. I brought him 60 pots of Mama Noodles so he could trade them for any water he could find. Andy told me that the prison had run out of water, and that he had a system in place with the B2 that meant they could ask for anything they needed. I had no idea how his 'system' was set up or how the B2 could ask for anything as they had little to no contact with the outside world. Andy assured me that he would follow up this complaint with the prison staff. I told Andy that Zaw had told me he cried every day. I told Zaw that when he felt like crying, he should think about how cold it would be in the UK when I took him there after his release. This was to make him feel less hot and to give him some sort of focus on the future or at least make him think he had one. I had lied to Zaw Lin and told him that I lived only a few meters from the prison. I wanted him to feel that I was always close to him. I also told him we would write a book about his experiences and use the money to help him and his family; he seemed to like that idea.

I told Andy that Zaw and I seemed to be forming a very strong bond and it might be a good idea if I went to visit more often. My visits were still being thwarted by Wan, whose heart was in the right place of course, but I felt Zaw and I had a connection. Andy said that he had hired a moped for Wan, so it was easy for her to get to the prison. He said we could discuss this the following week when he would be in Samui. I thought it would be a good idea if Wan and I could go to the prison together to see the B2. The way her visits were arranged meant that she would visit both men in one visiting booth, so they would have to share a phone. If we went together and each asked to visit the B2 separately, we could have two booths and the men would be able to speak for the full 15-minute visit. Andy said, "I need to check up on Wan's progress and activities as well as some case things so open to discuss how to best organize this. I need to discuss with MWRN team and Wan too so everybody is happy".

There was a new commander in the prison at this time. Andy assured me he would pass on that Zaw Lin was looking very tired, was suffering from headaches, and was looking unwell. He asked me to let him get back to his "Temple activities" for two more days then he would turn his attention back to the case.

On the 14th of May 2015, I found out that the father of Wai Phyo had died. This was dreadful news. I asked Andy if Wan could get a contact visit to tell Wai Phyo in private. I also was desperate for Wai Phyo's mum to visit him and asked Andy if she would need funds. Andy said he was in touch with the department of corrections and was doing all he could to sort something out. Andy said he would try to get a contact visit via official and unofficial channels. I urged him to do this, as, to hear your father has died in front of other prisoners in the bustling prison visiting room where it was hard to hear anything over 20 other visits would be dreadful. I got the phone number of the prison governor,

Pornthip Rattanachairit, and gave it to Andy; I hoped he could reach her. I also suggested we get hold of the previous governor, Som Pot, who had done at lot of work with the Rotary who had done a lot for the prison especially the women's side.

The rotary had built a room for new mothers in the prison so they did not have to sleep with the general population, where they had little space to care for their newborns, who, in turn, would often keep other prisoners awake. They had also built a fully functioning bakery where the female inmates could learn new skills that would give them employment opportunities once they were free. Later that day, I was horrified to see that the death of Wai Phyo's father had made national TV on a channel called *Coconuts*. I asked Andy if he had spoken to them. Andy told me, "Cannot control that as Myanmar media has released news already since earlier this morning, but doubt Thai media will follow up". I knew he was lying as the media had quoted Andy Hall as the source of the information.

I was furious because there was a TV in the jail, and I was terrified Wai Phyo would find out about his father's death on national television. I discovered that Andy had broken the news on his Facebook page, which was probably how the media got hold of it. I told him, "They are quoting you Andy. This really should not have been put in the public domain until Wai Phyo was informed. How did they get the information? Because it looks to me like it came directly off your Facebook Page. This is diabolical. No human should have to find out their father passed away on TV when they are in a cell with no access to a phone. Let us pray to God that this does not make the Thai press". My message went unanswered.

As it turned out, Wan did manage to get a private visit to tell Wai Phyo the awful news in the morning. I was able to visit him in the afternoon. He was devastated and had been crying a great deal. His tear-stained face broke my heart when I saw him. He was small, so childlike, his face so angelic. All of a sudden, he looked even tinier than he really was, and the grey prison behind him seemed to loom over him like a monster ready to swallow him whole. All I could do was assure him that now his father would never leave his side, and that we would take care of his mother, and that we would also be there for him no matter what.

I was really annoyed that Andy had let the cat out of the bag and that he seemed to be using any breaking info he could get his hands on about the case to bring himself publicity. His brazen attempts at fame were being done with little thought or consideration as to how it might affect anybody else, let alone the precarious position of the two scapegoats trapped in the prison system.

In the meantime, Heidi Anna had taken it upon herself to form a new group on Facebook for visits to the B2. She noted on that group that there would be no visits to the B2 the week following the 23rd of May 2015. She did not say why. I asked Andy and he said that week would be taken up by visits from caseworkers. I asked him to let us know who was going during the first week of June and he said there was nothing planned. By 26thof May 2015, Andy was publicly trying to raise more money and posting that the funds he had were almost gone. I asked him what was needed, and which costs were outstanding and he said, "Maybe the lawyer's flights" and left it that.

My English teaching friend and I had been having a problem with Heidi who it seemed to me was still trying to take over the prison visits and effectively keep us from visiting. By the 1st of June 2015, she had booted us off the Facebook group. We had no clue who was visiting and, if we did make the hour journey to the prison, if we would be able to visit. I told Andy this was an unworkable system. He had no solution.

Before Andy came along, I had a good relationship with the owner of the hotel where he stayed and considered her a good friend. I was also friends with her close friend from Sweden, Nina, who had a heart of gold and was happy to help with donations when she could. I was also friends with another girl named Tracey, who had a health food shop in the same village as the hotel and my villa. These characters were very much in the background and liked to help 'undercover' as there was still a huge risk factor involved with being seen to be involved in the case and the plight of the B2. Since I had started to question what Andy was actually doing with regards to the legal case, my relationship with them became strained. I shared my fears with them that Andy had never found any witnesses. He seemed to have very little information about the case. The lead lawyer he employed was a civil lawyer. He was being less than transparent about where the donated funds were going. He was becoming increasingly rude to me. He was still spending a vast amount of time swimming and having two-hour massages and often disappeared to a temple for days at a time. They didn't share my concerns and only had good things to say about Andy.

My relationship with Mel, the lady who ran the prison support network, was becoming stronger. She shared my concerns about the behavior of Heidi Anna. As Andy and Heidi tried to freeze me out of the prison visits, and any information on the B2 case, I noted that Andy had blocked me from his Facebook page. Mel had also been blocked. I also noted that now, the hotel owner was really being off hand with me as was Nina and as was Tracey. They were all now taking a far more active role in the case and had clearly joined forces with Andy. None of them knew anything about the law in Thailand. None of them knew the B2. None of them knew the mafia on Koh Tao and what they were dealing with. They all seemed to be under some kind of spell. To me, it seemed like a bit of a cult with Andy at the helm. I had no idea what they were playing at, but in my mind, it was nothing that was going to help the B2, or their case or anything other than Andy's ego.

I started to spend more time with the Burmese community at their temple in Chaweng. They had once welcomed Andy with open arms, but they seemed to have fewer good things to say about him as of late. I had asked Andy many times about finding funds and ways to help the B2's mothers. He seemed very uninterested and repeatedly told me that he was only interested in the legal case. The families of the B2, he said, were the responsibility of Htoo Chit and the Myanmar government. I spent hours every day trying to find a way to help the B2, asking questions and looking for evidence, but did not come up with a great deal.

With the court case approaching, I turned my attentions in the direction of Htoo Chit, who was busy organizing visas for the B2's mothers. I offered him and them my support and started fundraising to ensure they could live and eat and get to and from the prison when they arrived in Koh Samui. We found them a place to stay and made preparations for their visit.

On the 23rd of June 2015, after weeks of silence, Andy sent me a message that said, "Who organized Zaw Lin and Wai Phyo families to Samui? Confirmed? Budget"? I didn't bother to respond.

When I met the mothers, like their sons, I was amazed at how small they were. Despite having no common language, I immediately bonded with them. They held me a lot and always wanted to hold my hand. I took them to the market so they could buy what they needed while they stayed in Samui. They seemed to instinctively know I wanted to do all I could to help. I had never experienced a situation where so much warmth, love, and information passed between three women who were unable to verbally communicate.

Wai Phyo's mother was cute, like him. She giggled and smiled a lot when she was not deep in thought, worried about her son's future. She was fun to be with and I could see she would light up anyone's life if they were lucky enough to know her. I was very drawn to her. Zaw Lin's mother was far more reserved. Like her son, she had a more serious attitude towards life. She was friendly and warm but always looked deeply troubled as if her mind were thousands of miles from where we were standing. From day one until now, I feel a very strong bond with these women, they have never left my mind.

CHAPTER 33 – THE TRIAL

The Trial of the B2 ended up lasting from July 2015 to October 2015.

I was having nothing to do with Andy at this stage and, in turn, he was having nothing to do with the B2's mothers. He was not prepared to raise any funds for the mothers. Taking care of them was left to me, a lady called Evelyne who has been regularly visiting and supporting the B2, and an organization called CSI MM that consisted of Burmese people who had also been investigating the case on their Facebook page. CSI MM was the Burmese equivalent of CSI LA. They had also initially started out working alongside Andy, but like me had given up on him. We had been collaborating and sharing information regularly since the B2 were first arrested.

Between us, we managed to rent the mothers a safe house on Koh Samui. We were worried about their safety on the island. When the mothers first arrived, I used to take them to see their sons in the prison. We spent a lot of time driving to and from the prison and waiting around at the prison for the visits to start. With the court case looming, we made a roster to get them to the court and back every day. It turned out to be harder than we thought as some days the court would start at 8 a.m. and not conclude until 1 a.m. the following morning. The mothers had the support of delegates of the Burmese Embassy who attended the trial every day.

I arrived at the court early on Wednesday, the 8th of July 2015. I could tell it was going to be a very hot day. There was a strange sense of calm around the courthouse. As I sat on the imposing looking steps, the media started to arrive and set up cameras. The quiet was broken by a screaming and wailing May Thein, the mother of Wai Phyo, she was beside herself and the press was all over her, lapping up the drama. As the truck carrying the B2 arrived from the prison, the press pack ran after it. The truck went around the back of the court to the court cells where the accused would sit waiting to be called. The B2 were manhandled out of the back of the van and into the court building by some very intimidating and angry looking officers. I was often shocked at how rough the police were with the B2 during their court appearances. Thankfully Sar, who was not in the least bit intimidated by them, regularly pushed them out of the way and kept the B2 close to her.

The press was not allowed into the court and nobody in the court was allowed to take notes. I sat in my now familiar spot on the right-hand side on the bench behind where the B2 would sit. I saw the families of Hannah and David come in and wondered what on earth was going through their minds as they looked over to see who was sitting on the defense side of the court. I can remember Mr. Witheridge giving me a really hard stare. When the B2 came in, he gave them a long, hard, stare. I wondered if his first impression of the tiny men was the same as mine when I first saw them hobble into the courtroom finding it hard to walk in shackles and metal chains. The atmosphere was tense. I was lucky I got into the court; the court ushers still assumed I was there as a human rights advocate and not as part of the press. We all had to sit with our arms down and our ankles crossed and were told not to move on the hard wooden benches. It was like waiting for a bomb to go off.

The prosecution brought in all the physical evidence in a shopping trolley. The trolley was wheeled to the front of the court below the judges. Zaw Lin's guitar was in there. It all felt very surreal.

Also present in court were observers from the Solicitors' International Human Rights Group (SIHRG) who monitored the case.

The case for the prosecution started by them calling police Lieutenant Jakrapan Kaewkao. He talked the court through his role in the investigation and told the court how he received a call at around 6.15 a.m. on the morning of the 15th of September 2014, informing him that two bodies had been found.

The DNA evidence was discussed. At that point we expected a decision to be announced with regards to it being re-tested by an independent laboratory.

On the first day I was struggling with a bad toothache. I had arranged to go to the dentist at 3 p.m. but it was difficult to keep up with what was being said. My understanding of the Thai language is reasonable, but with a shaky start and with all the testimony being translated from Thai to Burmese and back again it was hard going trying to keep up. I made my exit at around 2 p.m. and left the courtroom through the big wooden doors that opened onto a long balcony-style outdoor corridor that was flanked with benches.

Sitting right in my line of vision was Montriwat Toovichien and his brother Worapan. I could not believe my eyes. I wanted to get word back into the courtroom that they were there, but I could not go back in. I stared at Mon. He stared right back at me, and my blood went from cold to boiling. I thought of the B2 on the other side of the wall and wanted to throw him off the face of the earth. I could feel their eyes burning into the back of my head as I made my way along the corridor to the steps that lead down to the ground floor and headed off to the dentist.

I remember nothing about having my tooth pulled out. All I could think about was the look on Mon's face and how much he utterly repulsed me. According to *Thai PBS*

Mon had been arrested for these crimes. He had been seen stomping all over the crime scene. He had blatantly stepped over the rope that was there to cordon off the crime scene. He was the brother of the island head man, Worapan. He had threatened to hang Sean McAnna and there he was waiting to give testimony and be a witness for the prosecution. I was devastated to have missed his testimony, but miss it I did.

The defense team made their concerns known about the DNA evidence that was to be used against their clients, specifically how it was collected, stored, and tested. A police officer for the prosecution told the court that no independent testing could be carried out as all of the DNA on the cigarette had been 'used up' and was 'finished' and that the other samples were only fit for one test or had been lost.

On day two the defense team said there had been a dramatic development when it appeared that evidence provided by the British authorities could prove the innocence of the B2. At that stage, the defense could only confirm that there had been recent significant information received from the UK that highlighted the important contradictions in the prosecution evidence, but they were not able to elaborate on what that evidence might be.

The same day, a 45-year-old woman was invited to take the stand by the prosecution. She had been working on Koh Tao at the time of the murders. She recalled some people playing guitar on the beach but was unable to say who they were or even if the songs that they were playing were Thai or Burmese. She admitted to having beers in several bars before urinating on the beach from where she said she saw the B2. She had nothing in the way of any information to give. The defense asked her if she often urinated on the beach and was she the kind of person who held on to her urine until she had no option but to go wherever she was when she could no longer hold it. I thought it was a total joke. By the look on the faces of the judges they did too.

The B2 looked tired. The day before they had not got back to the jail until 7.45 p.m., a time too late to have their shackles removed. Both complained of not being able to get much sleep.

On day three, the police forensics officer gave his evidence and graphic photos of the bodies were shown and bite marks on Hannah's body were discussed. Two of Hannah's family members had to leave the courtroom finding the evidence too unsettling to sit through. One female member of the Migrant Workers' Rights Network also had to leave when she was overcome with emotion due to Hannah's family's distress. The expert who had carried out the postmortems on Hannah and David told the court that David had serious head wounds that were likely to have been caused by a hoe. I found this odd as to me the injuries looked nothing like being caused by a hoe and far more likely to have been caused by a punch knife. The size of the defendants was discussed as both of the B2 are around 5 feet tall and David was over 6 feet.

The man who had carried out the postmortems said he was of the opinion that men of the B2's stature could have caused the injuries. I nearly fell off my pew. The DNA was still under contention. Outside the court, the doctor who took the DNA swabs from Hannah said the DNA was all used up. The defense did not agree. They maintained the swab could certainly be used more than once. When it became clear that there would be no chance to retest the DNA the *AFP* news organization questioned lead defense lawyer Nakhon asking him, "How disappointed were you that you could not retest the DNA"? Laughing, he replied, "I just prepare myself and prepare my mind about this ha ha not that disappointed".

AFP asked, "Do you think it is a major problem for their case"?

"Urr Maybe a little bit, because there is so many thing to present but um it will take time. I think it is not enough time for all witness to present I think so".

Later that day, outside the courtroom, David Miller's family told reporters they had visited Koh Tao for one day before the trial. It was a trip they found very hard indeed.

A few things struck me about the trial. One was that they said both of the B2 were working illegally in Thailand. The prosecution looked pretty stupid when Zaw Lin produced his passport.

When asked about this by the *AA News* publication, Nakhon Chompuchat, the head of the defense legal team said, "It weakens the prosecution case a little bit, and it severely discredits the investigation work". Sadly, it did not do this enough.

Another thing that struck me was that the public prosecutor, fell asleep many times during the trial as did the female judge who sat on the left of the lead male judge in the case. The female judge to his right seemed to be paying the most attention. Throughout the trial the lead male judge often simply got up and walked out.

Probably the saddest part for me was when the prosecution questioned a policeman about what he thought with regards to Hannah's vagina. He was showing photographs of it and Mr. Witheridge struggled to hold it together overcome by grief and the horror of his daughter's final moments. The look on his face is something I will never forget. I can never comprehend what he and his family went through but my heart wept for him and still does.

Each day I left the court and went down the stairs to exit. I saw the refectory area was full of media on their laptops all waiting for information to publish, upset that they were not allowed in.

The key evidence hinged on the fact that both men had initially confessed to the crimes and the finding of their DNA inside Hannah Witheridge.

CCTV showed that at a quarter past midnight on the 15th of September 2014, Ms. Witheridge entered a bar situated close to where she was murdered. She was not seen again on CCTV. At 2.08 a.m., David Miller is shown on the same CCTV entering the bar and is not seen again. It was concluded from this that the pair left the bar sometime after 2.08 a.m. via the back entrance that leads directly to the beach and is not covered by CCTV. It was established that Zaw Lin, Wai Phyo, and their friend Mau Mau, had been sitting on a tree branch on the beach at around 2 a.m. and it was concluded that the victims would have walked past the defendants. However, the defendants stated that they did not see the victims.

It was established that the murder weapon was a garden hoe. The blood of both victims was found on it. The bloodied hoe was found in semi-darkness by one Mr. O. who believed it was his and took it back to his garden. He was instructed by his employer to put it back where he found it, near the tree the defendants had been sitting on. Mr. O. was never a suspect and did not have his DNA tested.

The victims' bodies were sent to the Police National Headquarters in Bangkok for examination. Apart from the DNA of Ms. Witheridge, the DNA of another was found in her vagina. It was presumed this was from semen. The DNA of two others, apart from Ms. Witheridge, was found in her rectum. This was also presumed to be semen.

Cigarette butts found nearby on the beach yielded the DNA of three persons.

Mau Mau had been brought in for questioning on the 1st of October 2014. His statement about who he was with that night lead to the apprehension of the defendants. Zaw Lin was arrested at his dwelling and Wai Phyo was arrested on a ferry that had docked at the mainland port of Surat Thani. The prosecution said he had been hiding on the boat. Wai Phyo said he was travelling to Surat Thani to start a new job that had been arranged for him by a friend.

Without the provision of independent legal advice at any stage of the investigation, the defendants were first interrogated as witnesses, then as accused persons. They incriminated themselves in all of the crimes when they confessed and undertook a 'reenactment' of the murders at the crime scene on the 3rd of October 2014. Both police and international media organizations recorded the event. On the 2nd of October 2014, Wai Phyo told the police he had found David Miller's mobile phone and taken it to the home of his friend, Ren Ren. The police went to the home of Ren Ren and found the phone. David Miller's father and friends, Chris Ware and Alan Ware, established that it was the phone that belonged to David. This was later confirmed by the UK's National Crime Agency, who in 2017 formally acknowledged that it acted unlawfully in providing assistance with the ownership of the phone to help secure the death sentences of Zaw Lin and Wai Phyo.

After the retraction of his confession, Wai Phyo stated that he had found the phone on the beach, although Ren Ren stated in an out of court statement that Wai Phyo told him he had found it at a bar. All of the bars on Sairee Beach are on the beach so both of these statements could have been true.

It was established that during the investigation, Buccal swabs for DNA analysis were taken from the defendants, with or without consent. The defendants asserted that the interpreters attending the police station during the investigation did not explain the document that they signed regarding 'taking consent'. It did emerge that the interpreters recruited were not professional and could not read the Thai alphabet. However, the court determined that the defendants had given consent required by paragraph 131 of the Thailand criminal code. The court indicated that even if the consent had not been given, the court had the discretion to admit the evidence in view of the importance of the evidence to the case.

The court was relying on the following provision of the Thai Criminal Code:

Where it appears to the court that any evidence is just per se but it has been obtained by an unjust act or by result of an information produced or obtained through an unjust act, the court shall exclude it, save where the admittance of such evidence would be more beneficial to the carriage of justice than detrimental to the criminal justice standard or fundamental rights and liberties of the people.

In exercising its discretion as to whether evidence under paragraph 1 is admissible, the court shall be mindful of all circumstances of the case, including without limitation: (1) The value of provability, significance and reliability of such evidence; (2) The circumstances and gravity of the offence charged; (3) The nature of, and the injury caused by, the unjust act; (4) The fact as to whether and how much the person committing the unjust act whereby such evidence has been obtained has been punished.

Police Colonel Watee Atsawutmangkur, a scientist and director of the Blood Biochemistry and Gunshot Residue Analysis Unit, Forensic Institute, Thailand National Police Department, testified that the DNA found in semen from Ms. Witheridge's vagina matched Wai Phyo's DNA, and the DNA found in the rectum matched the DNA of both defendants. The basis for the expert's belief that the DNA was from semen was not apparent.

The SIHRG (Solicitors International Human Rights Group) report says that it was established during the court hearing that the defendants' later denial of any involvement with Ms. Witheridge must be a lie. However, that denial may not have been a lie if their DNA was planted in Ms. Witheridge or by some other fraud such as their DNA being supplanted by the actual samples taken. The SIHRG noted that on the *evidence presented to the court* they could not suggest that the conclusions of the court on the identity of the DNA inside Ms. Witheridge were not properly founded. They went on to say that whether it was right to accept that the biological source of the DNA was semen may be open to question. It's open to question it may cast doubt upon the convictions for rape but it does not follow that in all the circumstances of the case any question mark on the biological origin of the swabs negate the case against the defendants for murder. On any view the presence of their DNA in intimate areas must be regarded as powerful evidence of serious sexual assaults, even if falling short of penile rape. The same motive for both murders would be established as it was considered relevant to the case where rape was proven.

While I am not a lawyer, I have a fairly good understanding of the law. I have three concerns about the DNA evidence. As was rightly pointed out by the report, it is possible that the DNA was planted inside Hannah. It is also possible that the DNA samples were switched. And even if neither is true, rape does not prove murder. With the defendants' DNA not matching the DNA of the murder weapon, I fail to see how it is possible to sentence anyone to death for the crime of capital murder without their DNA being present on the murder weapon and without a single witness to the crime, let alone a motive, or any previous criminal history.

In line with my fears, the defense team argued that various international forensic standards applicable to DNA cases were not met. These included the need to thoroughly document the chain of custody of the swabs, to apply match probabilities to an opinion as to the identity of the DNA, the provision of database used in the analysis and the requirement to produce full laboratory case notes. Each failure should have cast doubt on the opinion evidence of the prosecution's DNA expert.

The SIHRG noted, "We are of the view that the Court was entitled to be persuaded by the prosecution expert on the evidence presented by the parties in an adversarial contest. Though this opinion is subject to resolution of the impact of apparent failures by the Prosecution to disclose documentation about the DNA handling and testing to the defense at all or in sufficient time for a defense to be prepared."

Jane Taupin, an Australian expert on DNA, flew to Koh Samui to testify at the trial. She is one of the world's foremost experts on DNA profiling and has worked as an internal laboratory auditor. She has written books on the use of forensic evidence in courtrooms. Her testimony, with regards to the DNA which the prosecution was relying upon to find the men guilty, would without a doubt have changed the outcome. She had noted that the DNA evidence had handwritten alterations on it and was not stamped with the laboratory stamp which would have been present had the DNA been tested in a laboratory which complied with international testing standards.

Despite Andy Hall asking Jane Taupin to attend the trial to support the defense lawyer's case, she was never called to the stand and the defense lawyers chose not to highlight her findings.

In news reports, Jane Taupin said:

"Crime scenes, she said, are notoriously difficult to gather quality DNA samples from. Cases like the one on Koh Tao, which deal with mixed samples, are fraught with danger: complex and sometimes unreliable statistical calculations must be carried out to determine the probability that someone other than the accused could match the recovered sample". Yet no statistical analysis was made available to the defense team or the court. Instead, the judges were simply told by prosecution witnesses the evidence "confirmed" that DNA recovered from the crime scene belonged to the two accused, a claim Ms. Taupin said is not strictly possible to make; instead, a probability ratio must be given. Whichever way you want to determine the statistics, they've got to be validated in your laboratory, and you've got to have them. But Thailand doesn't have them. Not at all," she said.

"DNA profiling is predicated on statistics, that's the whole point. You don't just say it's a match. It's not fingerprinting. You need to give significance to that match".

The SIHRG report notes:

"We must emphasize that the proceedings were adversarial and not inquisitorial. The court noted that the defense commissioned an independent comparison of the Defendants' DNA with the prosecution's DNA results from the swabs taken from Ms Witheridge. For this defense test, the Defendants' DNA was obtained from swabs taken from the Defendants in Court during the trial. The results were not disclosed to the Court by the defense. Assuming the reason for this non-disclosure was that the results were unhelpful to the Defendants, then, if the Defendants still were not involved with Ms. Witheridge, we would have to believe theories that the Defendants' DNA was planted in Ms. Witheridge. Or, that the samples that their DNA was compared with were not from Ms. Witheridge but had been taken from some other place. There was no evidence to support such possibilities. If such police or laboratory frauds/mistakes had taken place, then such frauds/mistakes have been successful in misleading the Court. It may well be the case that the documentation of the chain of custody of swabs in criminal cases is an issue that must be addressed by the Thai authorities. It appears that the Court relied on a combination of documentary records and oral testimony to establish the chain of custody of the vital swabs. The question of the standards applicable to opinion formation in DNA cases should be addressed also. It is generally not acceptable for scientists to express 100% certainties, even in DNA cases, as occurred here. Rather, reasoned match probabilities should be provided.

Everyone has the right to an appeal against conviction. In death penalty cases, the appeal court should review both the facts and procedural and other legal rulings of the trial court. We urge the Appeal Court of Thailand to review the evidence with the greatest care. The Appeal Court should be prepared to accept into evidence further expertise on DNA science. Even if on the merits the convictions are upheld the Appeal Court should issue clear guidelines to trial courts on current international scientific standards relating to DNA opinion evidence. DNA found on the cigarette butts matched the Defendants and their Burmese friend Mau Mau but Mau Mau's DNA was not implicated in the crimes".

Years later when I decided to study DNA, it became clear to me that the laboratory in Thailand had taken one strand of DNA and amplified it, a process that involves heating up and cooling it down, so it reproduces. Every human being has a 99.9% match to every other human being and only .1% of our DNA is different. The DNA codes repeat themselves other than the part that makes us unique. For example, I could be AAAAsBBBuCCCCCzDDDDy and you could be AAAAtBBBoCCCCmDDDDy. The way it works in simple terms is an enzyme is put into the DNA to remove the repetitive code, so you end up with 'suzy' and 'tomy' to compare. With the DNA samples from Hannah, there would be her DNA and the DNA of the two perpetrators in a mixed sample. This makes things more complicated. One way to understand this is to think of the code that is left as a bowl of alphabet spaghetti; the code pulled from that could indeed match 'suzy' and 'tomy', but it could also match 'somy', 'sumy', 'suzy', 'tuzy', and so on. With only one sample amplified and the rest of the DNA being used up or lost there would be no way to run multiple tests over multiple samples to ensure a match. This is why there was no point in the defense team independently testing the only sample the lab had left, an amplified sample that matched the defendants, but could also have matched millions of other people who did not contribute. It's simple, it's totally unethical, its genius and also totally not admissible in a court of law in any country. (wbp.bz/curseturtlegallery)

On the 21st of August 2015 a case was heard in the High Court of Justice Queen Bench Division at the Royal Courts of Justice, London before Mr Justice Green between Zaw Lin and Wai Phyo and the Commissioner of Police for the Metropolis.

The case concerned the application by the B2 for disclosure to them for personal data held by the Commissioner of Police for the Metropolis. The data was contained in a confidential report prepared by the MPS into the murder inquiry conducted in Thailand.

The matter was brought before the court as a matter of urgency as the trial was already underway.

In his extensive post trial report Mr Justice Green said "The stakes are very high for both sides. For the Claimants they could hardly be higher: Life or death"

With regard to the deployment of DCI Lyons of the MPS to Thailand and the concerns expressed by the MPS about confidentiality the report stated:

"The misgivings raised were sufficient for the Prime Minister to engage in discussion with the Prime Minister of Thailand with the consequence that the two reached agreement that The Commissioner of the Police for the Metropolis (MPS) would send a team led by a senior officer to Thailand to conduct an independent inquiry. That senior officer was DCI Lyons."

Ms Cressida Dick, an Assistant Commissioner with the MPC explained "the Commissioner of the RTP (Royal Thai Police) has sought and obtained express agreement from DCI Lyons at the outset that his observations of the deployment as set out in the Report, would only be shared with the Miller and the Witheridge families, and would not be disclosed any further." She stated "It would be significant and I believe a damaging step to provide the Report or parts of it to the suspects to use in their defence when we are not willing to give it to the Thai authorities. I believe that it would significantly undermine the Thai authorities' relationship with UK law enforcement, if not the wider relationship between two governments given the high-profile nature of the case".

The MPS refused the request on the basis that the Disputed Information that was held by the MPS which would otherwise be subject to disclosure was exempt from disclosure under section 29 DPA 1988 and moreover made it very clear that it will not provide the Report voluntarily to the Claimants."

Mr Justice Green ended by saying "In coming to this end result I nonetheless feel very considerable unease."[2]

---

2. https://www.judiciary.uk/wp-content/uploads/2015/08/hq_15X0311_final.pdf
See more at: http://wbp.bz/curseturtlegallery

CHAPTER 34 – THE LAST FEW DAYS OF THE TRIAL

With the last few days of the trial being set for October, I was in a bit of a dilemma. My mum's birthday is in October. Having put my parents through so much worry since the murders, I felt that I had to go to the UK and spent some quality time with them. While they were proud of what I was doing, they had spent enough time in Thailand to know what the consequences of my investigation might be. I am sure they lost far more nights' sleep over it than they let on. However, I did not want to miss anything that was said in court, and I did not want to let Zaw Lin down. In the end, I chose to go to the UK as I knew I needed a break. It was all so harrowing and seemed so hopeless. I was exhausted having lived and breathed the case for so long and spent so many hours up all night dissecting every last bit of information and trawling the CSI LA page for anything we could go on trying to find the missing link that would nail the real killers.

I went to visit Zaw Lin and Wai Phyo in jail to let them know I would be away for three weeks. At first Zaw Lin did not seem to understand why I was leaving and looked very frightened and scared. I explained to him that it was my mum's birthday and I had to be there with her to celebrate. When the message finally sunk in, no mean feat with the language barrier, the look of relief on his face was tangible!

"Oh", he said. "I understand, you go to England for happy birthday for your mum and then you come back Thailand".

I smiled and reached my hand out to touch the Perspex that separated us. He did the same and said, "Yes, I go come back"!

What he said next touched me. "Su, can you do something for me"?

I had no idea what he was going to ask.

"Can you give your mum happy birthday from Zaw Lin"?

I didn't hesitate to say yes. He asked me how old my mum was and what we would do for her birthday. I tried to explain to him how cold it would be in the UK. Before our visit ended, he looked worried again. I asked him what was wrong. He said that he was worried that if the verdict came back before I did and he was sent back to Burma, he would not be able to find me. I reassured him that I would find him in Burma. He again reiterated his fear and said he did not want to lose me from his life. I told him not to worry and that I would track him down and find a way to find him. I told him to get the address of the PO box we used to help the other foreign inmates correspond with their families and write to me if he was free by the time I came home. He did not doubt he would be found not guilty for one second. Zaw Lin would not have understood much of the court case. He had his translator, Sar, but most of it was a mystery to him. He was not educated and could not keep up. He was only going on what he knew, that he was innocent and there was no reason for him to stay in jail. This was all just a huge misunderstanding that would be resolved. On so many of my visits, Wai Phyo had asked how much longer they had to stay in jail. It didn't seem to occur to either of them they may never leave alive, and we certainly never made mention of it.

It was an odd feeling to fly out of Thailand. I felt safe on the plane, a feeling I had not had for a long time. My partner and I arrived to very wet weather in the UK. I had such mixed feelings; part of me desperately wanted to be away from the darkness of it all and part of me wanted to rush back and see the B2 and keep looking for a way to save them.

My mum's birthday was a big occasion with a jazz band and close to 100 people, all of whom knew about the case and had seen it on the TV. While home I talked nonstop about the case and worked on it as much as I could online. I think my parents got fed up with me talking about it. My mum said on more than one occasion that I had risked enough in helping the B2 and it was time to let someone else take over; but who else was there? How could I walk away? The truth was I had no intention of walking away and don't to this day.

The court had heard that on the 21st and 24th of October 2014, the defendants made statements alleging that their confessions and crime re-enactments had been obtained through torture and threats. They were questioned again on the 6th of November 2014, by a policeman. Zaw Lin alleged non-marking methods were used in his torture such as a bag being placed over his head so that he was very close to the point of suffocation. Wai Phyo alleged that he was subjected to severe physical beatings including to the head. The court was told that a doctor examined the defendants on the 3rd of October 2014, but found no sign of injury to either of the B2. The defendants told the court their examinations were not thorough.

With regards to the way in which the trial was conducted, the SIHRG noted:

"The procedure at the trial for taking evidence was the same method as was practiced by Magistrates Courts enquiring into indictable offences before committing a defendant for trial by jury in England and Wales. These "old-style committals" were abolished by the Criminal

Procedure and Investigations Act of 1996. The witness would be questioned in the traditional order: examination in chief, cross examination, and re-examination. The witness's answers would be written down (conveying the true sense with the question answered). At the end of the witness's testimony, the written version of his or her evidence would be read back to the witness in court. The prosecution and defense advocates, the witness, and magistrates could seek to revise the written version if anyone of them did not agree it was accurate. Any suggested correction could itself be subject to further questioning of the witness to clarify the point. The written version might remain unaltered or be amended according to the final ruling of the magistrate after hearing submissions. Finally, the witness would sign the written document known as a deposition. In the Koh Samui Provincial Court this process was followed. One of the judges quietly dictated into a small voice recorder his or her comprehension of the witness's answers. Then the recorder would be provided to a typist for typing and production of the written version of the testimony. Then it would be read aloud in court for agreement and then signature by the witness. The trial process of deposition taking has strengths and weaknesses depending on one's viewpoint of the relative importance of a witness's demeanor when assessing the reliability of that witness. The deposition process stresses the greater importance of the words spoken by the witness rather than the manner in which those words are delivered. Some of the judges in the Koh Samui Provincial Court clearly placed little if any weight upon the demeanor of some witnesses. This was evidenced by the fact that on occasions during the trial a judge left the courtroom all together. It would be wrong to accuse a judge who did this of inattentiveness unless it was regarded as a trial right for all judges to observe the demeanor of all witnesses at all times. The judges in this case granted themselves the period between 11th of October, and 24th of December 2015 to consider all the out of court statements submitted by agreement of the parties, all the documentary exhibits and all the witness testimony given in court during the trial".

The SIHRG notes continued:

"We took the precaution of writing in advance from the UK to the Court applying for permission to observe the proceedings. Written permission was granted. Subsequently we have been advised by Andy Hall of Migrants Watch (who has practical experience of such matters) that in practice, foreign observers are not prevented from entering Thai courts at will. We had explained in the letter our role as neutral international observers. We very much regret the decision of the Court not to permit us to make contemporaneous notes during the observation. This was a blow to our mission and brought into question whether we should continue with the observation at all. Jastine Barrett pressed the matter via the Court Clerk on the first day of the trial and was rebuffed with the message that the judge did not want any reports containing inaccurate information being published before the end of the trial. Observers, Nigel Dodds and Alexandra Zernova, pressed further oral applications to the Court to permit them to make notes but the judges declined. The reason stated was to avoid the risk of witness contamination. The further justification for the refusal was the correct statement of the process; that all testimony would be reduced to writing and be available through the court at the end of the trial anyway. However, in considering that we would only be interested in witness testimony shows that the Judges failed to appreciate the wider interests of a trial observer. The conduct of the judges towards the parties, witnesses, and defendants and procedural rulings are also of interest to the trial observer. Notwithstanding the ban on note taking (which applied equally to the media), we decided on balance to continue, relying on short breaks to catch up on note taking outside the courtroom and at the end of the days' hearings and into the night.

Many days hearings did turn into the night as the court sat very long hours on most days. The court had agreed with the parties in December 2014 or early 2015 to set a rigid timetable for the trial with regard to witnesses. Though in the end witnesses did not appear from overseas, when the timetable was set, consideration was given to this possibility. Additionally, in fairness to the families of the deceased, it was reasonable to provide trial dates with certainty in view of the time and cost of travel from the United Kingdom to Thailand. Though 10+ hour hearings in a day must be criticized as too long for most participants to concentrate and fully participate. The interests of the victims' families, the interests of the Defendants' lawyers who had to make advance travel arrangements from Bangkok. There is the deposition-taking nature of the proceedings. The latter point meaning that memory of what a witness had said is of less importance as it would be in a traditional jury trial to which the observers are accustomed. Depositions can be read and re-read at leisure before a judgment is reached. The Defendants were present in the court for the duration of the hearings. They were each individually shackled at the ankles by heavy metal shackles. They each wore a standard issue orange suit of top and trousers. Few criminal courts can entirely remove the stigma of association of a Defendant with guilt through the conditions in which he appears in the courtroom, whether that is his or her position in a raised dock or a cage or other special place in the court. Under international law, a Defendant is to be presumed to be innocent until proven guilty after a fair trial. His or her guilt must be established to a high standard and in a murder case attracting the death penalty a very high standard indeed. The requirement to prevent escape of Defendants appearing for their trial from custody must be addressed. If the Defendants were not shackled then alternative measures would be required to prevent escape attempts. That might mean excessive security at the door of the court becoming an obstacle to entry and egress for public, press and observers. It may mean using a court with a secure dock that itself would do little to remove the stigma suggested. The use of shackles was unfortunate and must have been uncomfortable for the Defendants, especially as they faced very long court hearings most days of the trial. However, the use of shackles as opposed to a secure dock (if one was available, there was no such furniture in the trial court used,) allowed the Defendants to sit very close to their lawyers. If faced with the choice of on the one hand a more distant court dock that physically lessens the inclination to communicate with your lawyer and for your lawyer to communicate with you and on the other hand wearing shackles that allow you to sit closely to your lawyer, it would not be unreasonable to opt for shackles and take advantage of close proximity to your lawyers, the witnesses and judges. So, as we say, the use of shackles was unfortunate but in all the circumstances, and those circumstances include a recognition of the fact that the Defendants were facing an accusation on strong evidence of the most horrific violence, we cannot impugn the trial on the grounds that the conditions in which the Defendants appeared at their trial was wrong. Having said that, we are of the view that the imposition of these heavy shackles was undignifying for the Defendants. In this context we note the 2007 Thailand Constitution Part 4: Rights in Administration of Justice Section 39. Before the passing of a final judgment convicting a person of having committed an offence, such person shall not be treated as a convict. It would be highly inappropriate to parade defendants before a jury in this way. Apart from the indignity, it would be highly suggestive of guilt. It was in this case inappropriate to parade the Defendants before press and public shackled in the way they were. However, we observed the judges and we saw or heard nothing from their demeanor or conduct of the case suggesting that they were prejudiced against the Defendants on account of the manner in which they appeared before the Court. We assume that the judges were likely to be accustomed to the appearance of defendants before them shackled in this way and wearing orange prison garb. We must give the judges the benefit of the doubt that their professionalism would be good enough not to be swayed by such matters. The judges, we presume, understand that this is the norm for the production of a remand prisoner on trial. Our thoughts on this would differ if it was established that the use of the shackles was unusual or unprecedented. We do not have direct experience of other trials in Koh Samui or elsewhere in Thailand to take the point further".

The SIHRG made a very interesting and worrying observation in their report:

"The prosecution claimed that the Defendants first confessed when being questioned as witnesses. Mau Mau having told the police earlier that the Defendants were also on the beach. If only being questioned as witnesses one presumes that as potential prosecution witnesses (why not prosecution at that stage?), Zaw Win and Wai Phyo would have been treated with a degree of respect not necessarily afforded to rape and murder suspects. It is thus curious, to put it mildly, that without any undue pressures being applied to them, they should both voluntarily confess to very serious crimes. One may also safely assume that they did so knowing, as any sane person would, that such crimes would attract at least very lengthy terms of imprisonment. It does seem hard to believe that under such circumstances, free confessions to the most serious crimes would be given. Detention by the police may trigger in a guilty detainee heavy remorse or a recognition that the "game was up". If they are guilty, they may well have reasoned, from the known DNA sampling of various persons that had been taking place on the island, that the criminals' DNA had been obtained at the crime scene or on the victims. Thus proof of their guilt would be inevitable. If they had not succumbed to sudden remorse or realisation that the game was up, the circumstances suggest that some irresistible pressure was applied to them to obtain such otherwise remarkable confessions".

They went on to say:
"The Court, in its judgment, did not find that the confessions were obtained improperly. We note that Mau Mau was the first to admit being on the beach that same night and was the first to be detained by police. No evidence was adduced by the Defense that Mau Mau had been forced to confess to crimes or tortured. He would have been in the same position as the two Defendants in respect of the sequence of confession followed by DNA results rather than a sequence of DNA results followed by confession. Myanmar Embassy officials gave evidence at the trial that Mau Mau had gone to their Embassy and was scared of being accused. The notes we have do not suggest that he complained to them of being tortured by Thai police. The judgment states that if the confessions were disregarded the other evidence, including the DNA evidence against the Defendants, was sufficient to establish their guilt".

However, what they did not mention in their report was that Mau Mau was a staff member of the Toovichien family!

The report continued:
"Everyone charged with a criminal offence has the right to be tried in his or her presence so that they can hear and rebut the prosecution case and present a defense. In principle, the accused should not be tried in absentia. Defendants may be tried in absentia in certain exceptional circumstances in the interests of the proper administration of justice, for example, when defendants have been given sufficient advance notice of their trial and they decide to

waive their right to attend or refuse to do so. We identify two relevant elements to the right to presence: Physical presence and mental presence. The right to an interpreter is essential to mental presence as are the conditions of the courtroom and duration of the sittings. The Defendants were physically present throughout (see the section on the Courtroom dynamics on the page above for more details.) Presence is meaningless if you do not understand the proceedings through a language barrier. Each defendant had an interpreter assigned. It was impossible for us to judge the adequacy of the interpretation. The rights under this heading of presence and the right to an interpreter were met as qualified by our observations concerning the length of court sittings. Our observers noted the times the court started and ended each day. The court usually took a one-hour break for lunch and occasionally there were other short breaks. Nearly half of the 21 sittings, discounting the lunch hour, exceeded 10 hours. Interpreters, lawyers and judges were often noted to be dozing. Though our observers did not note the Defendants dozing, that is not to say they had not lost concentration during lengthy hearings. Our observers were seated in rows of seating that were always behind the Defendants. Thus, the state of their composure could not be fully seen. There were occasions when defense lawyers requested the judges to rise for the day (or night actually), so that they could get a decent night's sleep and prepare. Such requests were denied. The Court was determined to keep to the pre-ordained timetable. This is a table of the sitting lengths. The lunch hour is not computed in the table".

"The trial timetable had been determined at pre-trial hearings. Even if it is right to assume that the parties had agreed the timetable before the trial started the defense's consent to the timetable does not excuse the excessive length of the court sittings. Judges must ensure sittings are not of excessive length and that lawyers have adequate time to prepare between successive days' court sittings. Judges presiding over any criminal trial, especially a trial that may lead to a substantial term of imprisonment or the death penalty, must be prepared to adjust a timetable if the original time estimate proves to be inadequate to the requirements of a fair trial".

The trial was not compliant with the right to be "present" because most sitting days were of excessive length. As a consequence, the rights of the Defendants to follow proceedings, to adequate representation and interpretation were likely to have been compromised to their detriment".

With regards to legal representation, it was noted in the report:

"During the investigation stage the Defendants were not provided with independent legal assistance in clear contravention of the Thai Criminal Code. After they had been questioned and incriminated themselves they were further questioned in the presence of a lawyer. Each when questioned in the presence of the same lawyer. This lawyer's role is described as being to ensure the legality of the process. This appointment was not to provide "legal assistance" to the Defendants. More it was to authenticate what the police were doing, which is a different role. The lawyer was not assigned as the 'defendants' lawyer.' He was under no professional duty towards the Defendants. They were not his clients. He owed them no duty of confidentiality. He gave evidence against them at their trial as to their confessions. They would not have waived a legal privilege of confidentiality for him to do so if one existed".

It continued:

"After charge the Defendants were assigned independent lawyers dedicated to their interests. Shortly after the appointment of their own lawyers the Defendants made statements dated 21st and 24th October 2014, respectively complaining that their self-incriminatory statements had been obtained through police and interpreter threats and torture. A complaint was lodged with the authorities and consequently the police re-interviewed the Defendants on the 6th November 2014 when they protested their innocence, claiming not to have seen Mr. Miller or Ms. Witheridge at all on the beach that night. The Defendants had full legal representation throughout the trial. We cannot comment upon the adequacy or competence of that legal representation without a detailed evaluation of the evidence. We have received comments from third parties to the effect that a number of important areas were not subjected to appropriate cross-examination. Our impression was that some cross-examinations appeared perhaps to be rather brief. However, we cannot go behind any restraints that might have been acting upon their advocacy that only a breach of confidentiality with their clients might explain. However, the adequacy of representation is likely to have been compromised by the excessively long court sittings that most probably impacted on the mental ability of defense lawyers to maintain appropriate levels of alertness.

We do not know the full details of the remuneration of the lawyers assigned and whether this was adequate for a case of such gravity. We are aware that the State was not providing the funds to assist the defense in relation to the instruction of a foreign expert, Ms. Taupin (an Australian DNA expert who was in attendance but not called by the defense), and other measures thought necessary in preparing the defense. These supports were funded or secured through the efforts of Migrants Watch in liaison, we presume, with the defense lawyers. The uncertainty of funding sources for the defense to match the resources of a Thailand State prosecution means that whether 'equality of arms' is achieved in Thailand in any given case is a quite random affair.

There was a clear breach of the right to independent legal advice at the investigation stage. The exercise of such a right may have avoided the circumstances in which it was contended that confessions were obtained by threats and torture. Either because the Defendants would have been advised to remain silent, or their exculpatory statements would have been advised to be given immediately. Or if the confessions were voluntary and desired by the Defendants to be given then if given in the presence of an independent lawyer acting for them it would have been less likely that at a later stage the Defendants would claim the confessions were false. Thus, it can be seen to be in the wider interests of justice that Thailand develops a proper right of access to legal advice at police stations when suspects are detained for questioning. The Defendants appear to have had adequate legal representation at trial but we cannot evaluate the competency of that representation nor the probable impact on the excessively long sittings on their alertness. It appears to us that perhaps greater training is required of Thai lawyers in trial advocacy including cross-examination".

We arrived back in Thailand to find that Wai Phyo and Zaw Lin were not out of jail. Zaw Lin was very happy to see me on my next visit but was dismayed that he was still incarcerated. Heidi was still monopolizing the prison visits on my return and did all she could to keep me away from the B2. For a few weeks I did stay away. Battling with the Thai courts and corrupt systems was one thing but having endless drama with other westerners who all should have been working together was becoming exhausting.

I kept fundraising and trying to help the B2 and the mothers and often popped to the prison to deposit funds even when visits were impossible. As the weeks went on, I started to really panic for the B2. The verdict was going to be back soon, and I knew they would be found guilty.

We were told the verdict would come on Christmas Eve. Once we had the date the international press started to hound me for information. I begged them all to keep it out of the press so the Thai people would be given an opportunity to do the right thing and not go on some face-saving exercise. Most news groups respected this and kept it out of the press. I knew the less hype there was in the press the more chance there was of a positive outcome, although I knew in my heart it would never happen. As the dreadful day of judgment grew closer, I battled to make sure I got visits with the B2 and tried to reassure them that a guilty verdict was not the end; it was only the start of the next stage which would be the appeal. The mothers, who had gone to spend some time in Burma, came back to the island. Through my Burmese friends, I tried to reiterate to them too, that this would not be the end. I knew that the Burmese community wanted to remain positive and found my constant reassurance that this was not the end pessimistic, but I did not believe in false hope and thought it important to prepare them for what I knew was coming.

The prison visits were getting tense. Most of the B2's visitors were starting to get excited about their possible imminent release. I was often scorned for being what I thought was realistic. Although even I had to admit there was a tiny part of me that focused on how amazing it would be for them to be free and what an incredible feeling it would be to see them out of their cages. My western mind told me it would not be possible for a nation to allow two innocent men to be put to death or even found guilty. Andy Hall didn't agree with my pessimism, by all accounts he was confident and trying to kick up the exact sort of media storm that I was trying to avoid.

CHAPTER 35 – CSI LA POST TRIAL INVESTIGATIONS

The public prosecutor released a report. The report is in Thai so I could not read it, but an excerpt of it in English appeared on the CSI LA Facebook page.

"On September 15, 2014, the 2 defendants intended to kill David William Miller by using a hoe as weapon. They willfully smashed and chopped Mr. Miller's face and head many times, which resulted in his death. The details of Mr. Miller's autopsy are provided by physicians and the forensic team from The Police Hospital".

Another one that was published in the UK's *Guardian* on the 9th of July 2015, covered the second day of the trial and read:

"A Thai court hearing the case of two Burmese men accused of murdering two British backpackers stalled on the second day of a three-month trial after a police officer failed to present what the defense says is key DNA evidence.

The head judge on a panel of three in a court on the tropical holiday-making island of Koh Samui said that he would rule on the matter on Thursday, when Police Lieutenant Colonel Somsak Nurod, who is believed to hold evidence related to the case, would appear to testify.

But Nurod spent only a few minutes in the court, where he showed the judge of list of evidence exhibits.

This included the alleged murder weapon, a hoe, which was used to kill Hannah Witheridge, 23, from Norfolk and David Miller, 24, from Jersey on Sairee beach on the nearby Koh Tao Island on September 15.

He left shortly after to recheck what other evidence was available. It was not immediately clear if DNA evidence, collected from sperm and cigarette found at the crime scene, would be provided to the defense.

Nurod appeared confused in court when asked to provide forensic evidence. He said the samples may have been destroyed.

Lead defense lawyer Nakhon Chompuchat said that the police officer will ring the defence later today to confirm what evidence he has.

"Some of the forensic with him has already been used up. Some things he is not sure about," he said.

Asked if he is disappointed that it appears that key DNA evidence may be missing or unusable, Chompuchat said: "We expected this before".

He added that it was important that the court acknowledges these facts, which cast doubts on the fairness of the trial and the reliability of the evidence.

Another judge had ruled in April that the DNA evidence be re-examined but later said the defense should request the order on the first day of trial.

A verdict is expected during October for the criminal trial of Zaw Lin and Wai Phyo, two Burmese migrants who worked in a bar on a restaurant on Koh Toa . Witnesses, including police, doctors and people living on the island, are not due to testify until September 25.

Andy Hall, a migrants' rights activist from Britain who is working for the defense, has told the Guardian that recent information provided by UK authorities has raised "a lot of very important inconsistencies between the Thai evidence and the evidence from the UK".

He did not give details on what evidence UK authorities had provided. But Metropolitan police detectives were sent to Thailand in 2014 to look over the case and report back to officials and the families.

"For this case to rest, it's very important to re-examine that DNA material and find out whose DNA profile it really is", Hall said.

The legal team representing the 22-year-old bar workers is made up of pro-bono lawyers who also criticize Thai police for improperly collecting evidence at the crime scene, intimidation and abuse of witnesses. These claims have been denied by the Thai police. Human rights groups including Amnesty International have become involved in the trial, noting that Burmese migrant workers, of whom there are about 2.5 million, have previously been wrongly accused of crimes by Thai police.

On Wednesday, the defense cross-examined another police officer who was second on the scene in the early hours of the day of the crime. They asked him why he took so long to call a medic and seal of the area. He was also asked why he moved Miller's body. He said he was concern the deceased would float in the current.

Doctor Chasit Yoohat, 51, a doctor on Koh Tao, also testified. He said that he observed the crime scene on the day of the murder, and found both had been brutally attacked. On Thursday, Steve Mitchell, a bar owner who was the last person to photograph the deceased appeared at court. He told reporters outside that he photographs tourists to promote the bar on the website.

The two defendants said last night their shackles were not removed, speaking during a break in the hearings on Thursday. "I didn't sleep all night", Wai Phyo said.

The authorities had been under pressure to solve this particular murder case quickly as it threatens the country's vital tourism industry.

The family of Miller said in a statement on Wednesday: "The act which ended David's life devastated our family and his friends. Just hours before he died, David was talking to us with his usual enthusiasm, describing the beauty of Koh Tao and the friendliness of the Thai people".

"Over the coming weeks we hope to gain a better understanding as to how such a wonderful young man lost his life in such idyllic surroundings in such a horrible way".

A post from Consul Myanmar, Mr. Htoo Chit from his Facebook page, was also quoted on the CSI LA Facebook page with regards to Mr. Vin and Mr. SEO from the Burmese Embassy.

"The Burmese consul has teamed up with the Thailand Lawyer Council to assist Mr. Vin and Mr. SEO. He said that the Burmese people at the turtle island were stated as villains after the incident of David and Hannah's murder.

According to the information that the consul has been given, the Burmese workers were attacked, tortured and forced to test DNA after Mr. Vin and Mr. SEO admitted to confess to the government of Myanmar, Myanmar and the people of the world. No one believes that the 2 people did it all.

Burmese people have been taken hostage and exploited in Thailand for a long time but the Burmese Military Government has historically not shown a great deal of interest, however, this has now changed and the Government are taking an interest. The people of Myanmar along with people around the world worry that the Burmese consul will not be able to find a team of lawyers and experts to represent these young men.

The Thai Lawyer Council has also told the Burmese officials about the case in Koh Tao and the arrest of the two Myanmar citizens. We believe their arrest is due to the corruption of Thai police and the Thai justice system and not due to wrongdoing by the Burmese men.

There are 3 million Burmese citizens in Thailand, so I want the government of Myanmar, including the opposition and the people of Myanmar, to stand up to help us see justice and be transparent with the Koh Tao case and find the person responsible for the Koh Tao case.

It came to light that in December 2014, a Thai taxi driver admitted to the press that he had been bribed to be a witness. On the 2nd of October 2014, an article in *The Thaiger* by Legacy Phuket Gazette said "A taxi driver on Koh Tao, off the Surat Thani coast, yesterday went public with his accusation that police investigating the murders of two British tourists had tried to intimidate him into providing false testimony. In a media interview yesterday, Prasit Sukdam also accused the police of giving him a large sum of money in exchange for false testimony to frame the wrong people. He claimed the money was taken from the Bt700,000 offered as a reward by Koh Tao residents for information leading to the arrest of the killers. Separately, Prime Minister Prayut Chan-o-cha dismissed reports that tourists will be encouraged to wear wristbands or register electronically upon arrival in addition to passport verification at the airport. "We can't make them wear any chip-embedded device. We want them to keep visiting Thailand", he added. Meanwhile, Prasit brought the issue up with Assawin sae-Phoo, head of the local taxi drivers on the tourist island, citing "fear for his life after turning down the offer". Assawin later took Prasit's complaint to Korbchai Saowalak, the Kamnam (government official) of tambon Koh Tao. Korbchai then spoke publicly to the police, calling on them not to work in the case in an aggressive manner and not find scapegoats. "Don't harm innocent people or frighten them", he said. Speaking later to reporters, Prasit said: "I don't want to take any action against policemen, but want to demonstrate my innocence and I will cooperate with other requests in the future. Just don't force me to acknowledge [something] I never knew [about]", he said.

CHAPTER 36 – THE DREADFUL DAY OF JUDGMENT

I was not sure what I was going to do for Christmas. I knew I would not really be in much of a mood to celebrate as I was convinced that the verdict would be guilty. In the end, I decided to book a Christmas dinner at a bar owned by a friend of mine on the beach. I hoped with all my heart that I would be doing back flips on the sand but the dark shadow in my heart never stopped pulling me down. The week before the verdict I visited the B2 three times and was both heartened and saddened to see them getting so excited about going home. They told me not to put more money into their accounts as they would not need it. I had to scream at them to stop giving what little resources they had in jail to other inmates. I went to visit Darren, a guy from New Zealand who was serving a long stretch and had taken the B2 under his wing. He told me that all of the inmates thought they would get a not guilty verdict so less well-off prisoners were around them like vultures, getting what they could from them. I asked Darren to look out for them and try to get them to keep what they had. He was convinced they were going home and told me the guards were too and it was almost a party atmosphere in there. It was a concept I found hard to visualize. As it turned out, they were right to give it all away but not for the reasons they had in mind.

The night before the verdict I stayed out late. There was no way I was going to sleep. I think I managed to sleep for about an hour. My partner at the time agreed to come to court with me, He always previously stayed in the background, partly because I worried about his safety and partly because he didn't want to get that involved. He was sick of living and breathing the case; everyone close to me was. Nothing else mattered. It was like my life depended on justice. I had never felt such a sense of purpose in my life, although I had always kept my name out of the press to protect myself and my loved ones. I told my partner that I needed him to be there because I didn't know how I would cope with a guilty verdict and would need his support. I don't think he really wanted to be there, but he knew had he not our future would be marred by it. When we arrived at the court, we made our way up the seemingly endless steps to the top to watch over who would be arriving in the car park. The first to arrive were the Miller family. They were smiling, which if found odd. I wondered what was going through the minds of the bereaved family. They were accompanied by their very young-looking female Thai translator. Michael Miller spotted the cameras and gave them a smile.

The mothers then turned up. May Thein was wearing a pretty pink top. I heard her before I saw her. She was wailing and screaming in Burmese. She was hysterical. By the time she had arrived at the court, the paparazzi presence was starting to increase. I ran to her, desperate to give her some comfort. I had been determined to keep my face away from the cameras for my own safety. This resolve left my mind as I saw her distress. She wailed, "Please release my son, please, my son did not do this, my son is not that kind of person, my son did not do this, I beg for justice". Her distress made me feel sick to my stomach.

The prison van arrived. A few paparazzi cameras could be heard clicking as the white van with its red stripe and metal mesh sides made its way to the rear of the court where the prisoner's entrance is. The doors to the back of the truck opened. I could hear the rattle of the chains as more than a dozen prisoners inside stood up from the wooden benches ready to exit. The first man, a Thai, got out carrying a large see-through plastic bag that held lots of little plastic bags tied at the top with red elastic bands containing the prisoners' food for their lunch. On the front of his tunic was his number, 090. The second man out was falang. He paused for a second to look up to see where all of the clicking came from. He looked perturbed and then got out of the vehicle. The third prisoner was Zaw Lin, looking very solemn. As he disembarked, the clicking became fast and furious. I could see he was being blinded by the flashes from the cameras despite it being an already very hot and sunny day. He didn't look up once. Next was Wai Phyo, who not only did not look up but held his head dropped low as he struggled with the weight of his chains.

I held onto May Thein tight as she made her way into the court. Like every time I had visited, I handed in my passport in return for a visitors pass but this time I was denied. Never before had I been denied entry to the court. It was interesting that every news reporter this time, on the day of the verdict, was allowed entry, having been denied entry on every single day of the trial. I had always gone into the court as support for the B2 and never as a journalist. This time, when they needed me the most, I was turned away and told to wait outside. The court filled up with journalists from all over the world as the B2's head lawyer, Nakhon, gave an interview to the press stating he was confident there would be a positive outcome. Andy Hall arrived at the court and asked why I was not inside, when the two other falang women who had helped to comfort the mothers were allowed in. Despite our relationship having long since broken down, to give Andy his credit, he tried to get me in. He may have had no regard for me whatsoever, but he knew what I meant to the B2. For the first time, I felt he had done the right thing, but to no avail, they singled me out and refused me entry. I hoped that someone would tell the B2 I was there, but I found out later they didn't.

There was nothing I could do but wait outside the court. My partner and I sat in the small café under the steps that lead up to the imposing building and had a very hot curry. I remember saying that maybe there was a chance that justice would prevail and maybe they would go home. I don't know where those thoughts came from. Then, just shy of an hour later, a very dark feeling suddenly came over me and I had the most horrendous feeling of foreboding. I felt sick to my stomach and felt the curry I had eaten creep up the back of my throat. My partner said I went white.

I remember saying, "What am I thinking? This is hopeless. They have been found guilty and sentenced to death". I ran to the steps of the court to see Liz Luxton, the translator for the Witheridge family, coming towards me. I remember thinking, 'why is she out of the court? Why is she not translating'? I realized it was over. I asked her what happened. As I looked around, I saw a semi-circle of cameras poised around the entrance to the court. She said in her pronounced German accent "They were found guilty and were given the death penalty". I asked her to repeat it which she did. She looked crestfallen.

I had imagined this scene so many times, only I would have been in the court. In my imaginings my knees buckled, and my world fell in and my partner had to hold me up, but it was not like that. I felt utter rage.

I needed to see May Thein. I raced up the steps and burst into the court foyer to see her in a state no human ever should have to be in, surrounded by the Burmese Embassy officials on a bench on the right of the long corridor that led to the steps that take you up to the courtroom. I called to her, and she looked up and simply held out her arms like a lost child motioning to me to come. As I reached her, I put my arms around her and felt the heat coming off her like a furnace. She was shaking and wanted my arms. She pushed everyone else away as she held on to me like a drowning child. I remember thinking it was amazing that of all the arms open to her she wanted to be in mine. It was both the humblest, and most proud, moment of my life. To mean that much to a woman who didn't even share a common language with me and a woman with whom the only common words I had shared were 'crazy' and '*mingalabha*' (a Burmese greeting) is an indescribable feeling and one that will haunt me to my grave. May Thien had learned the word crazy from me shouting at reckless drivers on our many trips to the prison in my car.

I was shaken out of being immersed in her grief by the sounds of whooping and cheering. A sound that was so alien to the surroundings. I looked round to see Ian Miller and his son, Michael. My immediate thoughts were ones of dismay, even if you are happy with the verdict, these two women's sons have just been sentenced to death. I was sorry for, what seemed like, a lack of empathy for the mothers of the boys condemned to die. I later found out the mothers thought their sons would be taken off and killed the same day. They had such little understanding of courts and appeals and anything beyond their lives as subsistence farmers living in abject poverty. They had little idea that they were now being screened on TVs in homes in just about every corner of the globe. As the Miller family made their way outside, I became aware of the clicking of the cameras outside pervading its way into the court building like the round of applause at the funeral of Princess Diana after her brother made his famous speech condemning the British monarchy.

After the Millers left, the wails of May Thien became so frenzied the usher asked us to leave the court. We had to go via the front door and into the glare of the world's media in order to collect our passports. The paparazzi that were all focused on the Miller family immediately changed focus to us and came in like a pack of hungry wolves; it was unnerving. I held tightly onto May Thien as we tried to make our way down the steps. Two photographers fell over as they tried to keep their invasive lenses in our faces by negotiating the steps backwards. We went to the far end of the court car park where I found a seat from which I tried to console a now utterly hysterical May Thein. The cameras were all over us. I felt hemmed in, hot and desperate for May Thein but oddly totally numb in terms of my own feelings. My partner came over and told me Michael Miller had made speech outside the court, the content of which had surprised him. After what seemed like hours the court car park emptied, and the mothers were taken to their rental house and sedated. I felt lost and flat and desperately wished I could see the B2. Instead, I drove back home to watch the Michael Miller speech for myself online.

I also found Michael's speech surprising. He found the evidence presented in the trial to be compelling. His speech read:

"We believe that after a difficult start the Royal Thai police conducted a methodical and thorough investigation. Having listened carefully to all the evidence, and despite what their lawyers say, it is our opinion that the evidence against Wai Phyo and Zaw Lin is absolutely overwhelming. They raped to satisfy their selfish desires and murdered to cover up that fact. They have shown no remorse during the trial. Initially they confessed for almost two weeks and then recanted in an attempt to avoid justice. We hope the campaigners who have relentlessly publicized this case will respect the process of law and the decision of the court. We believe the correct verdict has been reached. Finally, we would like to thank everyone who has supported us over the last year. Our thoughts are also with the Witheridge family and the horrors they are also enduring with so much dignity. Our lives have been changed forever. Nothing brings David home; no last hugs, no goodbyes; but whatever our anguish, the love we have for David can never be taken away. Our twenty-four years of memories and his beaming smile will always be cherished. David was intelligent and hardworking, he was caring, inclusive, and enthusiastic and fun. He is irreplaceable to us. Our hearts will always be filled with the brightness he brought to our lives. We remain so proud of him. We and his friends miss him terribly".

His speech was drowned out with the cries of May Thien. Mrs. Miller later accused me of deliberately dragging the mothers out of the court to ruin her son's speech.

I considered Michael's opinion that the B2 had showed no remorse. The B2 had both told me they felt very sorry for the victims and their families. If they had been wrongly convicted, and had not, in fact, committed the crimes they would have nothing to be remorseful about. I considered Michael's view that the B2 had raped to satisfy their desires and then murdered to cover up the rape. From the photographs of the crime scene, I couldn't agree the rape had been covered up. Hannah was naked from the waist down and had been left spread-eagled on the beach. I was unsure if Michael had known the B2 maintained that they were tortured into confessing to the crimes, confessions they retracted as soon as they had legal representation. The confession document they signed was in Thai which neither of the B2 could read. While Michael seemed convinced the B2 had retracted their confession to escape justice, I am of the opinion that leaving the island, and disappearing to Myanmar, would have been a better strategy. While news reports had stated that Koh Tao had been locked down after the murders, so nobody could leave, I had witnessed many boats coming and going between Koh Samui and Koh Tao that were full of tourists. Michael Miller said he listened carefully to the evidence. It can't have been easy when it was in Thai, even with a translator.

It was hard to know what to do that evening, Christmas Eve. I got two messages that upset me. The first one was from the owner of the bar I had planned to go to on Christmas Day. She said that she was sorry that the case had gone badly and knew how upset I would be with the death penalty. She wondered if it was a bad idea for me to go to the Christmas party as everybody would be wanting to have a good time and not be around me if I was upset. She wanted the focus of the party to be on Christmas and not the B2 case. I felt very hurt by this, but it was too late to arrange to do anything else. I simply reassured her that I would be fine and promised not to talk about it unless someone asked me, and then I would decline to comment other than saying it was a bad outcome.

The second message was from Andy saying that he and his legal team would be flying back to Bangkok that evening and would it be possible for me to visit the B2 the following day, Christmas, as there would be no one else going to see them. I could hardly believe what I was reading. I asked him what the hell he meant by neither he nor his legal team would be going to see the B2. They had just lost the case and as far as I was concerned, they needed to go and see the B2 and explain the appeals process. I thought this was a really gutless move on his part. Aside from him, the rest of the team were Thai and Buddhist so they could hardly use it being Christmas Day as an excuse. I decided I had wasted enough of my precious energy on Andy Hall and just told him that I would go and see them. I asked a good friend of mine to come with me. He had been visiting the B2 and had grown very fond of them. He was an older gentleman from the same hometown as me and I knew he would not only be willing to come to see the B2 but would support me if I got upset and how could I not? This would be my first visit to the B2 as convicted men. I had no idea how I was going to 'pass off' the disappearance of Andy and his legal team. The B2 would undoubtedly question his absence.

I then had to explain to my partner, who was already very weary of the case and my endless involvement, that I would not be around on Christmas morning as I was going back to the prison. He was not happy but understood that I had to go. How could I not?

On the 25th of December 2015, a press statement was released on the Judgment of the Koh Samui Provincial Court on the Koh Tao Murder Case.

The Koh Samui Provincial Prosecutor, brought a case against the two defendants, namely Mr. Zaw Lin (also known as Zoren), no surname, the first defendant and Mr. Wai Phyo (also known as Win), no surname, the second defendant, in Criminal Case (Black Case) No. 2040/2557 at the Koh Samui Provincial Court. Today, as the date of the hearing, the Court has rendered judgment which can be summarized as follows:

"The Prosecutor accused that the defendants committed the offences of illegal entry and residing in the Kingdom of Thailand: jointly murdering Mr. David William Miller, the first victim; and jointly gang raping Mrs. Hannah Witheridge, the second victim; and jointly murdering the second victim for the purpose of concealing other offences committed by the defendants and that the second defendant wrongfully committed and offence of theft by stealing the first victim's mobile phone and sunglasses. The offences were committed at Koh Tao Sub-district, Phangan District, Surat Thani Province and thus the Prosecutor requested the Court to render punishment on the defendants according to Sections 83, 91, 276, 288, 289, 334, and 335 of the Criminal Code and Sections 4, 5, 7, 11, 12, 38, 58, 62 and 83 of the Immigration Act, to order the second defendant to return or to reimburse Baht 16.000 to the descendants of the first victim and return the exhibits i.e. the mobile phone and hoe.

The first defendant pleaded not guilty.

The second defendant pleaded guilty to only one of the chargers of illegal entry and illegally residing in the Kingdom of Thailand.

The Court considered evidence from both the Prosecutor and the defendants and found the place where both defendants were sitting being not far from the crime scene and that from such a place it was possible to see both victims walking to where the crime transpired. The medical examiner conducted an autopsy on the bodies of both victims and found the DNA of more than one offender in her vagina and rectum of the second victim. This evidence is commonly accepted under international standards as being an effective proof of a person's identity and the evidence arose, existed and was obtained legally before the arrest of the defendants, therefore the DNA testing result can link and prove the identity of the offenders. By comparing the DNA from such evidence with the defendants' DNA, the DNA found in the vagina of the second victim matched the DNA of the second defendant while the DNA found in the rectum of the second victim matched with the DNA of both defendants. According to the DNA testing result in Document Jor- 12 which compares DNA of the offenders with the DNA of the defendants, there are more than 16 matchings of DNA, thus, under the commonly accepted international standard, this DNA testing result is beyond reasonable doubt persuasive and evidentially proves the offenders identities. The Prosecutor's witness who collected and tested the tissue specimen of the defendants testifies that the specimen had been collected and sent to the lab for testing immediately after the event and thus there was no opportunity for the police officers, medical examiners, and the scientists who tested the DNA of the offenders to bring semen and seminal fluid deep inside the defendant's body and put them in the vagina and rectum of the victim. Moreover, the Prosecutor also presented a witness who testified that the second defendant brought the first victim's mobile phone to the witness not so long after criminal incident and this is thus part of the evidence that establishes that the second defendant was involved in the incident. The Prosecutor's evidence of both the DNA testing result, where the DNA of both defendants matched with the DNA of the offenders, and the material evidence at the crime scene as well as the circumstantial evidence both before and after the incident are relevant and valid as they can prove beyond reasonable doubt that both of the defendants were the offenders who raped the second victim even without considering any other facts or circumstances such as the defendants confessions following arrest and at the interrogation stages.

Even though the case presented by the Prosecutor does not explicitly identify which of the defendants was the first who raped the second victim, the testimony of an expert witness, Pol. Col. Dr. Pawat MD., revealed that a tear wound at her vulva was bleeding. This indicated that the second victim was not yet dead while being raped and that such wound must have occurred before the fatal wound to her head, which caused immediate death. The forensic result certainly indicated that both defendants raped the second victim until ejaculation. Moreover, their actions and circumstances indicated that they conspired in advance to take turns raping the second victim. Therefore, their actions were considered the offence of jointly committing rape upon a non-spousal woman in the form of gang rape. When considering the characteristics of the wounds at the head and the face of the second victim, it can be found that all wounds were serious and their marks matched with the blade and the edge of the exhibited hoe. There was also the finding of bloodstains of the second victim on the exhibited hoe. Thus, there is no doubt that they exhibited how the weapon was used to inflict harm on the second victim. The serious wounds on the face occurred after the tear wound at the vulva while being raped. This leads to the fact that after the second victim had been raped at the scene, she was then attacked using the exhibited hoe until deceased. These circumstances were undeniably a continuous action which closely linked to the fact that both defendants were offenders who used the exhibited hoe, as a weapon to harm and slash the second victim numerous times. This caused deep tear wounds, their depth reached the base of the brain and caused the forehead bone at the left eye socket to be broken and flattened to an abnormal shape. This indicated that both defendants jointly used the exhibited hoe to viciously strike the second victim to death with the intention to cause death. Thus, the actions of both defendants are the offence of jointly committing murder for the purpose of concealing other offences committed by the defendants. The facts and circumstances arising from the case presented by the Prosecutor appears that the first victim was harmed at the scene at almost the same period of time as the actions committed to the second victim and the first victim died subsequently. The characteristics of the wounds on the body of the first victim also matched the shape of the exhibited hoe. This circumstance therefore indicated that both defendants used the exhibited hoe as a weapon to harm the first victim, in order to facilitate committing the action of rape to the second victim. This is considered the offence of jointly committing murder as written in the plaint.

For the charges against the first defendant of being an alien entering into and residing in the Kingdom without permission as written on the plaint on Clauses 1.1 and 1.2, the case presented by the Prosecutor did not show any evidence that the first defendant was not granted permission to enter into and reside in the Kingdom at the time of the written plaint as the first defendant was able to present his passport to the Court, the fact from the first defendants statement could not thus be heard to penalize the first defendant under these two particular offences. For the offence of theft at night charged to the second defendant, the prosecutor had a witness, who confirmed that the second defendant brought an exhibited mobile phone to the witness after the incident, claiming that this mobile phone was forgotten by a foreigner, moreover, there was a witness who testified that the second defendant confessed in the interrogation stage that he took the mobile phone and sunglasses of the first victim after he caused harm and raped the second victim. The circumstances of the case therefore establish that the second defendant was the perpetrator who jointly harmed the first victim at the scene. To this, the second defendant had a chance to conveniently and opportunistically steal the mobile phone of the first victim at the scene. However, the prosecutor was not able to present the sunglasses of the first victim to be an exhibit in this case and there was no evidence to confirm that the second defendant had involvement in the possession of the sunglasses after the incident. The case only indicated that the second defendant wrongfully stole only the exhibited mobile phone. The arguments of both defendants on the DNA testing result, the Burmese interpreter, the provision of a lawyer, and the interrogation state of the claim that both defendants had been physically harmed and tortured for the confession at the arrest stage were lacking in evidence presented by the court. They were adjudged arguments without grounds and not sufficient to refuse the veracity of the evidence established by the Prosecutor with respect to the DNA testing result or thereby affect this Court's ruling. Evidence of neither defendant was thus sufficient to refute the evidence of the Prosecutor. With regards to the fact that the second defendant wrongfully stole the exhibited mobile phone of the first defendant, the actions of the second defendant can be considered the action of tort and the return of the stolen property of reimbursement of such property must be done to the descendants of the first victim by virtue of Section 438 paragraph two of the Civil and Commercial Code.

The Court sentenced that the defendants were found guilty of the Criminal Code Sections 288, 289 (7), 276 paragraph 3 and section 83. The second defendant was also found guilty of the Criminal Code Section 335 (1) paragraph 1 and the Immigration Act, B.E 2522 Sections 12

(1), 18 paragraph 2 and 62 paragraph 1. The actions of the two defendants were found guilty under several offences, according to Section 91 of the Criminal Code, the court had determined the punishment for each offence. For the offence of murder of the first victim, the penalty for both defendants is the death sentence. For the murder of the second victim for the purpose of concealing other offences committed by the defendants, the penalty for both defendants is the death sentence. For the offence of rape, the sentence of imprisonment for both defendants is 20 years. Of the offence of theft at night, the sentence of imprisonment for the second defendant is 2 years. For the offence of being an alien entering into the Kingdom not through legal channel, for the offence of being an alien entering into the Kingdom without a valid passport and without permission by law the examination of an immigration officer nor the filling of forms prescribed by law, an action with the same intention which falls within the s cope of those offences is one and the same action which concurrently violates different provisions of law and as each offence has the same scale of punishment, therefore, according to Section 90 of the Criminal Code, the punishment of the offence being an alien entering the Kingdom without permission shall be applied to the second defendant and the sentence of imprisonment for such offence is 6 months. For the offence of being an alien residing in the Kingdom without permission, the sentence of imprisonment for the second defendant is six months. However, as the second defendant had confessed for committing offences of being an alien entering into the Kingdom without permission and being an alien residing in the Kingdom without permission, this extenuating circumstance provided benefit to the trial and as a result the Court reduce punishment to be inflicted on the defendant for each offence to half. As a result, the sentence of imprisonment for the offence of being an alien entering into the Kingdom without permission is 3 months and the sentence of imprisonment for the offence of being an alien residing in the Kingdom without permission is 3 months. Regarding the second defendants confession made subsequent to an arrest for the offence of being theft at night which was of benefit to the investigation and which led to the seizure of the exhibited mobile phone, thus according to Section 78 of the Criminal Code, the court reduces the punishment to one-fourth and as a result, the sentence of the imprisonment for the offence of being theft at night for the second defendant is 1 year and 6 months. As both defendants have been sentenced to the death penalty, the sentences of imprisonment on other offences cannot be thus included for both defendants and as a result the Court only imposes the death penalty on both defendants. The Court also ordered the defendants to return the exhibited hoe as well as ordered the second defendant to reimburse Baht 16,000 value of the mobile phone to the descendants of the first victim and requests were dismissed".

This is a redacted translation and is for information purposes only. Reference should be made to the official full transcript of the Court's judgement.

CHAPTER 37 - A VISIT WITH THE NOW CONVICTED AND CONDEMNED MEN

I woke up on Christmas morning and as I got in the shower my partner put on the TV. Immediately he got me out of the shower to see the news. There were massive protests on the Thai Burmese border. The Burmese had come out by the thousands to protest the guilty verdict and the death penalty for the B2. There were hundreds of vans driving up and down the border adorned with giant posters on the side of them. Many of the pictures were of the B2 and of me. They were everywhere. I had always promised my partner I would keep my name off all of the articles I wrote for my publication and had always done so, despite endless complaints that there was never a byline on my articles. I also promised I would keep my face out of the papers and local and international news. All that had changed at the court when I needed to support the mothers and now my face was everywhere. My partner said, "What the hell have you gone and done now"? I just looked at him with the most innocent facial expression I could muster and said, "Ooops"!

I don't think he saw the funny side of it. I was glad they were protesting and standing up for their fellow men but part of me was thinking this was getting well out of hand. This protest was a huge political statement and now it would be impossible for me to be seen by the Thai people as just a caring humanitarian. I was part of the circus.

I got ready to go to the prison and drove to the other end of the island. I picked up my friend who lived about a ten-minute drive from the prison. He was devastated at the outcome and we both discussed what on earth we would say to the B2. I said that we had to be positive and say that the appeal was being worked on even though it was Christmas, and use that as an excuse as to why Andy and his legal team had cut and run. For the first time in the history of my visits to the Samui Provincial Prison, I was apprehensive.

We went through the usual procedure at the prison and waited for what seemed like an eternity for the iron bar gate to open so we could walk down the little corridor and see them. I took a sharp intake of breath when I saw their faces, eyes red and swollen from crying. I was glad they were Buddhist and Christmas meant nothing to them as there would be no visit from their mothers, both of whom were still being sedated back at the safe house that we had rented for them.

The visit was the most difficult I had ever had with Zaw Lin and Wai Phyo. I didn't know what to say. They seemed too stunned to speak. They could not understand what had gone wrong. I knew in their hearts they had fully expected to be in Myanmar at that moment and not talking to me through the Perspex window that I wished with all my heart would melt away so I could hold them tight and give them the love that I had in my heart for them both. I have never worked so hard to fight back tears before. Their faces touched my heart and my soul. I have never felt more helpless and hopeless and more disgusted with a corrupt nation who, at that point, I hated with a passion. It is a feeling I still battle with.

I explained the best I could to Zaw Lin and Wai Phyo that this was not the end. It was either a mistake or a face-saving exercise and that they would not be executed anytime soon. We had an appeal to get through and if that failed, we would appeal to the Supreme Court. I told them all about the protests on the border and reassured them that the whole world knew that this was wrong. I said that justice had not been served and that we had a massive international following that would ensure that in the end justice would be served. I told them not to give up and that they must fight, and they must try to remember more information about that night. I told them in no uncertain terms that if we could not prove they did not commit this crime then we had no choice but to prove that someone else did. They must start to write down every last thing they could think of to give me every last lead to follow up. Andy had told me to never discuss the case with them and to only be there as their friend and not confuse me with the legal case. At this point, I no longer cared about him or anything he had to say. He had let them down and made huge mistakes that could cost these two young and very frightened boys their lives. I was mad as hell with him for not only for his mistakes but for leaving it to me to see them and try to give them hope. Nothing in your life prepares you to face two condemned men and it gut-wrenching.

Before we said our goodbyes, I assured the B2 that I would be back to visit in a few days. I had no idea at the time that this would not happen.

Outside the jail, my friend and I started to discuss what hope the B2 had of ever being free. It was bleak. I knew the first appeal would go before the very same judges who had passed down the death sentence in the first place, so the chances of them winning that one were zero. I didn't know what to think about the Supreme Court, but in view of the protests on the border and the wide international press coverage, I thought the chances were pretty slim. I could see no way Thailand could admit they had this wrong without losing more face than they would ever be prepared to lose. They would never live it down and even if they did admit it, who would they pin it on next? There was no way the real culprits would ever be brought to justice so logically the B2 were screwed. At this point, I started to think the only way these men would ever be free would be if we got them out of jail by less than legitimate means. A massive feeling that I can only describe as maternal instinct came over me outside the prison in the baking sun. I looked up at the prison and said to my friend, "These kids are going to be executed and we have to stop it. We can't bank on the appeal. We have to do something, and we have to do it soon."

As mad as it might sound to anyone reading this who has not lived in Thailand, I suddenly decided to take matters into my own hands. I could not stand by and watch these two men be strapped down to a gurney and have lethal injections forced into their arms. I was incensed and was in a state of panic. I told my friend that we had to get the B2 out; he looked quizzically at me and asked how we could do that, as storming the prison was not really practical or realistic. I agreed; however, the B2 would have to be transferred to Bangkok now that their fate was death row. To me, compared to death row in one of the world's most notorious prisons, one van with one driver, one guard, and two Burmese did not seem at all insurmountable. It may have been a totally mad plan, but to me, at that time, we had one chance to save these men and I was damn sure going to try to take it. I called Andy and told him. He thought I was mad and said that we had to trust in the law and wait for the appeal. I had no intention of trusting in the law. Where had that got us? I had no faith whatsoever that the defense team lead by a civil lawyer had the capacity to win an appeal. Once the B2 were safely behind the impenetrable walls of Bangkwang, we would have no options left. I figured out that I had about a month before the men would be transferred and started to make some enquiries to people I knew who knew "people". It would not be easy, and it would not be cheap, but it was possible. I started to ask myself if I had the guts to do it. I then asked myself if I had the guts not to do it and sit helplessly by and watch these two men languish on death for years for murders they did not commit before being murdered themselves.

I had nagging doubts in the back of my mind about the consequences of such radical action, but I didn't have to worry about it for long because the very next day the men were woken up at 4 a.m. and whisked off out of the prison. However, they were not sent to Bangkwang in the nation's capital, they were sent to a nasty prison on the mainland in a mafia-run town called Nakhon Si Thammarat. I could have found out when the men were leaving Samui prison but there was not a cat's chance in hell I could find out when they would leave Nakhon Si Thammarat to be transferred to Bangkwang. All bets were off. I still question if I would have taken that option if it had been available. It would be a very different ending to this book that is for certain.

After my trip to the prison on Christmas, I went to the party at the pub and got through it without letting on how devastated I was. I called my parents at around 3 p.m. to wish them Happy Christmas. While talking to my dad, he told me how nice it had been to see me on Christmas. Thinking he must have got dementia, and nobody had bothered to tell me, I explained to him that I was on the beach in Koh Samui and had not seen him that day to which he replied, "Well I have seen you. You were on the BBC news coming out of the court yesterday". My heart sank. This would not go down well with the Thai people who, after the protests on the Burmese border, must be cottoning on to the fact I had spent over a year trying to find the truth. Spending over a year reporting on what was going on in my newspaper and leaking information to the international press.

I shivered a bit and suddenly felt very unsafe, a fact I did not share with my parents during that phone call. I left the party and went to a few other bars to see people I knew who would want to discuss the case. There was a feeling of sadness from everyone I encountered all shocked at the outcome. I got a lot of hugs that night from fellow expats and got a lot of hard stares from the Thai people, or was that just paranoia? It turned out not to be.

The protests on the Thai-Burmese borders were still in full swing and on the 28th of December 2015 this article was published by the *VOA (Voice of America)*

Murder Conviction in Thailand Prompts Protests, Tension With Myanmar

BANGKOK - Thailand is calling on officials in neighboring Myanmar to contain protests against a Thai court's controversial death sentence verdict for two migrant workers from Myanmar last week.

Thai Foreign minister Don Pramudwinai told reporters on Monday that authorities have been in touch with their counterparts as the protests continued to spread beyond the capital.

Last Thursday a Thai court convicted two Myanmar migrant workers for the murders of a young British couple on a resort island. The case had been criticized by outside legal and rights groups amid widespread allegations that the evidence used to link the two suspects to the killings was insufficient or tainted.

Protests Grow

Since Saturday, there have been reports of several border crossing closures because of demonstrations by angry Myanmar nationals.

"We will come and protest here every day until they get a justice and are freed", OakkanTha, a monk from the Rakhine Monastery, at the Three Pagoda Pass border crossing told VOA on Monday.

Thailand has also stopped offering consular services at its Embassy in Yangon, the largest city in Myanmar.

The consular section will be closed from Monday through Wednesday "due to unexpected and prolonged demonstrations around the Embassy, following

Thailand's Koh Samui Provincial Court's recent judgment on Koh Tao murder case, which have caused difficulties in access to the compound of the Royal Thai Embassy", read a statement distributed to reporters by the Thai Ministry of Foreign Affairs.

"We cannot accept that these Myanmar boys were given death sentences although they didn't commit the murder", said student KhineWai Linn on Sunday in front of the Thai embassy in Yangon. "This is totally unfair Thai treatment of migrants from Myanmar".

Demonstrators also went to the lakeside Yangon home of Aung San Suu Kyi on Sunday, asking her to make a plea to authorities in Thailand.

The National League for Democracy president will help the defendants receive justice, said one of her senior staffers, Win Htein.

The NLD won a landslide victory in Myanmar's national election last month but for now the army-dominated government remains in power.

Myanmar's army chief, General Min Aung Hlain, has asked Thailand to review the evidence in the case, according to the government-owned newspaper New Light of Myanmar.

Protesters display messages near the Thai Embassy in Yangon, Myanmar, Friday, Dec. 25, 2015.

Thai junta leader defends decision
The protests have clearly upset the boss of Thailand's junta, Prime Minister Prayuth Chan-ocha, who said the verdict needs to be respected and angrily asked reporters on Monday whether "We should release all people when pressured"?

The two defendants have a right to appeal in Thailand, noted the retired army chief.

The Lawyers Council of Thailand, which represented the defendants, Zai and WaiPhyo, during their trial at the request of Myanmar's embassy, has called for their supporters to remain calm and have faith in the appeals process in the Thai judicial system.

Human rights groups have called for an independent investigation amid widespread skepticism about the case the Thai authorities used to convict 22-year-old suspects.

The two, who worked at a bar on Koh Tao, retracted confessions of killing Hannah Witheridge and David Miller on the Thai island in September 2014.

"We are innocent and we were not involved in this horrific crime, we didn't kill. We want freedom", the duo was quoted in a statement released by Andy Hall, a British human rights defender based in Thailand, after he visited them in prison on Monday.

Hall, on Twitter, said the two men have access to television in their cell and are "encouraged by seeing protests underway in support of overturning their convictions".

The defendants have claimed they were tortured into giving confessions, as well as being threatened with death by interrogators, following their arrests two weeks after the killings.

Police have denied any coercion and have been on the defensive since the protests over the verdict.

Investigators based their case on DNA evidence which linked the two suspects to the crime scene, police major general Piyaphan Pingmuang told reporters in Bangkok on Sunday.

"The DNA evidence cannot lie", he said in rejecting the possibility the case could be reopened.

The police major general also blamed the protests on unnamed groups he said are trying to politicize the verdict.

Myanmar migrants Win Zaw Htun, right, and Zaw Lin, left, both 22, are escorted by officials after their guilty verdict at court in Koh Samui, Thailand, Thursday, Dec. 24, 2015.

Thailand's tourism sector under pressure

Thailand's government has been under the control of a military junta since a May 2014 coup ousted the civilian leadership.

The coup, and a previous period of sometimes violent political demonstrations on the streets of Bangkok, affected Thailand's tourism sector. And the killings of the two young British backpackers, Hannah Witheridge and David Miller, on Koh Tao four months after the coup furthered weakened the tourism industry, which now accounts for more than 14 percent of the kingdom's economy, according to officials.

The crime was widely reported in the British media which recounted that the attractive couple had been in a quarrel with some islanders on the night they were murdered and the crime occurred a night after two British women were reported to have been mugged there by a Thai motorbike gang.

Both of the murder victims suffered head wounds and a coroner said Witheridge had been raped, for which an additional 20 year sentence was imposed by the provincial court last Thursday.

The subsequent police investigation was labeled a farce amid intense pressure on authorities to solve the case which had tarnished Thailand's image as a relatively safe tourism destination.

Human rights groups say it is not unusual for migrant workers in Thailand to be wrongly charged with crimes.

The kingdom hosts an estimated three million such workers – most of them from Myanmar, which is also known as Burma.

Zinlat Aung in Bangkok, Si Thu in Yangon and Nai Kun Enn at Three Pagodas Pass contributed to this report.

I felt a strange kind of emptiness now that I was unable to visit the B2. I missed being at the prison and around people who understood how passionate I felt about the plight of the

B2. I decided to go to the prison and visit Darren. He told me that the prison population was shocked, even the guards were aghast when the B2 came back to the jail having been found guilty.

CHAPTER 38 - IAN YARWOOD

Boxing Day and then the New Year came and went. I was feeling more and more uneasy on the island. My face had been in the media all around the globe and had been on the posters on the Burmese border. People were inclined to be seen out with me less and less and I found myself spending an increasing amount of time at home not wanting to go out. The mothers went back to Myanmar so there was little need to spend all day every day raising funds. I had no visits with the B2 and I felt lost and lonely and sad. I spent about 18 hours a day trawling through the CSI LA page looking for information to help Andy and the legal team prepare the first appeal. However, Andy was not interested.

I felt I had lost grip of the case, but then, on the 6th of January 2016, I got an email from an Australian lawyer who had been following the case. His name was Ian Yarwood.

Ian had supported Andy Hall financially in the past after learning about his troubles with the Natural Fruit Case. Ian said that he understood that Andy had used some of the funds to travel to Koh Samui in the early days to contact the B2.

Ian contacted a man by the name of Peter Sheridan, a retired American barrister living in Chiang Mai with whom Andy had consulted when preparing the defense case for the B2. During that conversation Peter had mentioned my name as somebody who was in touch with the B2 and owned and ran the *Samui Times*.

At this stage in the game, I was highly suspicious of anyone who was contacting me. I was not popular with a lot of Thai people, and especially the mafia, who were not averse to creating false profiles to spy on people or employing the services of westerners to gather information under false pretenses. I wrote a very short note back to Ian and checked him out online. He had a reasonable online footprint and seemed to be legit, but I remained cautious all the same.

I asked Ian what I could do for him. He told me that he had been reading through the draft translated judgment case from his office in Perth, Western Australia. He told me he discovered a whole host of people who had been involved with the defense team in one way or another including another retired barrister, Robert Holmes, an Australian who lived in Bangkok; Jane Taupin, the leading DNA expert also from Australia, and of course, Peter Sheridan. Ian enquired as to whether or not Heidi Anna worked with me. I confirmed that I did not work with Heidi Anna and I had never warmed to her. I outlined what I had done for the B2 and gave Ian an overview of how I got involved. I found it interesting he was in touch with Peter Sheridan and Robert Holmes. I had never met either of them or Jane Taupin, but I had done a lot of research into her and had tried and failed to find out why Andy had not called her to testify at the trial.

Ian shared my concerns about Jane not being called to testify. He informed me that he was the one who put Andy Hall and Jane Taupin in touch with each other. Ian said that not calling Jane Taupin to testify was "a very big mistake".

A few emails went back and forth before Ian and I agreed that it would be easier for us to speak on the phone. The decision to hand out my phone number was not one I took lightly in those days. These days I hand it out to no one.

I told Ian the whole sorry story about Andy and the defense team and about my suspicions that Andy had simply used the Koh Tao case to raise his own profile. I told him I was very unsure that the defense team had done a decent job, and, that I thought it was insane to have chosen a civil lawyer to head the team. Ian agreed.

The more I thought about the defense team the more I started to have grave concerns that the B2 had been incredibly badly defended. I wondered if there was anything we could do about it. I suggested to Ian that there might be a case for a retrial on the grounds of misrepresentation.

On the same day Ian put out a tweet:

"KOH TAO MURDERS: UNEXPLAINED EVIDENCE FROM DEFENCE DNA EXPERT THAT HELPED CONVICT TWO MIGRANT WORKERS

It is well known that the defense failed to call international DNA expert Jane Taupin to give evidence. She had travelled from Melbourne, Australia to the island of Samui at the request of the defense team and was available to give evidence.

Instead, the defense called Woravee Wiyawut MD who is described at page 38 of the judgment as a DNA specialist at the Forensic Institute (being Khunying Pornthip's workplace).

Khun Woravee gave evidence that both the Forensic Institute and the Central Forensic Bureau were accredited under ISO 17025 and that both institutions operate in accordance with international standards.

The court took comfort in that Khun Woravee's evidence and stated that it lends more plausibility that the plaintiff's evidence is beyond reasonable doubt.

I do not know whether the Central Forensic Bureau is accredited under ISO 17025 or not. This is an issue that both the prosecutor and the defense should have settled long before the trial commenced.

However, given that the Central Forensic Bureau failed to:

1. Keep original physical samples from Hannah's body;
2. Maintain adequate notes;
3. Have chain of custody documents;
4. Ensure its documents did not have handwritten corrections & incorrect dates; and
5. Have relevant stamps on its documents;

It is open to conclude that it did not operate in accordance with international standards and that it did not have ISO 17025 accreditation.

One might ask: "Why did Khun Woravee give evidence that appears to be untrue"?

Firstly, Khun Woravee might or might not have personal knowledge of whether the Central Forensic Bureau has ISO 17025 accreditation. He might honestly believe that it has this accreditation based on something he read or heard from another source. If Khun Woravee did not have personal knowledge but made his statement based on what he read or heard then his statement is "hearsay" evidence, which is normally inadmissible in most courts.

Secondly, it is important to note that in the Kingdom of Thailand the culture dictates that keeping face is of vital importance even if this is achieved at the expense of the truth. It is also important that one does not cause anyone else to lose face.

Therefore, there was tremendous pressure on Khun Woravee to refrain from saying anything publicly that might cause the Central Forensic Institute to lose face or for any of its staff to lose face. It might matter little that two migrant workers are on trial for their lives and that the family and friends of victims are looking for answers.

The international DNA expert Jane Taupin would have been under no such cultural constraints about providing an honest opinion on the Central Forensic Bureau's documents, evidence and procedures.

Notwithstanding Khun Woravee's evidence, and with the greatest respect to the court of Koh Samui, in my opinion the scrappy DNA summary and table submitted in evidence by the prosecutor should not have been admitted in evidence and the accused should have been acquitted.

Ian Yarwood
Solicitor
Perth, Western Australia"

After I had spoken to Ian on the phone, I remembered that on one occasion, the 30th of April 2015, Andy had gone to one of the court hearings to hold the B2 for another 12 days prior to the trial. He had taken along some of the ladies I used to be friends with before he enveloped them into what I referred to as his cult. He also took his parents. The ladies he took with him were Tracey from the UK, Nina from Norway, Maria from Sweden and Heidi from the USA. He told the court that the two Scandinavians were members of Hannah's family, and that Tracey was his parents' translator. The judge clearly knew, having seen their passports, this was a lie. I was not in court that day as I had to be in Malaysia, however, I did get Nina and Marie to tell me about their court hoax on my return. I taped our conversation.

I told Ian about this incident, and he told me:

"There are some critics of Andy's on Twitter who have raised this issue of Andy bringing in people who claimed to be family of a victim. That is an outrageously stupid thing for Andy to do. It will mean his credibility with the court is shot to ribbons. He then goes to testify for the boys but he has already lost credibility".

On the 9th of January 2016 I got wind of another death on Koh Tao. I was not sure who or why or what had happened this time, but it didn't take me long to find out; the latest death was Luke Miller, a British man from the Isle of Wight. My blood ran cold once again, another dead man with the surname Miller? What the hell had gone on this time?

CHAPTER 39 – LUKE MILLER

On the 8th of January 2016, the body of 26-year-old Luke Miller was found by a security guard at the bottom of a swimming pool at the Sunset Bar on Sairee Beach. Mr. Miller, a bricklayer, had travelled to Thailand with his friend, James Gissing, on the 22nd of December 2015. Luke Miller and James Gissing were joined by James's sister, Nichola, who arrived from Australia. Prior to his untimely death, Luke Miller posted on his Facebook page, "Can honestly say this New Year I am living the dream of going to the Full Moon Party on a speedboat drink cocktails, strawberry daiquiris living life to the full yolo so let's do this"

I immediately started to look into this latest death. The police account of events was that Luke had been out drinking and at some point in the early hours of the morning had decided to show off in front of a crowd at a party. The party was taking place at a resort that had a bar with a swimming pool. The police said that Luke had managed to climb on top of a DJ booth that was covered in barbed wire and then dived into the pool, an act that had caused not only severe head injuries, but his death. There were a couple of rather startling aspects to this version of events. If this had been the truth, then why was it that, once again, we did not have a single witness? Why was it that nobody called for help or called an ambulance? How was it that if anyone had seen this 'accident', they all simply went home and left his body in the swimming pool for the security guards to find the next day? Even more unfathomable was the fact that Luke could not swim and hated water. James Gissing told me, when I spoke to him days after Luke's death, that Luke only ever went for a paddle when James was there with him. The police had also been releasing information to the press that suggested, that prior to his death, Luke had been in a fight, and at one point they released information that suggested that, after the fight, Luke had indeed been murdered.

Regardless of what actually happened, Luke's body was quickly removed from the island and sent to the mainland. The Gissing siblings also rapidly left the island.

I spoke to Nichola Gissing very soon after Luke's body had been sent to Surat Thani for an autopsy. She was very scared. She and James were making their way to Bangkok where they were offered accommodation in a safe house via an Australian friend of mine, who had learned all about justice Thai style when her son was attacked in Koh Samui. Like me, she had also been working hard to save the hapless B2 and had followed all of the odd deaths on Koh Tao.

Nichola told me on the day of Luke's death, James and Nichola were visited by a policeman, he was asking for the password for Luke's phone that had gone missing. The policeman she was talking about was Ched, aka Big Ears, the very same man who was photographed by Sean McAnna with Montriwat Toovichien the night Sean said they told him he was going to hang himself.

Nichola told a friend that she had managed to get to see Luke's body after it had been transported to Surat Thani on the mainland for an autopsy. She had been shocked to discover hand-shaped bruises on both arms. Later Nichola told me that Luke's phone battery had been sent back to the UK, but the actual phone was never found. Despite having left Koh Tao, Nichola had been in touch with police officers on the island and one of them had taken to continually messaging her. It was the young officer who had been first officer to arrive at the murder scene of Hannah and David.

He had been trying to persuade the Gissing siblings to go back to Koh Tao suggesting that he was going to do a thorough investigation into the case. Nichola said she was almost fooled by this man but decided against returning to the island as she didn't trust him. She also told me, "Well, the Koh Tao police retracted the statement about him having a fight. I have photos of Luke's hands from the morgue. He has bruises on his knuckles, so they are lying, and none of the bruising was accounted for in the autopsy".

Within a couple of days, we found a GoFundMe site raising money to get the body of Luke Miller home. It was started by Aisling McConville, one of Luke's many friends from the Isle of Wight. It said:

"No word if the insurance company will pay for the repatriation as of yet. We are also going to be paying for the funeral costs by the looks of it out right , and be giving Luke Miller the send off he deserves. Any money left over will be donated on to another suitable trust or a charity. Already made arrangements with the family (in fact I am sat with now) I am happy for anyone to inbox me on Facebook and ask for my number".

According to a report by the BBC during the British inquest into the death of Luke Miller, Coroner Caroline Sumeray said: "It has been suggested this was a cover up by the Thai authorities but there has been a very thorough police report".

The coroner mentioned that the Gissing siblings had initially been told by local police that Luke Miller was seen to be assaulted in another bar before he was found dead and that they were treating his death as a murder. However, Ms. Sumeray said that the police contact who made that statement could not be relied upon, and there was not even any evidence that the policeman who suggested Luke was murdered was even a member of the police force.

In a statement read to the court, Mr. Gissing said he felt, "Police were covering up as it was the death of another foreigner on Koh Tao".

The hearing was told a witness described a man banging heads with another swimmer, but Ms. Sumeray said there was no evidence this was Mr. Miller.

The court also heard Mr. Miller had lost the key to his rented motorcycle in the Sunset Bar pool a few days before his death, and despite searches to find it had paid the 5,000 baht (£114) fee for its replacement.

A post-mortem examination in Thailand showed Mr. Miller had a number of small bruises on his face and legs and concluded he died as a result of head injuries and drowning, the inquest was told. Toxicology tests showed he was one-and-three-quarters above the [legal] UK alcohol drink-drive level and also had traces of the drug Ritalin in his system.

Ms. Sumeray said, "I can only record a conclusion based on the evidence before me. I cannot speculate about what may have happened".

At the conclusion, Mr. Miller's mother, Sara Cotton, wept and said: "I want my son".

The Thai people were angry. They had another suspicious death on their hands and more bad publicity in the media.

CHAPTER 40 – SUPPORT FOR THE B2 FROM UNLIKELY SOURCES

After the convictions of the B2, a friend of mine contacted a group called Anonymous, a decentralized international hacktivist group that is widely known for its various cyber attacks against several governments, government institutions and agencies, corporations, and the Church of Scientology. We sent them links to CSI LA and other forums where the guilt of the B2 was being questioned. Not only did they listen, but they decided to help and took responsibility for the hacking of fourteen Thai police websites in protest at the convictions of the B2. The affected websites included those of the Bangkok Metropolitan Police Bureau, the General Staff Division of Royal Thai Police, and regional police stations.

The words 'Failed Law', 'We Want Justice', and hashtag #BoycottThailand were displayed on some of the hacked sites, along with the name of the Myanmar-based 'Blink Hacker Group'. The Thai police confirmed the attack on its websites but said there was no confidential data on the public websites.

On the 10th of January 2016, Laura Witheridge, the sister of Hannah Witheridge, posted a scathing attack on Thailand to her Facebook page. It read:

"As some of you may have already seen there has been another death of yet another British National on Koh Tao.

I wasn't going to post anything. Not until I logged on here this morning to see that a friend has shared the link warning people not to go there….It wasn't the sharing of the link or the warning that triggered this lengthy status, as I hope people do share these things and try to warn people not to go… it was the ignorant comment someone had made about how Thailand is the most beautiful place in the world that frustrated me this morning. Aesthetically, on a postcard or a photograph maybe… However, literally…. I have to disagree. Lots of things look beautiful. You only have to consider a lion or a tiger, beautiful to look at, yes… but get too close and they will tear you apart and feed you to their young. My point being that aesthetic beauty can lure you into a very dangerous trap.

Since Hannah was taken from us, I am continually asked whether I will warn the World about the dangers of Thailand… I am asked if I will warn people because I might 'just save someone's life'. This person's comment serves as a perfect example of why I would be wasting my time. People can be ignorant and many, probably the majority, have very short memories. Countless times, I have logged in to Facebook and seen the status's made by people who know both Hannah and I who have gone out there anyway. They think it won't happen to them… well, guess what? Neither did we. No one is immune. Many Thai's hate westerners and they have little or no regard for human life. I don't say this lightly, or without reason. Let me share a few facts with you about this beautiful place you speak of.

Many of the Thai people have no regard for human life. My evidence for this statement firstly, some quotes of the things said to my bereaved, heartbroken family by the judges and court officials at the trial of the two Burmese migrants-

Why are you still here? Do you care? She is dead already

Why are you so bothered? Just go home and make another one

Why are you making such a fuss, she will be back in 30 days as something else and may have better luck next time.

Would it surprise you if I told you that the Thai's view drug possession as a more serious offence than rape or murder? Or that the vast majority of the Thai police force are corrupt?

What if I told you that when we went to Thailand to bring Hannah home, we were offered the opportunity to go to the Royal Thai police headquarters for an 'official update'… but that, on arrival, we were taken into a large room, left for 5 minutes before the door opened and around 200 journalists were allowed into the room and we were ambushed by this mob of hungry journalists shoving cameras in our faces…

The Thai police chief had no intentions of giving us an update… after all, the bungled investigation meant he had nothing to tell us. The invitation was so that he could make money out of our misery. The press had paid him generously for 5 minutes to capture photographs of our family. The photograph on this post serves as evidence of this: (photograph shown)

"What if I told you that since we lost Hannah there have been many more suspicious deaths on Koh Tao. You probably haven't heard of them all, as not all were British Nationals. The deaths, where possible, are covered up as suicides and accidents. This would have happened with Hannah, if it had not been for the hideous brutality of her passing.

Luke Miller latest casualty of Koh Tao

I highly suspect that with this latest tragedy, the Thai's will say that it was an accidental death caused by drugs. Hiding the truth and offering a story that suits, is something that they do often… My thoughts are with Luke Miller's family and friends.

What if I told you that I have had many death threats from Thai people since they murdered my sister? That they defaced photographs of me saying that the killers had only done 'half the job'… what if I told you that people commented on these photographs saying things like 'there is still time', and 'tick tock tick tock'. What if I told you that I have been sent crime scene photographs? What if I told you that I have been chased in my car?

What if I told you that the Thais offered us 'compensation' to try and keep us quiet? Obviously, we were absolutely appalled and told them to shove it.

What if I told you that I am now frightened of my own shadow? That I am constantly looking over my shoulder? That I am exhausted, but frightened to sleep because of the nightmares? I miss my sister desperately. My heart is heavy and my mind is tired.

Still think Thailand is beautiful? If your answer is still 'yes', then I would suggest you watch the following".

Laura put a link to the Anonymous video that will be written of in another chapter.

I was stunned, But I was not the only one; the Thai authorities were too and very keen to shut her up as soon as humanly possible. The news that the Thai police were going to sue Laura did not take very long to hit the international headlines. This article, written by Philip Sherwell, was posted *The Telegraph* on the 14th of January 2016:

"Thai police respond to scathing criticism from sister of Koh Tao murder victim.

Kingdom's judicial and police chiefs go on counter-offensive after blistering attack by sister of murdered British backpacker Hannah Witheridge.

Thai police chiefs and judicial officials have rejected a series of accusations from the sister of murdered British tourist Hannah Witheridge.

They responded to the criticism as hackers linked to the Anonymous cyber collective knocked nearly 300 Thai court and government websites offline in retaliation for the death sentences imposed on two Burmese men.

A spokesman for the Court of Justice said that the Office of the Judiciary had already conducted a preliminary investigation into the allegations made in a Facebook posting by Laura Witheridge.

Miss Witheridge dismissed the police investigation into the murders of her sister and fellow Briton David Miller on Koh Tao in Sept 2014 as "bungled".

She also alleged that court officials had made highly offensive comments to her family and linked to an Anonymous video accusing the Thai police of using the two Burmese men as "scapegoats".

The court official noted that the victims' relatives and representatives of the British embassy attended the trial of the two murder migrant workers, who were found guilty on Christmas Eve.

"Throughout the trial, neither complaint nor any improper conduct was brought up for immediate action to be taken against", said the spokesman.

"Moreover, all judges and court officials are consciously aware of the rights of the victim and her family afforded by law. We are under the legal duty to ensure those rights will be protected and that they will not be undermined by any action or person".

The spokesman invited relatives of the murdered woman to submit a formal complaint through the British embassy so that a full investigation could be conducted.

Thai police commanders also rejected Miss Witheridge's allegations, which included claims of widespread corruption and cover-ups of deaths of Western visitors.

Gen Chakthip Chaijinda, the national police chief, has ordered his force's legal affairs unit to examine her denunciations to decide whether to take legal action against her.

Miss Witheridge posted her lengthy comment – later removed – in the wake of a death of another young British tourist on Koh Tao.

The body of Luke Miller was found in a hotel swimming pool. Police said that they believed he had plunged into the water and struck his head while drunk, even before an autopsy was conducted.

Miss Witheridge said that she was speaking out in frustration after reading the "Ignorant comment" that Thailand is "The most beautiful place in the world" following the latest death.

Her comments put her at striking odds with the family of David Miller, who said they supported the police investigation and court hearings and were convinced of the guilt of the convicted men.

Zaw Lin and Wai Phyo were found guilty largely on the basis of disputed DNA evidence after retracting confessions that they were said were forced by torture.

Cyber-hackers have declared war on Thailand over the verdicts. A group, believed to be based in Burma and associated with Anonymous, first defaced and knocked offline several Thai police websites.

And this week, they launched their mass attack on Thai court websites, declaring the strike was "In protest over the Koh Tao murder verdict". The convictions have aroused anger in the men's home country, also known as Myanmar.

Suebpong Sripongkul, the Court of Justice spokesman, said the hacking would have no effect on the verdict and said it would pursue legal action under the computer crimes act against those responsible.

"The Court wishes to state that the attack will not result in the ruling on the Koh Tao case as the court issued a ruling based on the law", he said, noting that the two men could file an appeal.

The defense team is expected to lodge an appeal in coming weeks by contesting the DNA evidence that was used to convict the men".

The news in Thailand was full of it, and for a while, it actually looked like the Thai authorities were going to have Laura extradited to Thailand to face charges, but it fizzled out, as it would in another case, a year later. One that would see me and a young British rape victim under the same threat of extradition to face charges of computer crimes and damaging the reputation of Thailand.

CHAPTER 41 - ANONYMOUS

By the 11th of January 2016, word was travelling to every corner of the globe that Thailand had convicted two innocent Burmese men for the murders of Hannah and David. My friends and I invested hours trying to find ways to get justice. Then we got the news that Anonymous, who had taken on our cause, and jumped on board, were going to help the B2. We waited with bated breath for days as they investigated the case and put together a broadcast.

The following couple of weeks seemed like months, but eventually the days whittled down to hours then minutes then seconds—I refreshed my computer screen a million times before finally the broadcast was uploaded.

In the 37-minute broadcast by Anonymous, a masked presenter said that it had come to the attention of Anonymous that a Thai court had sentenced two Burmese migrant workers to be executed for the rape and murder of Hannah Witheridge and the murder of David Miller. He passed on his condolences to the families. He went on to say that it was the desire of Anonymous to seek truth and justice in the case. Their involvement had come about due to the large support network the B2 had online that suggested the B2 were scapegoats. Anonymous had learned that Thai police had accused innocent people before and would rather blame foreigners or migrants for such crimes to protect their lucrative tourist industry. He continued stating Anonymous had carefully viewed many documents and had gone over many facts and found there had been many similarities between this and past cases in Thailand. Their concerns were stated as "biased sentencing for westerners and migrants for crimes". Anonymous said they were against any government who used prisoners for any kind of publicity stunt for whatever purpose.

They went on to discuss the rape and attempted murder of Sheri McFarline and the murder of her boyfriend Kelvin on the 3rd of February 2000. This crime took place in northern Thailand when, again, the police were under much pressure to solve the case quickly. In this case, the Thai police had blamed the crimes on Mr. Sangthom See Yang and Mr. Enthorn See Jong, both of Chinese descent. They were both found guilty and sentenced to death, despite having photographic alibis. Anonymous accused the Thai police of lying, falsifying facts and evidence, ignoring the alibis, bungling DNA evidence, and threatening to kill the families of the men if they did not admit to the crimes. They went on to say that not only had the police ignored the DNA evidence, but they had also even had the lower court suppress the suspects DNA being compared to the DNA the police submitted to the court. However, due to pressure and support from locals, who were prepared to stand up against injustice, the case was reheard by Thailand's Supreme Court. The judge in this court had found that the DNA taken from Sheri McFarland and Kelvin did not match the DNA of the two Chinese migrant suspects who were previously found guilty and sentenced to death by the lower court. The judge had acquitted them both and demanded that they be released as free men immediately. To this day, the case has never been solved.

The next case they discussed was that of Kirsty Jones, a British woman who was raped and murdered in a guest house in Chiang Mai in the north of Thailand, also in the year 2000. Anonymous pointed out that the police had also bungled this investigation by failing to secure the crime scene, allowing vital evidence to become contaminated. In this case, the police arrested a non-Thai national, Andrew Gill, and charged him with the rape and murder alongside another suspect they could not name. He was later released as they had no DNA evidence to link him to the crime. They then turned their attention to a tour guide who claimed he was tortured into confession and was forced to masturbate to produce semen to be inserted into the crime scene. Fortunately for the guide the Guides Association of Chiang Mai marched to the police station to demand his release and the charges were later dropped.

Over some time, Sue Jones, Kirsty's mother had applied to view all of the documents involving her daughter's rape and murder only to be denied the documents by the Thai police. She then approached her own country's officials who said that they had supported the decision not to give her all corresponding documents and it was for the benefit of good relations between the UK and Thailand governments. However, not giving up, Sue Jones had finally attained the requested documents only to find that names had been deleted from police reports. A breakthrough had occurred when two senior officers from the Dyfed Powis police in the UK had found DNA and semen on Kirsty's sarong that was used to strangle her. That DNA was noted as being of a Thai national which cleared all previous suspects who were accused of the crime to which Lieutenant General Suthep Dragsuan, commissioner of the Fifth Region Police, comprising most of northern Thailand, had stated that the Asian DNA was planted. This case is also remains unsolved. Mention is then made that General Powitwongsuwan claimed that Thailand's judicial process is trustworthy, adding that their authorities cannot reinvestigate the current case involving Wai Phyo and Zaw Lin, the two Burmese migrants, since this would mean that the judicial process has been incompetent. Anonymous stated that nothing could be further from the truth, and with this specific case in mind, as saying that the Thai police had been incompetent would be an understatement.

Their investigations then turned to the cases of Nick Pearson, Christina Annesley and Dimitre Povse. They came to the same conclusions that I had and suggested that the Thai police lie, fabricate evidence, do poor police investigating, contaminate crime scenes, lose DNA and evidence, accuse non-Thai nationals, and refuse to believe truth and evidence that would clear their preferred suspects and refuse to believe that their own Thai locals are responsible for any wrongdoing. Anonymous, after an in-depth look at the case of Hannah and David, concluded, "if the DNA from the murder weapon was not a match to the two Burmese migrants, then how can they have been found guilty of murder. They stated that this conviction was exactly as the previous false conviction, of that above, that saw two Chinese migrants set up for the rape of Sheri McFarline and murder of Kelvin back in 2000". The Anonymous presentation then showed a video of the Thai military beating up a Burmese migrant by repeatedly hitting him over the head and kicking him in the face.

Going back to the Hannah and David case, Anonymous stated: "It is interesting that Mon's brother, the island headman, Mr. Worapan Toovichien, had offered a substantial reward if anybody could implicate his family members to the crime. This was more like a challenge if anything. If Mr. Worapan was any real island headman, one would think that he would offer a reward to find the killers and those responsible, not for successfully implicating his family members, again we see here what is of main concern on this island, their good name and not justice. These victims are foreigners and experience has shown that the Thai police do not really care about foreigners, they only care about their own good name and their tourist industry. In conclusion, Anonymous has seen so many flaws in this case, so many incompetent officials involved. The DNA cannot be trusted.

Statements have not been taken seriously or investigated thoroughly. CCTV footage is missing or was refused to be handed over, people leaving the island without having been investigated, and Koh Tao travel and mobile phone records ignored and not investigated regarding suspects. It seems like the island of Koh Tao is an island that tourists should avoid. We do not believe the two Burmese migrants are the actual culprits of this horrific case and our thoughts go out to the families of every case we have mentioned in this video and offer our sincere condolences. Truth and justice is what Anonymous desires and we encourage the Supreme Court in Thailand, that has shown integrity in the past, to demand a thorough investigation into the deaths of those in Koh Tao. We encourage the Thai government to investigate the allegations of Mafia drug dealing, date rape cocktails of female tourists in Koh Tao, the DNA of the two rape cases dating back to 2000, and offer as much help and support to the still grieving parents who do not yet have closure to the deaths of their children. Anonymous would like to see the Thai government allow foreign police investigators have more power and control over serious rape and murder cases in Thailand that involve foreigners. We do not like the facts in this recent Koh Tao case. We do not believe the Thai court has convicted the actual murderers of the crime and Anonymous calls for this case to be reinvestigated with credible forensic specialists such as Dr. Pornthip, who clearly has much respect in the eyes of the Thai people, migrants, and foreigners. Anonymous will post all of the corresponding links to the facts of this video and this specific case. Lastly, Anonymous would warn foreigners from preferring Thailand as their first option for a holiday until such a time as the Thai police make many changes in the way they handle rape and murder cases involving foreigners and migrants and show more respect to deceased victims. If you feel this case warrants another investigation, feel free to sign the change.org petition via the link provide below in the description. Anonymous at this point supports #boycottThailand until such time as changes are made as to how Thai police handle investigations involving foreign tourists".

CHAPTER 42 - THE KEY TO
THE CASE IS THE DNA

Things were looking bleak for the B2. The key to saving their lives seemed to hinge on the DNA evidence. Ian and I decided the only option left open to us was to discredit the DNA. In order to do this, we needed to know if the laboratory that tested it was accredited to do so. If this was the case, we could go after the governing bodies. We initially hoped we could persuade the legal team to do this. In order to do that, Ian approached Robert Holmes, the retired Australian barrister who had been aiding the legal team. The plan was to attack the Thai laboratories through the governing body BLQS, which is under the auspices of APLAC in Australia. This would ensure that BLQS would be forced to undertake an investigation of the labs concerned. To not do so would put them in breach of its agreement with APLAC and ILAC which in turn would have international implications for Thailand.

Around this time, the CSI MM group, who had also invested a great deal of time investigating the case, were getting very upset about the way the case had been handled. They told me that there were seven witnesses, three of whom were friends of Zaw Lin, who were all accused and tortured in relation to the Koh Tao case. Their names and details were passed on to Andy Hall and the Migrant Workers Rights Network (MWRN) who put this information into the hands of Sein Htay, the head of MWRN, who passed the details onto the lead lawyer, Nakhorn. However, CSI MM had discovered that the defense team had not contacted a single one of them. I could have wept for the B2.

I had been back in contact with Htoo Chit who had been involved in the case as a member of the Burmese government. He was in touch with CSI MM and had as little regard for Andy and the defense team as did I. I outlined our plan to take civil action against the lab and all parties agreed it was the way forward. In view of the fact that the defense team had lost a winnable case, we also decided it would be a good idea to put the appeal process in the hands of a different legal team. We all suspected that the current team were either grossly incompetent or had been 'got at'.

Both of these plans would involve enlisting the help of the existing legal team as we would need the case files. We decided on Robert Holmes, whom Ian Yarwood contacted. Coincidently he had also come up with a plan to sue the DNA lab. Holmes was happy to advise a new team once he had secured an affidavit of Pornthip's testimony. Pornthip testified at the trial as a DNA expert and her testimony stated that the DNA on the murder weapon matched neither Zaw Lin nor Wai Phyo. Holmes also said he needed to seek more legal advice before announcing to the world that civil action would be taken against the lab. Finally, it seemed like we had a plan that did not involve Andy Hall and that everyone was on board. However, it didn't last.

Robert being part of this new team put him at odds with the existing legal team who had no idea about our plans. To pull this off, Robert needed a lot of documents and translations from the existing team. On the 19th of January 2016, Ian decided to call ILAC, the International Laboratory Accreditation Cooperation, but did not manage to get hold of anyone so he left a message. Things then started to go wrong. The CSI MM team, who were in on the new plan, had discussed our intentions with Heidi Anna who in turn told Andy Hall. The cat was out of the bag and Andy was furious and had no intention of letting go of the appeal. At this point, I really had had enough. There were too many people at odds in the whole case that was turning into a total circus. I was ready to simply walk away knowing I was beaten. With the appeal date looming, it looked as if the legal team was going to miss the deadline. To me it was essential they were sacked, and a new team were brought in for the appeal.

I recalled a conversation I had with Andy on the 24th of December 2015 when he said that he and the defense team would be taking some much needed holiday time and that he would be asking for a 60 to 90 day extension for the appeal to be lodged. I hoped that Andy could get the extension and asked Robert to confirm this would be the case. He confirmed that in Thailand there has to be an appeal pursuant to the criminal code in Thailand in the case of death penalty sentences and a delay to file an appeal would be granted.

Not deterred by Andy's refusal to give up the case, we started to think about the costs involved in hiring a new team to handle the appeal and sue the lab. Robert suggested it would be between $15,000 and $40,000 US.

Ian and I had also discussed the possibility of going for a retrial as we believed the B2 had a possible case against the legal team for misrepresentation. We decided it was time we took a harder look at Andy Hall and how he had handled the case. All attempts by me and Ian to get any information out of Andy with regards to the appeal failed.

In the meantime, concerned about the welfare of the B2, who had now been shipped to the notorious Bangkwang, AKA Bangkok Hilton Prison, I had contacted a prison support group in the nation's capital. We established that prison bank accounts had been set up for the B2 and that even though they were in separate buildings in the notorious Thai prison, they were not confined to their cells or shackled.

By the 22nd of February 2016, I had just about given up on being personally involved in helping the B2, despite knowing that they wanted me on board. Zaw Lin and Wai Phyo had had no say in who defended them, and decisions were being made for them by people such as Robert Holmes who they didn't even know. The way Andy had run the defense, without transparency of what he was doing, or who was involved, to my mind was an abuse of the human rights of the B2. Pretty ironic when he was meant to be a human rights activist.

On the 24th of February 2016, I got a letter from Wai Phyo.

"Dear Sister Su

Thank you very much for your letters that I received on 18.02.16. I am so appreciate for sharing your time to write a long and beautiful letter to us even you are so busy with your own. Your writing is so beautiful and clear that I can see all of your activities in it. Moreover it gives me so optimistic views to see the vissitutes of life. As you said, many people round the world are more suffering than us. My body is locked up in prison but my mind is still free to think. I am so lucky because my mind is never locked up in any dogmatic belief. For some people, life seems to be mysterious, but in Buddhism everything is happening under the law of cause and effect. When bad things happen to the best people and good things happen to the worst people, you may doubt the law of cause and effect. Many of the results we experience in this life are the results of actions created in previous lives, and many of the actions we perform in this life will open in the future. Therefore I am in prison even though I have never committed the crime because of some bad actions in my previous life. Some people become sick in prison and some warders become prisoners. My friends in prison said that I am so lucky because many people take care of us even our government (Burmese prisoners have never get embassy to visit Thailand) IT is sure that I am luckier than the Scottish man who died elephant trekking , so it is difficult to decide about the falling and rising of good and bad fortune in a life. I agree one thing with you about the animals is that they wild must stay in the wild. The wildlife must be preserved, but allowed for business reasons. I think that trekking on an elephant back is safer than travelling by plane with a suicide bomber. Nowadays all prisons situations are changed. We all inmates from building 5 come to building 2 and vice versa. So I am in B2 and Zaw Lin is in B5 now.

I am not sure you can visit us at the same time. Please ask the lawyer for visiting information and please pass this message to sister Evelyne. I forgot to write to her about the visiting days and new buildings.

In this new building we have to pray twice a day and exercise for half an hour every day as prison activities. Exercise is not a problem but to force somebody to pray is very strange as in Buddhism. Buddha has never asked anyone to worship him. He showed the way to Nirvana and encourages people to follow it. How can be peaceful for those who are praying with an angry mind? Finally, I want to say thank you again for believing my innocence. I promise you for staying strong to show my gratitude to those who help and believe us. Moreover, I want to describe to the world the true stories of the migrant workers in Thailand and how badly treated we are. Take care of yourself and I wish you body fitting soon so you don't need to go to the gym anymore. Please give my best regards to all the members of your family and friends. I love you like my own sister, with love Wai Phyo. Please write your address in your next letter".

There was no way I was going to write my address in any letter that went anywhere near the prison. I was glad we had a PO box. It made me smile that Wai Phyo hope my body fitted soon so I did not have to go to the gym anymore. He was writing with regards to the elephant after I told him of the sad death of a tourist who was killed by the elephant he was trekking on in Samui. I felt that wildlife should be wild and not broken for tourist pleasure, but Wai Phyo was right, it would be safer to be on an elephant than on a plane with a suicide bomber. Wai Phyo had obviously found a friend who could translate a letter for him in prison and I was happy about that.

A few days later I got a letter from Zaw Lin:

"Happy Valentine's Day, my big sister Su and Evelyne. Compliment of the season. How about your present condition of your health and the atmospheric around you? I hope that everything is well with you. I so much thank you with all my heart and soul for your help towards my heinous condition. I don't know where to start thanking you because my heart is full of happiness and joy and time. I miss you so much. You did what my blood big sister cannot do for me. May the peace of joy, love, and happiness of God always be with you. I always think in my heart every day asking myself why God give me a lovely big sister care like you. Oh, very great thanks for given me yeah. I received your mail dated 27.02.2016 and thanks you so much for your letter. This new prison Bangkwang is better than other prisons that I have been. Lesser people here were 5 people in the room. But you have to comprehend that there is comfort in jail no matter how the prison looks like ha haha. Please I will like receiving your mail often. Please Sir do not forget me. For I have faith that I will get my freedom soon and see you face to face again. Sir my arms are always around you and I know that your arms are always around me and this way we can stay strong for as long as it takes and one day we will fly free together like birds. I will stop here until next time I will receive your reply. Thanks, take good care of yourself. Remain bless. Zaw Lin, you are in my heart forever".

CHAPTER 43 – THE BEGINNING OF THE END OF MY DAYS IN THAILAND

By the end of February 2016, my relationship with my partner was starting to suffer and so was my health. I was living and breathing the case and it was mentally exhausting. As I was getting ready to give up, I was contacted by Tom Stone who was directing a Channel Four documentary on the case. He wondered if I would like to take part. I declined his offer. It was far too dangerous for me to be involved. More and more people were telling me I should leave the island for my own safety. I had been publishing information about Ian Yarwood's plans to discredit the DNA. However, I did agree to meet with him and his team to tell them all I knew.

I was starting to feel really unsafe on the island. My partner moved out for a while to catch his breath. Being home alone was daunting. I was told the mafia had a list of people they were planning on dealing with, and my name was getting closer to the top. I was having trouble sleeping at this point, partly out of fear for my life but mainly out of fear for the B2 and the hell they were now living in on death row. One night when I woke up to use the bathroom and took my gun with me, it dawned on me that the life I was now living was anything but healthy. I thought I would be better off trying to help the B2 from the safety of the UK. There was so much I wanted to tell the world about what had really happened over the last couple of years, and I knew there would be no way I could do that from Thailand. Away from Thailand I would be free to tell the truth and not have to worry about going to jail or being bumped off.

I looked into rumors that five families had funded the political protests in Bangkok that brought down the government and put the Junta in charge in a military coup, and that the Toovichien family was one of the main contributors. I had never seen any evidence to suggest the rumors were true, but if they were, I was in serious trouble. On the other hand, leaving Thailand could be tricky. Nobody involved wanted me to have freedom of speech, so there was a possibility they could make it very hard for me to leave. I decided if I was going to go, it would have to be done very quietly. I knew I could not leave without telling the B2 so this meant a trip to Bangkok. My partner agreed to leave Thailand with me. At the time, I thought we had a future together. In retrospect, I think he was scared for me and possibly for himself. I think he could see how tired and exhausted I was. I was sick of the lack of justice and sick of pissing into the wind. I needed a change so we planned our escape. However, we didn't manage to get out before yet another suspicious death related to Koh Tao came to light.

CHAPTER 44 – YET ANOTHER SUSPICIOUS DEATH ON KOH TAO

In March 2016, Wai Phyo's mother had a lump removed from her neck. We had raised the money for her operation, but in the end, a wealthy Burmese businessman who had been following the case paid for it. I wrote to Wai Phyo to let him know the operation had been a success.

It was at this time I first came into contact with Steven Drylie, a British ex-serviceman and paramedic who lived on Koh Tao. Steve got in touch with me in my capacity as the editor of the *Samui Times*. He was looking for a French man called Jean-Francois Louet, a resident of Koh Tao who had gone missing. Drylie told me he did not know the missing man personally but was aware he had been reported missing by his girlfriend. It turned out the missing man owned some property on Koh Tao. He and his girlfriend had left the island for a visa run/ vacation to Indonesia.

On the 14th of March 2016, having completed their trip, he and his girlfriend made their way to Surat Thani and boarded the ferry back to Koh Tao. However, shortly after they boarded, CCTV evidence showed Jean-Francois Louet getting off the ferry and going to buy something from a 7-Eleven store nearby and then asking directions. It was reported to me, by Drylie, that Jean-Francois had no phone, money, or passport on him when he disembarked the ferry. Drylie relayed the story that the missing man's girlfriend had stayed on the ferry and continued her journey back to Koh

Tao without him. She suggested that the missing man may have gone to a local hospital in Surat Thani on the mainland and he had suffered a recurring infection in his arm and leg. Twelve days after he disembarked the departing ferry, he was still missing.

During our conversations over the next several days, Drylie let it slip that he knew this man personally and it later turned out he even rented his bungalow from him on Koh Tao.

The motives for his girlfriend, Lea Mezzianai, going back to Koh Tao without him were unclear. I put out several appeals in the *Samui Times* for anyone who had seen this man to come forward.

On the 29th of March 2016, the local police in Surat Thani found a body in a wooded area. The body, that I was sent photographs of, was completely black and looked as if it had been burned. The corpse was completely unrecognizable, but due to a necklace and a dive watch, the police thought it was the body of Jean-Francois Louet. It turned out, after DNA tests, they were right.

I later found out the man known as Jeff had been on a diving holiday to Indonesia with his girlfriend and while there had picked up an infection in his leg and arm. After taking medication for a fever and having had a deep dive to 60 meters, he lost his appetite and showed signs of illness and disorientation. I could not understand why the girlfriend of this man had simply left him wandering around Surat Thani with no money or passport or means of contacting her or surviving and simply went back to Koh Tao. Soon after his body was found, Drylie told me that she had gone back to France and no further information ever came to light about this very odd case. I wondered why Drylie had first chosen to tell me he didn't know this guy, but it was interesting to know a man that just happened to have been on the crime scene of Hannah Witheridge and David Miller and Luke Miller.

CHAPTER 45 - IAN YARWOOD STILL ON THE CASE AND I LEAVE THAILAND

Ian Yarwood had written to the B2 but was not getting any letters back from them. I was not sure why. From time to time the prison used to limit how many letters prisoners could send. I assumed that it was because they had to prioritise letters to their families and to those of us who had supported them in prison. Evelyne had put a letter from Wai Phyo on her Facebook page and Ian was very eager to post the letter to his Twitter account. I was not at all comfortable to publish the letters from the prison. I worried the B2, and all the other prisoners, would be at risk of the prison authorities stopping letters all together if they were going out in the public domain. Prison was hard enough without trying to serve your time with no contact with the outside world. During my written correspondence with them, the B2 confirmed that they were getting letters from Ian but were not sure who he was. I explained that he was being a great support to them.

My partner and I decided to leave Thailand in April 2016. I started to pack up the house as quietly as I could so as not to draw any attention to the fact we were leaving. I boxed up a lot of my personal possessions and posted them from various post offices around the island, again to not draw any attention to the fact we were getting ready to go. I felt very sad to not be able to take all of my things back to the UK. Shipping my furniture would have drawn attention that I just didn't want. Now it was a case of simply getting away without being seen.

We had two cats so I decided to book them onto a different flight from us as a bit of a decoy. If I was being traced, then it was important to lay a false trial. We decided it was safer to drive to Bangkok. We also had a lot of stuff and excess baggage would be a nightmare on the ridiculously expensive Bangkok Airways from Samui and would draw unnecessary attention. We would have no problem blending in at the bustling ferry pier. We hired a driver with a 4x4 and loaded what we could of our belongings, including my trusty mountain bike and two cats into it after sending six massive parcels to my parents' house in the UK.

When the day came to leave the island, we got on the early morning ferry that took ninety minutes to reach the mainland. We then embarked on a 12-hour drive into Bangkok to stay with my friend who lived in the safe house the Gissings had stayed in after the death of Luke Miller.

The following day I took the cats to the airport, very mindful of whether or not I was being followed. They had to have a worming tablet and see the vet and then stick around for 48 hours before being allowed to fly. The cats were booked onto a Thai Airways flight while we planned to get a flight down to Kuala Lumpur and leave from Malaysia on a Malaysian Airways flight, a route that took us in the opposite direction. The day before we left, the 7th of April 2016, I made my way to the Bangkwang Central Prison where I met Wan, the Burmese lady who visited the B2 in Koh Samui for Andy. She was at the prison with two of her colleagues who helped me through the booking-in process at the prison. I was curious to see the inside of the prison. I had seen the outside some years earlier when I was passing through Thailand, mainly because of that Nicole Kidman series *The Bangkok Hilton* in which it had featured. I remember taking photos of it, despite being told it was not allowed, and being threatened with arrest before jumping on a bus and getting the hell out of there. We booked in at a small booking-in area overlooking the river on the opposite side of the jail. Like Samui we had to hang around for hours waiting to be called. Eventually we were and we queued up outside before going through a door where we could put our personal belongings in lockers. We then had to queue up again to be filtered through a room with an x-ray machine our shoes had to go through.

We filed past the x-ray area and went through two gigantic gates that hung from walls two feet thick painted with gold paint. I remember thinking, "Holy crap, what am I doing in the Bangkok Hilton"! As we went through the gates the picture changed from frankly scary as hell and intimidating to light and airy as the sky was clearly visible above us in a courtyard that was neatly manicured and full of colorful tropical plants. We filtered off to the right of the courtyard and into a very long corridor that had chairs on one side of a window. Beyond the window was a foot-wide gap between another set of bars and windows on the other side of which were chairs for the death row inmates to sit on during their visit. It was a scorching hot day and the few fans on the walls did nothing much to cool us down.

In the prison in Koh Samui, when we wanted to visit the B2, we had two booths and they were next to each other allowing us to chat with both of them. This was not the case in Bangkwang. The two allotted spaces for the B2 were quite a way apart. We sat for what seemed like an age, then the door opened and the death row prisoners started to filter in, about thirty to forty of them. Some looked a bit like Zaw Lin and Wai Phyo, scared and horribly out of place. Others had all-over body and facial tattoos and looked as scary as hell. I watched them filtering in wondering what they had done to find themselves behind the bars of one of the world's most notorious prisons.

I saw Zaw Lin before he saw me and he did the most theatrical double-take you have ever seen. I was in the booth for Wai Phyo and heartbreakingly Zaw Lin thought it was his and sat down looking happier than I have ever seen him. I could have cried, having to wave him on to the booth further down but it was not long until I got to speak to him. He could not believe I was there and was in tears of joy as I was. He looked surprisingly healthy and smart in his white T-shirt and black jeans. Zaw Lin told me that he was ok and coping in the jail and he had all he needed and was just overwhelmed to see me. He asked how often I could visit him in Bangkwang and it was then that the lump in my throat nearly choked me as I had to tell him that I was going to the UK. I told him it was more than likely going to be for a while and said that I needed to go back for a year to take care of my parents.

It was not a total lie. I did want to spend some time with my parents after a quarter of a century away. I knew I had put them through a lot with this case and dreaded to think how many sleepless nights they had had knowing I was at risk in a country they had spent enough time in to know the risk was very real indeed. Zaw seemed to understand why I needed to go to my own country. I spent the rest of the visit assuring him that I would never give up on him and he must never give up on himself. I told him I would spend every waking hour trying to help him and impress upon him, while not scaring him, that I would be safer doing this from a country where I could not go to jail for telling the truth. I think he understood. I have feelings for both Zaw Lin and Wai Phyo, but found it a lot harder to leave Zaw, who had grown so much during his journey and for some reason held a place in my heart that no one else ever has and I doubt ever will.

My goodbyes over, I found the taxi that took me to the jail and got the driver to drop me off quite a long way from where I was staying and made damn sure he did not follow me. Scarily, he managed to get hold of me on the Line App, which is similar to WhatsApp, later that day and asked me how I was doing. To this day, I have no idea how he got my number but it made me very glad and very nervous to be leaving the next day. On our last night in Thailand, we had dinner with some friends who lived in Bangkok and then went off to say goodbye to the red-light district in Patpong. I was sad and relived to be going in equal measure but still somewhat unsure if I would actually get out alive.

CHAPTER 46 – 7th APRIL 2016 – THE DAY I LEFT THAILAND

We woke up early in the morning on what was to be the last day I would ever spend in Thailand. Of course, I didn't know that at the time. I knew I had no intention of going back but it never dawned on me that I would never see what I still consider to be home ever again. I went to several cash points to empty my bank account before we raced around in the morning trying to get water bottles for the cats' cages. We said goodbye to some friends and got to the airport with the cats and the mountain bike and all of our other belongings. We arrived at the cargo depot first to drop the cats off who were looking very bemused and a bit frightened. I arrived to find that it was a bank holiday, and it was shut. My heart sank. I could not leave the cats in Thailand and with all of our luggage and nowhere to stay rearranging our flights and the cats' flights was going to be a nightmare. Thankfully, there was someone on duty and he went through all of the paperwork for the cats and I left them after a fairly tearful goodbye. Things never really go to plan in Thailand and I honestly didn't know if I would see them again.

Once the cats had been dropped off, we made our way to Suvarmabumi airport and offloaded the rest of our luggage. The entire time I was in the airport, I was scared. I was looking around for any of the familiar mafia faces and anyone who was looking vaguely in our direction put the fear of God into my heart. My palms were sweating despite it being cold in the heavily air-conditioned airport. I had a sick feeling in my stomach. I kept my sunglasses on and wore my Australian bushwhacker hat. It was a disguise that would not have fooled anybody but I felt I had to do something to feel safer. I kept my head down, furtively looking around for any sign of danger.

I heard somebody call my partner's name and my heart sank and I froze. Time seemed to stop. Everyone in the airport seemed to stop. It was like watching a movie that goes into slow motion just before something huge and dramatic is about to happen. I felt nauseous and regretted travelling with my partner. What right did I have to put him in danger? I heard my partner's voice. It was as if he was talking down a tube. It said, "Hi Paul". I was snapped out of my slow motion-moment and felt a wave of relief to see it was a friend of ours, a long-term ex-pat who ran a popular bar in Koh Samui. Then I felt panic again. This guy was really well connected and although I trusted him as far as you can trust anyone on the islands, I wondered if he had been paid to follow us or had been frightened into doing it. I nodded to him and said we were going on holiday. I hoped that my partner would have the sense not to tell him where we were going or what we were doing at the airport, which was ridiculous as that is the only topic that is discussed when you bump into a friend you were not expecting to see at the airport.

My partner spoke to Paul while I went to check the departures board to find that it was the last call. I yelled to my partner, and we ran down to our gate. I asked what Paul said. He told me that Paul said he was very relieved we were leaving as he thought that I was in grave danger. I looked around to make sure he was not about and did not see which gate we were heading to and took in a thousand faces wondering if any of them knew me or where I was going. We boarded the plane, and I took my last look around Bangkok Airport runway. Every second before we took off felt like an hour. I have never willed a plane to take off so much in my life. I started to eye up the other passengers wondering if they were out to get me but told myself that we would be in transit at the other end and assassinations in transit would be pretty difficult. Eventually the plane took off for the short run down to Malaysia. I felt some relief, but I was still in Asia and in Asia anything is possible. The plane landed without event, and we killed a few hours in Kuala Lumpur airport, mainly in the smoking room. My nerves were still on edge. Eventually we boarded a gigantic Airbus A380 that we were told weighed over 500 tons. After what seemed like my entire lifetime, it took off and we were bound for Heathrow, in a civilized country where for the first time in a long time I would feel safe. A massive wave of relief came over me and I found myself laughing hysterically. We were free. We were safe. I thought of Zaw Lin and Wai Phyo stuck in jail and felt sick for leaving them, but I knew I was no use to them in Thailand. I would end up dead or in jail myself and that would not help them or me. After 14 hours, the plane landed in a cold and rainy Heathrow. I have never been so glad to see the dreary UK weather before in my life.

After hours of hanging around the pet welcome centre to get the cats and a wild goose chase trying to find my bike in one terminal and our tiny hire car in another, we were ready to leave. Having figured out how to get all of our belongings into a tiny car and having brought ten-pound SIM cards managed to get the sat nav on my phone working and we headed off to my friend's mobile home on the Thames that she had kindly agreed to let us stay in. It was pouring rain when we arrived. The cats were clearly distressed and cold. Disheveled, we arrived at reception and were shown the way to my friend's mobile home and given the key. It was freezing inside. We tried to turn on the heat, but discovered the boiler had been dismantled for the months between October and April when the park homes were not used.

After figuring out how to put the boiler together, we had a hot shower and got the heater on and put the cats next to the fire having stopped en route to get them food and a litter tray. Utterly exhausted, we walked to the local pub and had a steak. I was still eyeing everyone we came across with great suspicion. It was a hard habit to break. We made our way back to the mobile home and wrapped ourselves up in duvets, and for the first time in as long as I could remember, I slept like a baby.

CHAPTER 47 – THAILAND
FOLLOWS ME TO THE UK

We woke up on the 9th of April 2016, to a beautiful sunny day. We had some salami and cheese that we had brought for breakfast and went for a long walk into Marlow. I felt free and happy and as if the whole nightmare of Thailand had been just that, a nightmare that I had woken up from. I felt light and happy and as if I was in a totally different world. The dark world that I had been living in, with all its murky secrets and hidden black under belly of lies and corruption, was in my past. Or so I thought. Actually, it was far from over.

Later on in the day, I got a message from a friend in Samui to say that his Facebook account had been cloned, an imposter had set up an account to appear like it was him. Whoever cloned it was using it to upset the man's brother and other people on the island by sending them obscene messages. The cloner had spent hours putting these messages onto the public profiles of other Samui residents and it was not going down too well. I had no idea who was doing this but contacted a man on Samui called Jim to ask him. I had known Jim for some time despite never having met him. Jim was a volunteer for the Samui Rescue organization who were called out to accidents and incidents and attended to help the police. Jim contacted me when I first started the *Samui Times* and offered to give me information on accidents and incidents to publish in the paper. I was happy for the information but rather less happy with the very graphic photographs he sent along with the information. While in Thailand, it is normal for the media to include graphic pictures of accidents and murders and death, this was something I had always chosen not to do.

Jim told me he would look into the situation and get back to me. My partner was very upset with me, having believed we were leaving all of the drama in Thailand behind. I could tell he had had enough. I resolved to not get involved, but during the early hours of the 11th of April 2016, I had no choice as my own account was cloned. My cloned page was asking people for donations for the B2. I was furious. I knew people would donate. I got hold of Jim and told him finding out who was doing this was now a matter of urgency. He assured me he would find out and get back to me.

I took to my laptop and wrote this article for the *Samui Times*.

"Several imposter Facebook accounts have appeared online cloned from the Facebook accounts of Samui residents. The owner of these fake accounts has been using them to cause chaos among genuine Samui Facebook users who believe the rude and insulting messages being sent are from real Facebook users. Suzanne Buchanan , the editor of the *Samui Times*, Facebook page was hit in the early hours of this morning – the cloned page claims that she would like donations for the two Burmese men found guilty of the rape and murder of Hannah Witheridge and David Miller in Koh Tao in September 2014 and asks those who wish to donate to contact via personal message in order to be given a bank account to pay into. Local golf professional and Samui resident Alexander Lester's account was also cloned – several obscene personal and public messages have been sent including comments on the *Samui Times* own online page.

Ex Samui resident Adam Murphy's account has also been cloned and used to post obscene messages. Two more accounts in local residents names, who have not given us permission to publish have also fallen prey to imposter accounts.

A further Facebook account has appeared for the Burmese men – Donation for Wai Phyo and Zaw Linb – whoever created the account added the letter 'b' at the end of Zaw Lin's name – his motives for the extra letter are unclear.

The police have been informed of the imposter accounts as have Facebook. If anybody else has suffered from imposter accounts please contact the editor of the *Samui Times* by emailing editor@samuitimes.com

If anybody is receiving strange messages on Facebook or noticing strange comments under the articles of the *Samui Times* or any other group pages, please contact Facebook by reporting the comment and person responsible for it immediately".

I sent a message to my cloned account that read, "I would like to donate money, how do I do this"? A message came back 30 seconds later. "Send to yourself ahaha" . I sent another message. "Who are you"? Then later "What is the crack with this"? And later "What do you want"? I then told the cloner I had reported the incident to Facebook. That report promoted this message "Hey Suzanne Buchanan, I think this content is my intellectual property, and it can't be used without my permission. Could you please message me back about this or take it down". Neither happened.

On the 11th of April 2016, at 3.16 p.m. this message came in via the *Samui Times* messenger account:

"We require 2 payments to this account below the second payment via Western Union. You have 2 days to do this or this is just the start. We can close your website and release information all over the web. We can lock you down your devices and access accounts. Account name: S BACHE Account Number: 32284460 Sort Code: 30-80-88 Amount: USD 1200 Bank: Lloyds Second payment Western Union Chris Esterhuizen Amount USA 7000 Moutague Gardens Cape Town Western Cape South Africa. You have 2 days".

This message was followed by another at 2:15 GMT the following day.

"Haha trust me you do not know us. Please go and visit this man but he won't help you. We gather information from the web see arguments watch look for companies submitting tax returns. Fake emails, hack emails. We are the real deal, we want payments that's all. The target is you because we have seen that a lot of people trust you and we're hope to get funds from your name. Also noticed groups on Twitter against you on Facebook. The public shall believe what we want them to believe. So we will extend 1 week to get the money or we shall have a bot on your computer close you down. The good thing is with a scam like this is that everyone blames everyone. This can stop for a fee. We also know your financial records and we have people working in the banks and in governments around the world so don't even think on trying to scare us. You fucking wid da real nighas "!

It was a bizarre message as I had not messaged them. The only person I had spoken to was Jim. I had no idea if the threat was real or where it was coming from. I called my bank and told them to keep an eye on my account. I called Lloyds to try to find out if that was one of their sorting code numbers but of course, due to data protection, they couldn't tell me anything and advised me to call the police which I did and retold the entire story, which took hours. My partner looked fed up. I was fed up too. I had been able to relax for two days but now the nightmare had followed me to the UK.

On the 11th of April 2016, I had a message from a friend in Samui who told me there was a Facebook page called Boycott Samui Times and Fake Media Sites that was carrying the *Samui Times* logo. This page had posted, "Just read that the owner of the site has gone back to England. If that's the case, she should sell or close her website. This isn't a newspaper as no paper has ever been printed. This is a non professional gossip page. Looks like Suzanne is working with the Burmese government to cover up the murders of Muslims back in Burma".

When I read the part about the cover up of the murders of Muslims, I knew where this attack was coming from. Just prior to leaving Samui, I met a man who had been posting on the popular news site *ThaiVisa*. He told me that he had information that proved the B2 were guilty. I met up with him at his house and he told me that the B2 were involved in genocide in Myanmar and the rape of a Muslim woman that resulted in the displacement of an entire Muslim village. He was nuts and went onto my very long list of people I wanted to avoid for the rest of my natural life.

This man had met me using a false name, so it was not possible for me to name and shame him on Facebook, but I did know where he lived, having met him at his house. I had been changing my profile picture on Facebook continually, so my actual friends knew which account was mine. Unfortunately, no sooner had I changed my profile picture than the cloner did the same thing, so it was impossible for anyone to identify my genuine account except for digging deeper and looking at the post history or my number of friends.

I had a brainwave; I got onto Google maps and took a screen shot of an aerial image where this guy lived and posted that as my profile picture, thinking that I had well and truly outwitted him.

Two minutes later the cloned account picture changed as well. Why would this lunatic post his own address when plenty of people on the island were baying for his blood with the chaos he had caused on their fake Facebook pages?

I got a message from another man on Samui that read, "Hi Suzanne, would you kind to send me the address and the name of the prick who hacked Mr. Lester's account? Thank you so much". I told him that there was a map on my Facebook page. He came back and told me that he had seen the map, but he wanted the guy's name. He said he would love to have a civilized conversation with the man but wanted to know 100% that it was the right person. I told him that I had never been given the man's real name, but I knew that he owned part of the resort that was depicted in my profile picture. I said the man was a pest and the man on Samui agreed.

Jim continued to tell me he would go and see this guy. When he eventually went and saw him, he told me the man swore it was not him cloning my or anyone else's account and passed a message back to me begging me to take the photo of his property down as lots of people were hanging round outside his property and he was too scared to go out.

In the meantime, the articles in the *Samui Times* about the cloning prompted a lady to get in touch with me from an English language website called Thailand Justice who had also been closely following the case of the B2. The message read:

"I just read your article about the fake Facebook accounts and thought you should be aware of this".

'This' was a link to a Facebook page called Boycott Fake Media in Thailand that suggested that my and others' online publications were making up stories about Koh Tao. I believe this person to be someone who posted on ThaiVisa as "Tony121", and a number of other aliases, the latest being "DiscoDan". He is a British ex-pat resident of Koh Samui and now posts on Twitter as: https://twitter.com/samui_csi. I had to ban a number of people from my Facebook Community page last Saturday for making obscene comments and noticed that all these fake accounts had been set up around the same date the 8th of April 2016. One of them was Alexander Lester. I suspect the same person is behind all of this.

I thought she was right. Tony121 was the man I had met just before I left Samui who told me the preposterous story about the B2 and genocide. Alexander Lester was one of my friends on Samui whose Facebook account had also been cloned along with that of his brother.

Later on, she sent me this message:

"I run the Thailand Justice website and Facebook page. Tony121 sent us a series of vile messages through the website last August essentially threatening Andy Hall. OK, I know Andy is not the most popular person but these messages were sinister (even towards Mr. Hall's parents) and the British embassy in Bangkok became involved. We were never able to find out who he really is. Do you know his real name? I have been in contact with Adam Murphy but he doesn't know who Tony121 is either. Anyway, he needs stopping and the police should become involved".

Adam Murphy is a good friend of mine. Adam used to live in Koh Samui but had more recently been spending his time in Cambodia. Adam had been keenly following the case and also investigating it and was and still is one of the key members of my team.

I advised her that although I didn't know his real name, I had changed my profile picture to a screenshot from Google maps as to where he lived. The days passed with me scrambling around trying to find out who this guy was. On the 22nd of April 2016 I got a message via the *Samui Times* from Edward Martin telling me to be careful. I messaged him from my own Facebook page asking him what he meant. He never got back to me.

On the 26th of April 2016, I got an unexpected email from the father of Hannah Witheridge.

Hi Susanne

My names Tony Witheridge, Hannah's father. I believe you are now safely back in the UK. I really would like to speak with you regarding the murder of my daughter Hannah and of course David. If you could let me have your number or you could call me on 07********. I don't mind driving to wherever you now live and we can talk privately somewhere if you prefer. Anyway, if you could take the time to call me, I really would be most grateful. You hear so much rubbish concerning the case and as you know the family on that island. I thought I may get to some of the truth. It's not going to bring Hannah back, but I may be able to get some closure.

Kind regards

Tony Witheridge"

I called Tony Witheridge. We talked for about two hours that day and again the following day. I told him all I knew about the case. I honestly think he thought I knew exactly what had happened to his daughter and had nothing but regret that I could not give him the closure he so desperately wanted and deserves. To this day this man is one of my main motivations for uncovering the truth about what happened on Sairee Beach on Koh Tao on that dark night in September 2014. This man's pain is something that no one can imagine other than him and his family and of course the families of all of the other victims. I speak to them regularly and they have also become part of my motivation to find the truth to gain some kind of closure for each and every one of them.

I wanted to handle Tony Witheridge with kid gloves, but I also wanted him to be aware of all I had uncovered. On the 26th of April 2016 I sent him a document with some of my reports on it along with this email:

"Dear Mr. Witheridge,
I hope this email finds you well.

I wanted to just touch base to let you know that I have been thinking about you a great deal and I was hoping the latest CH4 documentary was not too upsetting for you. I have written a couple of articles in the *Samui Times* and am sorry if they caused you any distress. Sadly, reporting is the only way I can hope to find justice for all concerned. I face a moral battle in my mind every time I report and cringe at the very thought of hurting your family any further.

Since speaking to you, I am so upset that the Thais believe throwing you a couple of scapegoats is any kind of compensation. This to me is disrespect at its very worst. They must think we are all idiots if they expect you to be able to find any kind of closure in this way and I am disgusted you have to live without true justice.

A small team of us are doing our best to find a solution to this problem. We want to find justice and closure for the families of all of the victims who have fallen prey to crime in Thailand. We hope to find a way to persuade Thailand to 'man up' to the truth and start punishing and taking responsibility for the influential people who obstruct justice and, in our minds commit the kind of crimes that give the country such a bad name.

Through our research we now have concerns about the British Embassy and the Foreign Office and how they handle situations concerning British victims of crime and their families. They seem to be more interested in diplomatic relations between the two countries rather than demanding justice for our citizens.

I was speaking to Andrew Drummond about this (a Scottish journalist in Thailand also investigating the case) and mentioned the statement the Embassy issued on behalf of you and the Millers. I have not divulged the content of our conversation as it was between you and me and not for publication. However, Mr. Drummond has asked me to pass a letter on to you with regards to the Embassy as he wishes to look into what on earth is going on. Mr. Drummond works with the families of other victims and a pattern is starting to emerge. I have added the letter to this email as an attachment so you can choose if you wish to read it. The very last thing I want to do is add to your burden. I only want to find the justice and closure so many crave.

Thank you so much for talking to me last week. It was a pleasure to talk to you. You sound like such a lovely man and I wish I could do anything to ease your pain and give you the comfort you so obviously deserve. I have thought about you a great deal since our conversation.

With very warm and kind regards
Su."

I started thinking the only way we could get any kind of justice for the B2 would be heavy public pressure. The only way I could do that would be to get the whole sorry story out into the public eye and I needed a big outlet for the case. A friend of mine put me in touch with someone at the BBC who put me in touch with Celia Hatton in the BBC World Service. I had many lengthy phone conversations with Celia towards the end of April 2016. She was very interested in getting the handwriting of Dimitri Povse from his so-called suicide note analyzed and getting in touch with his family. She was looking for angles that had not been covered before and seemed very keen to do something and seemed to be investing a lot of time and the BBC's resources into some of the leads I gave her. She also invited me to go to the BBC in London, which I did and spent several hours giving a taped interview to Celia. We shared a lot of email correspondence before she went quiet.

CHAPTER 48 – THE CHANNEL 4 DOCUMENTARY

As I had mentioned to Mr. Witheridge in my email to him, by now the Channel 4 documentary, *Murder in Paradise*, had aired. It was the inside story of the murders of Hannah Witheridge and David Miller. I was very interested to see it as I had met with producer Tom Stone and the film crew in Samui.

Tom Stones' production made no secret of the fact that powerful local families were under suspicion for the murders and it was explained that these families know exactly who come and go on the island, they control money, and are very aware of any outsiders who may arrive on their shores to check up on them. Mention was also made that the Toovichien clan own more businesses on the island than any of the rival families who live there. Andy Hall also took part in the documentary and images were shown of photographs he was sent during the murder investigation that showed men with bruises and blisters under their armpits with allegations of torture from the Thai police. Some interesting previously unseen footage came out in the documentary of Wai Phyo being interviewed in the police station and being asked to recreate the murder with a plastic scoop. He seemed to have no idea what he was doing and an odd moment took place where a translator stroked his hair when asking him to tell the truth. Wai Phyo is visibly distressed and had no legal representation. Andy explained that prior to this footage Wai Phyo had been left naked in a very cold room. He had his testicles pinged, been photographed naked, and was sexually abused. Filming undercover in the prison, the B2 can been seen stating, through a translator, they had no knowledge of the crimes and had plastic bags put over their heads during their interrogation and were punched and kicked in the chest, being told they would have their hands and legs cut off and be thrown in the ocean and be tied up to burning car tyres. They both deny any involvement in the murders.

The local mayor, Chaiyan Turasakul, also took part and said that the tourists who have died are responsible for their own downfall. He said that, "These foreigners who come to Thailand they live the lifestyle they want to, without realizing it is not their country. They are not allowed to do as they wish, there is a difference between our culture and their culture so when these foreigners live according to their culture, this leads to accidents and risk to their lives." His examples were taking an overdose or driving a car or motorbike too fast, leading to an accident and going diving without taking any safety precautions and many other things. He said, "It all depends on fate, however, most of the incidents I come across, the foreigners were dead drunk and cannot even recall what happened. I would say this is one of the main problems".

Pornthip, the leading Thai DNA expert who testified at the trial, also took part, and explained that the police made a number of errors and failed to use a forensic doctor at the scene. She said that "the person who was examining the crime scene had no forensic knowledge. This case is very complicated. There are two dead bodies and lots of issues, how did they die? Where did they die? Did they die together? Were there other places (to investigate)? The investigator must be able to study the detail of the corpse that person must be a forensic doctor". She pointed out that the police also did not test blood on the rocks and sand or

Hannah's clothes. Dr. Pornthip states that she re-tested the garden hoe and found DNA from two men, David Miller and anther male who is not Zaw Lin or Wai Phyo. She went on to say, "From the pieces of evidence sent to me there is only one that is relevant and that is the hoe. There are two DNA profiles found on the hoe both are male but neither of them match the defendants' DNA". During the documentary, Andy agreed that it is a big problem when the murder weapon that needs to be gripped so hard does not have the DNA of the defendants. During his interview with Suwat Jangyodsuck, a major general in the Royal Thai Police, it was revealed he has no idea why people do not believe in the evidence. He states that the DNA was tested in a lab by a specialist and the equipment used 'came' from some European standards but he states clearly he has no idea what those standards are. In their undercover prison interview, the B2 said it was impossible their DNA was on the bodies or any part of the crime scene. The point is made that in Thailand there is no jury, just three judges.

On the 23rd of May 2016 the defense lawyers filed the first appeal for the B2.

CHAPTER 49 – APLAC AND ILAC [INTERNATIONAL LABORATORY ACCREDITATION COOPERATION]

On the 13th of January 2016, Ian Yarwood sent a fax to Khun Suthon Vongsheree based on his understanding that the Bureau of Laboratory Quality Standards (BLQS) granted accreditation to the laboratory who tested the DNA used to convict Wai Phyo and Zaw Lin. When Khun Vongsheree did not respond, Ian approached the secretary of the Asia Pacific Laboratory Accreditation Cooperation Inc (APLAC), Mr. Michael Fraser, who wrote to Vongsheree twice at Ian's request.

After 132 days, he finally got a reply from Vongsheree, who, in his response, cited the fact that Ian had written to the BLQS general address and not him directly as an excuse for his tardy response. In his response, Khun Vongsheree pointed out that he did not know who Ian was. In an open letter of complaint, Ian pointed out to Vongsheree that while the defendants were not his clients, he had express oral authority from them to write a notice of complaint. He had been advised by Mr. Fraser that oral consent would be sufficient, which was useful as gaining written consent from the B2 inside the imposing walls of Bangkwang would be impossible, let alone confidential. In the open letter, Ian stated that while, to the best of his knowledge, the B2's legal team would also, at some point, be submitting a complaint, he did not know how long that would take, and decided to take it upon himself to send a letter as, by this stage, the B2 had been "languishing in prison for more than 600 days". He went on to point out that the letter from the legal team was likely going to be more comprehensive than his letter as he was not permitted to have copies of the documents filed in court as evidence or a transcript from the trial.

This should not have posed much of a problem as Vongsheree would be able to conduct an investigation without the material and would also be able to obtain copies, if he wished, from the Accredited Laboratory's documents. It is worth noting at this point that there are no verbatim transcripts of proceedings in Thai courts, unlike those in the West, a fact Ian believed the secretaries of both ILAC and APLAC were unaware of until he brought it to the attention of Mr. Fraser in May 2016. Transcripts in Thai courts consist of what the relevant judge records and more often than not are a mere paraphrasing of the witness testimony with little to no actual context.

In the open letter, Ian pointed out that the most important document produced at the court was the DNA table which, according to the prosecution, demonstrated matches found between the DNA found on Hannah's body and that of the defendants. While Ian did not have a copy of the table, he had it on good authority from Jane Taupin that, in her expert opinion, it was "meaningless". He cited the reasons as being that the documents produced by the Accredited Laboratory for this trial lacked any stamps from the relevant accreditation body such as BLQS. Ian had been advised by the secretary of ILAC, Ms Jennifer Evans, that as such they could only be referred to as 'Unendorsed Reports' which may or may not have been produced under the auspices of the ISO 17025 accreditation. ISO 17025 accreditation can only be granted by an authorized accreditation body.

Accreditation means that the laboratory has met the Management Requirements and Technical Requirements of ISO17025 and is deemed technically competent to produce calibration and testing results. Ian pointed out to Vongsheree that his letter dated the 13th of January 2016 and this letter were to serve as a formal complaint to BLQS regarding the procedures of the Accredited Laboratory. In the letter, he pointed out that the defendants in the case were found guilty of murder at the Samui Provincial Court on the 24th of December 2015, and sentenced to death and the basis of their conviction depended on key DNA evidence and the interpretation and conclusions resulting from analysis conducted by the Accredited Laboratory, and that the defendants' complaint was that the procedures carried out and the interpretations were completely flawed and they did not comply with the international standards for DNA analysis as prescribed.

The particulars consisted of the fact that no original mixed semen samples were ever made available to the defense for independent examination, the police and prosecutor only ever made 'amplified DNA evidence' available to the defense but without the original samples one could not be sure of the original source. As only 5 microlitres of the original mixed semen would have been necessary for the test there was no valid reason that none was made available to the lawyers.

The Accredited Laboratory conducted a comparison of reference samples to medical samples from Hannah, and reached a conclusion there was a match despite there being no data regarding that match or even the provision of an explanation as to what criteria it relied on to reach such a conclusion. Ian's complaint went into more detail, but for the purpose of keeping this chapter readable I will leave it at that other than to say the entire analysis of the medical samples from Hannah were completed in only twelve hours which is utterly unrealistic if the relevant ISO 17025 and ILAC standards had been complied with. These revelations in Ian's letter did not only show how serious the matter was in terms of Zaw Lin and Wai Phyo's conviction but cast serious doubt on the operations of the Accredited Laboratory and its ability to conduct DNA analysis and interpret DNA profiles in criminal trials in Thailand, not to mention the conviction was in this case was based solely[3] on a 100% DNA match.

In his letter to Vongsharee, Ian asked him to advise whether or not the Accredited Laboratory conducted its testing in this matter under the auspices of its accreditation by BLQS given that the DNA table produced by the Accredited Laboratory was an Unendorsed Report, and whether he thought it appropriate for the Accredited Laboratory to produce Unendorsed Reports as evidence in trials of murder and rape. He ended by saying, "To that end, the defendants in this matter require you to investigate the facts in this case and to report your findings".

A few days later, we got a response from Vonsheree. He sent it to Ian, Michael Frazer, and 'Concerning ones'. He made a rather sarcastic apology for not getting back to Ian sooner and stated that the law in Thailand dictated that only an authorized person could give information to anyone who could demonstrate their official state and that person would need to submit their questions through official channels such as an embassy in Thailand, Canberra, Sydney, Brisbane, Adelaide, or Perth. The Embassy would need to contact the Ministry of Public Health, then the Department of Medical Sciences, and then and only then, would it go to BLQS. Vonsheree said that if such questions involved many Ministries then there would be more documented communication among the governmental offices and stated that he would not respond to Ian any further unless Ian followed that procedure. However, he went on to say that in his email to Ian dated the 24th of May 2016, he had given information of ISO/ICE 17025 accredited laboratories with

---

3. For more details on the DNA results wbp.bz/curseturtlegallery

a link that would show that The Laboratory of Toxicology Sub-division and Biochemistry Sub-division Institute of Forensic Medicine, Police General Hospital,

The Royal Thai Police got accreditation on the scope of DNA testing in January 2015, four months after the occurrence of the Koh Tao case. He went on to say that he had forwarded Ian's questions to the laboratory, but they had, to date, not answered him. He then went on to say that the fact the accreditation symbol was not present on the report used by the prosecution for the DNA evidence during the trial of Zaw Lin and Wai Phyo was not relevant as at that time the laboratory was NOT accredited for DNA testing. Therefore, there was no misconduct on the usage of the accreditation symbol of the laboratory. He ended his letter by saying he too hoped the truth would be found and that the court would give fair justice to everyone and reiterated that he would not be in communication again unless Ian went through the channels he had laid out.

The revelation that the laboratory who tested the DNA that resulted in two Burmese migrant workers was not even accredited at the time they did their investigations was shocking but also provided more problems.

Ian wrote to Michael Frazer, the secretary of APLAC, for clarification on what Vongsheree meant when he referred to someone needing official status when asking for information with regards to the lab because Michael Frazer had previously told Ian that verbal permission from the B2 would be enough to warrant Ian asking the questions. His second point was with regards to the date on which the lab was given accreditation, i.e., four months after the Koh Tao case. Evidence given at the trial suggested that the lab was in fact accredited at all times to carry out its DNA testing. The sticking point here was that one of the links provided to us showed the lab was in fact accredited at the time of the Koh Tao case. However, a different page appeared online when the lab item was clicked on and, that link indicated that the lab was accredited to carry out buccal swabs, vaginal swabs, blood stains, and other biological stains, but there was no specific mention of semen. It was not clear from the links to the website what the scope of the accreditation was between 2013 and January 2015.

What we wanted to know was if the lab had accreditation to test buccal swabs, vaginal swabs, blood, hair, saliva, and/or semen in 2014. It didn't take long for Michael to get back to Ian and he advised that he had been in touch with Vongsheree for clarification. He said that as the case was under appeal it would be illegal for anyone to interfere and basically it all had to be done via governmental channels. He also sent a table setting out what the labs were and were not accredited to do, the summarizing of which was:

The laboratory has not used STRs analysis in the Koh Tao case. The extend scope was not accredited during the scene. Tao case. Therefore, the facility did not use the BLQS DMSc endorsement on the DNA testing report as is the correct practice according to ISO/IEC 17011 clause 8.3.1.

The confusion had raised a catch-22 situation. If the lab did not have accreditation, then we had no recourse with BLQS who would basically tell us to go away. However, this also meant that the prosecution witness misled the court on this point that should lead to the original judgment against the accused being quashed. If the lab did have the accreditation, then they needed to investigate the complaint. We had no transparency at this point from either BLQS or the lab; the only way forward was for APLAC to conduct an investigation or an audit of BLQS and/ or the police laboratory. Michael tried again with Vongsheree who reiterated that he would not communicate with Ian unless it was via an embassy and that the B2 legal team could not communicate with him via the Ministry of Public Health and General Director of the Department of Medical Sciences or directly.

Once again, we were stumped. Vongsheree and his superiors were going to make it as difficult as possible for anyone to find the truth about the accreditation of the lab or the way it prepared its report for the court. Jane Taupin confirmed to Ian that it would be impossible for one Thai organization to properly audit another, and Thai culture would not allow it.

We could get nothing more out of Vongsheree. On the 21st of November, Michael Frazer checked out too with this letter to Ian:

"Dear Ian,
Thank you for your email(s).
I apologise for the delay in responding to you.
Following further communication with the APLAC Quality Manager I would like to reiterate the following:
As previously advised because the test facility was not accredited for the tests conducted at the time of testing the specimens by BLQS DMSc APLAC has no further role in this matter.
If you wish to investigate the matter further with BLQS DMSc as advised in my email dated 12 July 2016.
Point 1 This case is under the appealing court, it will be illegal if someone interferes with this case consideration. The attempt to reduce reliability of the evidence data, the testing reports, if they are likely to be misconducted shall be avoided. The official status, means one has to connect to the governmental officer, like Suthon, via the governmental channel (e.g. Thailand Embassy) in your country. This is our system to make sure that your presences are legally existing and can hold all legal responsibility. Ian Yarwood might be very well-known in your country, but he is not known in Thailand.
As intimated by Suthon Vongsheree, the best way forward would be for Thai Defense Team to request the information required directly from the test facility.

Notwithstanding the gravity of the situation, APLAC cannot consider any further correspondence on this issue.

Best regards
Michael Fraser
APLAC Secretary"

CHAPTER 50 – ROBERT GOES BALLISTIC

I am not sure what we expected to come out of this letter, but we certainly did not expect Robert Holmes to go ballistic. He expressed his anger towards Ian Yarwood in an email to the Thailand Justice team. In the letter, he confirmed that he had been an advisor to the B2's Thai defense team and had drafted the grounds of appeal against the B2's conviction with another leading Australian barrister, Mark Trowell QC. He told the Thailand Justice team that it had always been his view that the DNA evidence was seriously flawed from both a forensic science viewpoint and legally. He went on to say that he had no confidence that the appeals court would make a decision based on law or evidence and said that it was he who had come up with the novel approach of attacking the Thai laboratories through their governing body, BLQS, which is under the auspices of APLAC in Australia. Like Ian, he thought this would ensure that BLQS would be forced to undertake an investigation of the labs concerned and should they not take that step they would put themselves in breach of the agreement with APLAC and ILAC that would have international implications for Thailand.

He went on to say that he had drafted a complaint and handed it to the legal team and obtained an undertaking that the complaint would be made. He felt that it was wrong of Ian Yarwood to consider filing his own complaint and suggested that Ian had "zero evidence to support such a complaint". He said the only parties that had access to the evidence were him and Jane Taupin. However, Robert had sent Ian a draft copy of his complaint and was now accusing Ian of plagiarizing it and sending it to BLQS. Robert felt that this action by Ian was not only a serious breach of professional ethics but had put any negotiations between him and the legal team in jeopardy. He went on to say that now Ian had made his open letter of complaint public, the legal team would rightly abandon their plan to complain, and that Ian had made a fool of himself. He also said that Ian had no authority to make the complaint and had given the government "the perfect out" as a complaint made by a foreigner without supporting evidence would be detrimental to the case.

Of course, the truth was Ian did have permission from the B2 as I had written to them and they had given me written permission as well as verbal permission to my friend, Annie, who had visited them in prison. Ian and Robert had discussed making a complaint in January when Ian first contacted ILAC in Sydney to gather more information about the process. We had all hoped that the legal team would make the complaint but as time dragged on it looked increasingly unlikely and while Robert had sent Ian a copy of the draft complaint, Ian maintained he had never agreed to keep it confidential. Ian also maintained that an imperfect letter from him would be more effective than no letter from the legal team. The B2's appeal had been filed on the 23rd of May 2016, about the same time Ian questioned Robert again as to when the legal team would file the letter of complaint to BLQS.

On the 1st of June 2016, Robert told Ian that as the defense team were working pro bono, it was not high on their list of priorities. Ian asked Robert how much it would cost to pay the lawyers to file the complaint and Robert suggested $10,000.00—$15,000.00 AUD. Ian thought this was an extraordinary amount of money and offered to pay $5,000 and Robert said with these funds filing a complaint should take two to three weeks. Robert later told Ian that he had offered Nakhon 125,000 baht to file the complaint as a priority. Ian had hoped that a member of the legal team, Sana, would have been tasked with the complaint as he felt that Nakhon had not only been rude to Jane Taupin during the trial but had been badly prepared for it and lazy. Robert asked Ian to deposit the funds into his account so he would be able to pay for Nakhon once the work had been completed. The transfer was made on the 2nd of June 2016. Robert confirmed he had received the funds the following day. With no progress on the complaint, Ian sent Robert an email stating that if the letter was not sent by the 23rd of June 2016, he would seek the return of his funds as well as the international transfer costs. This timescale would represent three weeks from when the funds were sent.

CHAPTER 51 - THE TRUTH
ABOUT ROBERT HOLMES

While Ian was convalescing from a bout of ill health, he contacted Brisbane barrister Mark Plunkett to ask about Robert Holmes. After Ian sent pictures of Robert, Mark made some enquiries with other barristers and discovered Robert Holmes had been incarcerated for fraud. Ian called to tell me in shock. Could it really be that the retired barrister who had been advising the legal team of the B2 was a con man and a fraud? Once again, I took a deep breath and started to investigate. It transpired that, according to Deputy Registrar Lucy Barnes of the Supreme Court of Queensland, Robert John Holmes was admitted as a barrister on the 19th of May 1986. She had no records of criminal proceedings against him. However, according to the Bar Association of Queensland, there was no record of him being struck off. Ian continued his enquiries and sent me a message to say he was now in touch with four barristers who recalled Robert Holmes having a conviction for fraud. He also told me that Jonathan Head from the BBC had been in touch and had asked Ian for a copy of the letter of complaint he sent to BLQS.

We had a breakthrough in the investigation into Robert Holmes when Ian got wind that articles about Holmes' convictions had appeared in the *Brisbane Courier Mail*. He dug around a bit more and discovered there were three articles published.

The front-page headline of the article that appeared in the *Courier-Mail* on Friday, the 29th of January 1988 read, "BRISBANE BARRISTER SOUGHT OVER $1M FRAUD". It was written by Phil Dickie and read, "A BRISBANE barrister is being sought by police after defrauding banks, finance, legal and credit-card companies of more than $1 million". The publication had also discovered that at least one barrister had objected to his admission to the bar. It is most unusual for any barrister to make an objection to someone else's admission and objections tend to be based on grounds of poor character. From what we understood, Holmes began his crime spree in September 1986 just a few months after his admission to the bar. The *Courier-Mail* stated that among the companies defrauded are Westpac, ANZ, and the Bank of Queensland. Macquarie Bank did not comment. Finance companies were also stung, including Esanda, Hunter BNZ, Barclays, CUBE Finance, and Convenient Finance. The frauds were apparently committed in order to feed Holmes' gambling addiction. A board member of the Queensland Bar Association recalls that Holmes was a high roller at Jupiters Casino on the Gold Coast. The *Courier-Mail* explained that Holmes' technique seemed to have been "Never to let a cheque settle without having another cheque on its way or an overdraft ready". Holmes made use of generous overdraft facilities and entered multiple lease-back arrangements with different financiers over the same property simultaneously. This property included a $40,000.00 law library. On Christmas Eve 1987, "Holmes is believed to have taken more than $100,000.00 in a complicated sequence that included 'round robin' cheque deposits". It was suggested that Holmes had the arrogance to write to several bank managers wishing them "Merry Christmas".

Holmes then promptly fled Australia, buying tickets to three international destinations on his credit cards. Three years elapsed but Holmes was eventually deported from England on the weekend of the 23rd and 24th of March 1991 and faced Brisbane Magistrates Court on Monday the 25th of March 1991 whereupon he was remanded in custody.

He was finally convicted of fraud and served a term of imprisonment.

It was astonishing that Holmes was never struck off the roll of the Supreme Court back in 1991. A fact Ian made the Queensland Bar Association and the Queensland Legal Services Commission aware of. A board member of the Bar Association said that Holmes should now be struck off the roll adding that the Bar was "derelict" in failing to move for him to be struck off following the conviction. He added that the Bar has an important role in protecting the public and not just its own reputation.

The frauds were bound to have had a devastating impact on the careers of many honest bank officers. They would have also affected the profitability of the banks and the dividends that could be paid to ordinary honest shareholders.

In his letter to the Thailand Justice team, Robert had announced he was "a leading Australian barrister". This was a pretty outrageous claim if one considers that he practiced for only 18 months and during that time was preoccupied with fraud.

Ian was still trying to get his funds back from Robert who had still not managed to get the legal team to produce a letter of complaint. The revelations about his past now made sense of his requests for funds for the complaint letter and his idea to hire a new defense team behind the backs of the existing one.

Robert made no secret of the fact that he thought he was much smarter than members of the Thai defense team who he described as having 'vacuous minds', although he did rate Sana and Nad Bergman, who was married to an American millionaire gem dealer named Jeffery.

Interestingly, Jeffery had been commenting on my articles about the B2 in the *Samui Times*. Ian and I were keen to find out if the legal team was aware of Robert's criminal past. We wanted to know if Robert was part of the legal team or just an advisor. We also wanted to know if the relationship Robert with Nad and Jeffery Bergman was purely professional or if they were friends.

As Jeffery was married to a member of the legal team, we decided to send him an email. In his response to that email, he confirmed that he and his wife, Nad, were indeed personal friends of Robert. Jeffery told us that he had had several meetings with Robert over breakfast, coffee, and lunch. He went on to say, that Robert had attended a private New Year's party at their riverside condo in Bangkok.

In an email to me, Jeffery said, "A little birdie told me she was sitting in the window of a room where a judge and several defense attorneys were having a meeting immediately after the delivery of a guilty verdict in an internationally scrutinized and politically sensitive murder trial. The little birdie told me she heard the judge say the real killer was now laughing and that what the defense team needed was the case to be moved to another jurisdiction in order to have a hope of receiving justice". One can only assume he was talking about his wife. Who else did he know who could have been in that room?

Jonathan Head, the BBC correspondent for South East Asia around this time, had also been speaking to Celia Hatton from the BBC, the lady I had been speaking to with a view of making a documentary about the B2's case. It seemed she had decided, on the advice Jonathan gave her when he returned from covering the elections in the Philippines, that she was no longer interested.

My correspondence with Celia ended with this email from her where she explained that she had spoken at length with Jonathan Head, a few months ago. He was adamant that the case hinged on the DNA. She said Jonathan Head had confirmed to her that he had spoken to me at length, with regards to this matter. She said, "He seems invested in doing this story and knows much more about it than me. Unfortunately, unless you have some revelatory new information, I'll have to agree with Jonathan that the best outcome for the boys lies with the investigation into the DNA lab."

I was disappointed but not surprised. Ian and I decided to continue our investigations into Robert Holmes.

Jeffery Bergman seemed to share my concerns about Andy Hall. Jeffery asked me to disconnect my feelings and opinions about [Andy Hall] from the defense team. He told me, "None of the team members actually like working with him, but he was taken on as a necessary evil as he was willing to manage and accomplish many things the team could not by themselves. I could give you many examples but there is really no point as I am not trying to defend him in any manner. And please, don't let your justifiable anger and distain for [Andy Hall] taint your opinions of the defense team". To this day I cannot imagine what accomplishments Bergman was talking about when it came to Andy Hall's involvement in the case.

My heart was just bleeding for the B2. They had been very badly represented by a civil lawyer with no experience of handling a capital murder trial, Andy Hall who we had no proof even had a law degree, we had discovered that the man leading and advising the defense team was a con man, and now it seemed that even the judges knew who the real killers were!

CHAPTER 52 – THE FIRST
APPEAL COMES BACK

On the 1st of March 2017, the B2 got the results of their first appeal to the Region 8 judges. It was unsuccessful. The ruling was made secretly on the 23rd of February 2017. The Samui Court said evidence presented by the state in the original trial was adequate and reliable, and therefore declined to overturn the December 2015 verdict, condemning Zaw Lin and Wai Phyo to death.

According to a report in *Khaosod*, the ruling came as a total surprise to the defense lawyers who said they had no knowledge of the ruling that was made the previous week which was apparently relayed to the B2 without their notification. Nakhon Chompuchart said, "We will definitely petition the Supreme Court". He could not comment any further as he had not seen the decision.

I was not at all surprised they lost. In Thailand, no witnesses are called during the appeals process; the judges simply go over the material they were presented with in the first place. Why would they possibly have changed their minds?

CHAPTER 53 - ANOTHER MISSING PERSON ON KOH TAO

In the first week of March 2017, I was tipped off that a young Russian girl had gone missing from Koh Tao. There was nothing in the papers about this, so I checked out a few Facebook groups associated with the island and found out that the 23-year-old had gone missing on the 15th of February 2017. Valentina Novozhyonova had been staying at the Koh Tao Hostel and had been planning on leaving Koh Tao go to and spend some time in Koh Samui.

The Facebook appeal for the missing girl made note of the fact that the local Koh Tao police had found her belongings in her room along with her passport and phone, which the police had taken into their care.

Valentina was reported as being 170cm tall (5 feet 5 inches.) with light brown hair and a tattoo in the shape of a V on her wrist. Interestingly, even though she had been missing for three weeks, there had not been a single search party sent out for her. The story had also not made it into the press.

I published and broke the story, and the comments and online speculation went wild. It seemed that her disappearance was not even reported for the first two weeks and Koh Tao was being heavily criticized online for trying to cover up the story to prevent any more bad publicity on the island.

Online, Koh Tao was now being referred to as Death Island and this latest story was bringing the B2 back into the spotlight as more suspicion was being raised as to what the hell was happening on Turtle Island AKA Koh Tao. Many people on social media were suggesting there was a serial killer in Koh Tao and everyone there knew it but were just too scared to come forward and do anything about it.

On the 3rd of March 2017, the police bothered to start looking for the girl and started to ask the dive schools on the island if they had seen her. It had come to light that she was a free diver and had been free diving solo in Chalok Bay. It was said on one social media site that the depth of her last dive had been 22 meters. This information would have come from her dive watch/computer that would log all of her dives. This led me to believe that she had not gone missing while free diving as she would have been wearing her watch. Although it was possible the information came from a written dive log. The police thought she had gone missing while diving and three weeks after she went missing asked for volunteer divers to look for her.

By the fifth day of the search, nothing had turned up. The search party had consisted of over one hundred local officials and volunteers who searched the shore and by air with air force rescue planes. Thai and foreign divers had also scoured the ocean for her. The authorities were reporting that they thought she had gone diving and something had gone wrong. By now, the governor of Surat Thani had got wind of the situation and told all agencies concerned to carry out searches on the surface of the water, underwater, and to bring in modern technology to help with the search. He also said he planned to construct an observation tower with round the clock surveillance to ensure better safety for visitors. We discovered she had checked in at the hostel on the 11th.

By the 8th of March 2017, the authorities reported that they had sought the help of fortune tellers as they had got nowhere with the physical search. Three of Koh Tao's best mystics were contacted according to a report in the *Thairath* newspaper. All three said, independently, that she was in the sea. Surat governor Apichart Bunsrirort now asked the searchers to step up and planned to visit Koh Tao. We then discovered that there was CCTV of the missing girl outside a convenience store near the Koh Tao Hostel where she was staying at 6 a.m. on the 15th of February 2017.

I managed to get hold of a girl called Nikita, who was a friend of Valentina.

I asked her if she had any further information that might help us locate her and asked if she had been travelling alone, had ever had problems free diving, if she had ever gone missing before, when she was due home and if she could think of anything else that we could go on. She got back to me and told me that she had been travelling alone and had never mentioned any problems in the past about her free diving. However, she said that some publications had made mention that Valentina had a psychotherapist who was quoted as saying that she had some phobia that could have caused the girl issues when she was diving.

On the 12th of March 2017, reports were appearing in the press suggesting the missing girl's mother suspected she had gone missing due to a diving accident and her only previous free-diving experience was in a swimming pool where she had been taking lessons for four years. It was also reported that she was epileptic and suffered from asthma.

Nikita confirmed to me that Valentina did suffer from asthma, as far as she knew. She also confirmed that Valentina did have experience of diving in the ocean in Crimea where she dived to 24 meters and said she was no novice when it came to diving. Nikita confided in me that she feared something was being covered up and was concerned at the false information about her being a novice in the press.

The press coverage was confusing me because it mentioned that Valentina was diving with a dive buddy. This also turned out not to be true.

By now, the Russian press were reporting that body parts had been found in the waters of Koh Tao. DNA test on the body parts, a hip and arm bone, revealed they did not belong to the missing girl and later it was released to the press that the body parts were not even human!

I wondered how these sorts of mistakes could be made.

If Koh Tao had hoped to keep this story out of the press, they were out of luck. The missing girl was making the news all over the world and not for the first time I felt happy I was not in Thailand as I was the only reason it had got into the international press.

A few days later, as the police continued to scratch their heads, Valentina's mother arrived on the island. The story of the dive buddy was still in the press. This nameless person had apparently gone to Malaysia and the police were waiting for him or her to return to Thailand. A breakthrough was then announced by the police who had found a flip-flop that they thought belonged to the missing girl. I found this utterly ludicrous as there are hundreds of flip-flops on the beaches of Thailand and found it highly unlikely anybody would be able to identify who it was once owned by. The missing girl's mother gave a sample of her DNA to help in the investigation.

Surat Gov. Apichart Bunsrirot, held a video conference with police from all over the province of Surat Thani to discuss a way forward. Missing person posters were going up all over Koh Tao and Koh Phangan.

By the 14th of March 2017 the missing girl's mother was distraught and was begging the authorities not to give up on their search. She met with chief of the governor of Surat Thani at Bans diving resort on Sairee Beach. She was shown the CCTV footage from the convenience store and confirmed that was her daughter. Remarkably the mother of the missing woman also reached out to a fortune teller, this time a Russian one who told her that her daughter was alive but trapped. Mother Vavara was taken around the island by police to take pictures and had sent them to the fortune teller. Then the Koh Tao police announced that an ocean expert Juliang Pheungworiyaton had told them that he had been contacted by a boat operator who told him that he saw a female tourist on the 15th or 16th of February swimming out to sea. They also mentioned that that girl could have been Russian and was wearing a bikini.

By the 28th of March 2017, the police had given up and called off the search. They then started to tell the local media that they believed the girl had mental health issues. This is not in the least bit uncommon. Just about every foreigner who dies on Thailand's shores is accused of having mental health issues.

Ian and I got on the case and discovered that far from never having dived in open water before, Valentina had experience of free diving in the Black Sea. We also found out she did not have a dive buddy who had left the island. She possibly had some mental health issues but had never been suicidal as had been suggested in some media outlets.

CHAPTER 54 - KOH TAO KILLS
AGAIN - ELISE DALLEMAGNE

I kept my eye on social media and Koh Tao Facebook groups who had long since blocked my personal Facebook page. They did not have the intelligence to envisage that as an investigative journalist I might have more than one account. By the 23rd of May 2017, rumors started to emerge that the body of a young girl was found partially burnt, partially eaten by animals and what was left was wrapped in T-shirts. Unsurprisingly, this information had never been passed onto the victim's family or made public at all. Was this the missing Russian diver?

A quick check of the Facebook page of Nomsod showed me that he was on the island of Koh Tao when the Russian girl went missing.

It turned out that the story about the body being found was in fact true and not just a rumor. But it was not the body of Valentina. It was the body of another girl, this time from Belgium. Elise Dallemagne was 30 years old and was found on the 27th of April 2017. She had been living on Koh Phangan. On the 17th of April 2017, she had contacted her mother by Skype to say that after 18 months of travelling she had decided to return home to Belgium. She had arrived on Koh Tao on the 19th of April 2017.

We started to make enquires and discovered that she had checked into the Triple B Bungalows in Koh Tao's port town of Mae Haad. During her first night, three of the bungalows, including the one she had been staying in, caught fire. The owner of the bungalows said that the fire had started by an electrical fault and had nothing to do with Elise, who fled the scene. It seemed that the girl then walked several kilometers to Tanote Bay where she had a meal and booked herself a ticket to Bangkok via Chumphon for the 24th of April 2017. She went so far as to put her luggage on the boat. Her luggage arrived in Chumpon; Elise did not. She was found several days later, dead, on a rock, in the jungle above Tanote Bay partially eaten by animals, her remains wrapped up in T-shirts. This girl's mother told the press that her body had been taken to Surat Thani by the Koh Tao rescue team. However, our friend, Steven Drylie, told me that the girl had not died on Koh Tao at all but had died on Koh Phangan, although he did tell me that he knew she had been on Koh Tao. He also told me that the police had put her death down to suicide. I was not at all surprised and waited for news reports to say she was mentally ill to emerge. I really had to wonder why so many suicidal people from all over the world would decide to book two-way tickets to Thailand, where they planned to end their lives, and how anybody could buy a story that a girl who was going to kill herself would bother to call her mother and tell her that she was on her way home, bother to buy a ticket to Bangkok, and bother to put her luggage on the boat.

An autopsy was performed at the hospital in Surat Thani and then again at the Institute of Forensic Medicine Police Hospital in Bangkok. The girl's body was identified by her teeth and x-ray pictures provided by her mother from Belgium. Her body was cremated in Bangkok 14 days after her remains were found.

From what we could gather from her mother, Elise had been travelling for two and a half years in India, Australia, and New Zealand. During that time, she often visited Thailand. She was said to have spent more than a year on Koh Phangan where she was part of the yoga/yantra-Community. She was also an active member of SACRED, an Indian sect run by the notorious Sathya Sai Baba Cult movement who reside and practice on Koh Phangan between Thong Sala and the Hin Kong Village. According to her mother she lived there for three months with Guru Raaman Andreas from Germany and two female Thai friends, Nuri and Raani.

We will never know why she got off the ferry on the 19th of April 2017, or booked herself into a small bungalow for 250 baht a night at the Triple B Mae Haad. Like the mother of Valentina, Elise's mother went to Koh Tao looking for answers. She said that she spoke to the owner of the Triple B who was angry and did not want to be associated with her daughter's death.

Elise was spotted at the Poseidon Resort in Tanote Bay and booked a second ticket home scheduled for the 24th of April 2017. Her body was discovered by some tourists who had been watching a big monitor lizard walking backwards and forwards to the same tree in the jungle. When they went to investigate, they found her decayed, half-eaten corpse.

The police did carry out an investigation and told the girl's mother, Michelle, that she had committed suicide and hanged herself in a tree. An eyewitness told the *Samui Times* that her body was wrapped up in old T-shirts and a fuel bottle was found nearby. The girl's mother didn't accept that her daughter would have killed herself, and said she was acting rationally and normally during their last conversation.

This, like all of the other cases, raises serious questions about police investigations in Koh Tao. In this case, there are many unanswered questions, such as why did she get off the boat on the 19th and the 24th of April 2017? Why, on the last trip did she leave her luggage on the boat and only take her cell phone and a small rucksack? Why did she leave Mae Haad and go to the other side of the island? Why did the police never question taxi drivers and motorbike taxi drivers as it would have been too far for her to walk? Why was no CCTV found?

Cases of female hangings are incredibly rare. I discovered through research women almost always kill themselves by overdose or by cutting their wrists. He had never had a single case in his career where a young woman took a rope and hanged herself. Why did the police keep this body so quiet? Why did it not make the news until her mother screamed out for help? Why was it being mentioned on social media, but no news outlets covered the story?

The mother of Elise was never given her autopsy reports and will never know why her daughter was found dead in a remote part of what is known now as Death Island.

Elise's mother has her ashes and has taken them back to Belgium but she does not have, and never will have, answers. She seriously doubts the police's version of events and has publicly asked for help to solve the case on more than one occasion.

I, of course, wrote about this latest death and some interesting comments appeared below my articles.

"RIP Elise, yet another 'suicide'… normally people planning on taking their own lives don't book plane tickets to travel, Koh Tao may have a serial murderer".

"They do have 'one' [a serial killer] but certain residents with vested interests and or fear the perpetrators are in disingenuous denial – and they don't want word out to the world that they are even more murders there".

"I have lived in Thailand for five years and those kinds of headlines are an average thing. Especially on the islands where there is a massive mafia presence and any shady deaths can be attributed to suicide or Burmese labor immigrants".

"Amazing how often authorities will just say suicide and its case closed".

The Koh Tao residents were not at all happy about more headlines and of course I got the blame for letting the stories out into the wider world. One woman, Claire Wyndham, runs a school on Koh Tao, I am told (due to her involvement with the mafia) with no paperwork or work permits. Ms. Wyndham started up a petition for Koh Tao residents calling for my arrest. In her comments on the article, she tries to defend the death and defends Steven Drylie who lied about the location of the body.

"I'm just after facts. There are no direct quotes here except from Koh Tao Rescue denying they ever dealt with the matter. If this girl died on Koh Tao, I want to know the direct sources of information. I'm not criticizing , I'm genuinely interested as a resident. No one I know on this very small island has mentioned it at all. Writing without proper sources i.e.-names of police officers, direct quotes and the fact no other media seem to have had much to say, makes me naturally question the credibility of the information. If this girl died here, I want to know. The poor young thing, it's terrible".

I responded to Ms. Wyndham and explained we had confirmation of the tragic death from her mother. Ms. Wyndham went on to ask me why I had not quoted the girl's mother in my articles or the names of the police who had been in attendance. She tried to tell me that if Steven Drylie said she has not been found dead on the island, then 'she' needed proof that the girl had been found on the island. I suspected this was to protect the reputation of the island more than out of consideration for the actual site of the girls' death. Ms. Wyndham clearly had a great deal more trust in Drylie than I did. I knew he had lied about the circumstances of Luke Millers death. I was about to construct a public response to her questions, but my German friend and fellow journalist did it for me.

"Claire Wyndham - Confirmation by police and the mother that Elise died in Koh Tao, Tanote Bay, is a matter of fact. We also received the same information and we could prove it while doing further research. The case was just silenced because nobody wanted to read about another fatal case there. Mother Michele confirmed several times that it was Koh Tao and she and her husband visited the island in May to get some more information. Police told her, quoting the mother, that Elise had hanged herself in a tree in the jungle on top of the hills of Tanote Bay. They - till today - have never received a final autopsy report and that was the reason why they desperately went public and why they hope to find some people who have seen Elise Dallemagne during her last weeks on Phangan or Koh Tao".

I didn't hear from Ms Wyndham again but somebody else posted a link to an article about the death of Elise Dallemagne in the UK's *Mirror* with this note "Ain't just *Samui Times* reporting it! It's everywhere! Might be time for some people to start fessing up".

It seemed to me that most people weren't buying the stories assumed to be leaked to the press by the police other than those who had a vested interest in Koh Tao.

Koh Tao hit the headlines again on the 17th of June 2017 when a fit and healthy German man was found dead at his bungalow in the heart of the jungle. Thai authorities said Bernd Grotsch, 47, died of either a heart attack or a snake bite, but his family believed there was more behind the death. The family never received an autopsy report and complained that his body was sent to the same Bangkok hospital that carried out the botched reports on the bodies of Hannah Witheridge and David Miller. Immediately after his death, the family of Mr. Grotsch were told his body had been moved to Surat Thani on the mainland, but days later when they checked again, they found he was still at a temple on Koh Tao. It was alleged that the family put a lot of pressure on the German Embassy and eventually his body was moved to Bangkok. Word on the street told us that

Mr. Grotsch had once lived on Koh Tao and had recently returned to the island to tie up some loose ends on a twenty-year-old motorbike business he owned there.

In a surprise twist, on the 30th of June 2017, Deputy Surat Thani Police, Chief Pol. Col. Preecha Kladsawad directed investigators at the Koh Tao police station to re-open the investigation into the death of Elise Dallemagne after her story was run in the *Samui Times* and was then shared by the CSI LA Facebook account. Although the local police said it was suicide, Koh Tao Police Chief Pol. Lt. Chokchai Suttimkek gave some different accounts. He said that her body was found on Koh Tao on the 27th of April 2017, but he denied part of it had been eaten or it was wrapped up. He said the body of Elise Dallemagne was found with a rope tied to her neck in a tree and the evidence suggested that she had died on either the 23rd or the 24th of April. He said that the autopsy had confirmed that she died from lack of oxygen as a result of the rope. He said that the police informed the Belgian Embassy in Bangkok, and her mother, before cremating her in the presence of the embassy staff. He went on to say that her mother had come to Thailand to collect her daughter's belongings and denied that any of them had arrived in Chumphon.

The island of Koh Tao was making headlines on a regular basis around the world but in the UK especially. On 27th July 2017, Elaine Dickinson, a writer for the UK's *Independent*, who used to live in Thailand, wrote about the island's 'dark side' and strongly urged tourists to avoid the holiday destination. In her article she said:

"Resting in the Gulf of Thailand, a two-hour ferry ride north of Koh Samui, Koh Tao is best known for its incredible marine life, which over the years has attracted a small but buoyant expat community of around 2,000 people, many of whom run dive centers, restaurants and B&B's. But my requests to long-time residents and business owners were met with fear, as they made it quite clear they felt their lives would be in danger if they spoke on the record. Off the record, however, they told of an island held in the iron grip of a mafia family, who demanded protection money, controlled the local police force and were not above attacking or burning down the homes and businesses of people who crossed them".

At around the same time, *The Sun* ran a story about Sean McAnna bringing up once again the murders of Hannah Witheridge and David Miller. *The Sun* writer said that he had also been to Koh Tao and echoed the statement made by *The Independent* writer when he said he would never return to Koh Tao.

By the 7th of July 2017, residents of Koh Tao were getting angry and Claire Wyndham created a change.org petition entitled "Hold *SAMUI TIMES* responsible for destroying Koh Tao's tourist trade". She described herself as the owner and manager of the Koh Tao International Primary School and Koh Tao resident.

She said:

"The *Samui Times* has continuously made false and inaccurate statements about Koh Tao Island that have been quoted and shared by international news sources all over the world. We are asking all Koh Tao residents to sign a petition that can be presented to the authorities reporting ourselves as the victims of the Samui Times illegal activity".

I felt it was a very interesting statement because I thought the victims were the young travelers who had all lost their lives on the island and not Claire, who ran a school that was not financially dependent on tourism. I was constantly being told by Koh Tao residents both directly, and on social media posts, that the deaths had had no impact on tourist numbers and that the island continued to thrive.

I fought back in my paper:

"What Claire Wyndham fails to mention are the family members of actual victims who tragically lost their lives on Koh Tao and how they deserve satisfactory investigations into their loved ones deaths and have a right to information and answers. This attitude is common on Koh Tao among residents who announce on social media platforms that their concern is for their income and not the wellbeing of visitors to the island or the wellbeing of the loved ones of those who died.

Imagine what it is like to not be provided with an autopsy report when your daughter dies in the case of Elise, the young Belgium girl found dead in Koh Tao. It is hard to imagine what it is like to have no trace of your daughter who was last seen in Koh Tao in the case of young Russian girl Valentina. It is hard to imagine spending your life convinced your son was murdered in the case of Nick, a Brit who was found dead while on vacation with his family. It is hard to imagine how you feel when the police did not contact the last person who saw your daughter alive in the case of Christina, a young British girl found dead in her resort. It is hard to imagine seeing your friend dead with suspicious bruises and being sure of foul play in the case of Luke. It is even harder to imagine the reality that your sons' or daughters' lives were brutally cut short in a horrific double murder in the case of David and Hannah. However, it seems the residents are not even trying to imagine what the families and friends of these poor souls are going through and only imagine silencing the press. If there is nothing to hide then why should the press be silenced? Why should the press be responsible for suspicions being cast over the island and not the deaths or the unhappy relatives themselves? If the number of deaths, according to the Koh Tao residents, is nothing unusual, then why object to them being reported on.

Perhaps what makes the press suspect something is amiss are conversations such as the one the *Samui Times* had with the British Paramedic and Koh Tao rescue worker who was at the scene of the horrific murders of British Hannah Withering and David Miller. Just after the murders when asked about Sean McAnna, the man who claims the mafia were going to kill him and frame him for the murders, Steve Drylie said, "I think the ones who did it saw him and thought he was a witness so ran after him". When the *Samui Times* asked him how he thought Sean could sleep at night when he may have information that could saves the lives of the Burmese after they were convicted and sentenced to death, he responded, "Thai people cannot keep their mouths shut".

Koh Tao residents shout unfair and inaccurate reporting. If the conviction of the Burmese men is sound, why on earth is somebody who works with the Koh Tao rescue and Koh Tao police telling the local paper that "The truth will come out one day" and in another conversation described the police as having less skills than "cub scouts on an explorer badge" when discussing a body that was found washed up on Koh Phangan.

We may not have answers to the reasons for every death on Koh Tao and we many never know the truth. However, one truth we do know is that hundreds of thousands of people have questioned the guilt of the Burmese men who stand to be executed for a crime they may not have committed and many of the families of those who have died in Koh Tao do not trust the police or their investigations. We do know that the local authorities have announced they will sue this publication for its reporting and that Koh Tao residents blame the *Samui Times* for the decline in tourism and not the deaths of young, innocent travelers whose life came to an end on their shores".

By the 16th of July 2018 the victims' families in the UK had had enough. Pat Harrington, the mother of Ben Harrington, decided she would start a petition to take to the UK government asking them to look into the suspicious deaths. By now, all of the families had found each other in the UK and had started chatting online about their shared experiences of the Royal Thai Police and their issues with the investigations that had so much in common. In her petition that she started on Change.org, Pat said:

"My son was killed on Koh Tao Thailand in 2012. They say he had an accident but things have never added up. The coroner in the UK would not use the word 'accident'. Statistics from the *Farang* Death Database, out of 562 deaths between 2008 and 2017, 95 are British, 106 are reported as road traffic accidents and 56 from falling and 89 from drowning, 87.37% are male. The Crime Suppression Division have now taken over the investigation into the latest death on the Island. The British Government need to take notice of what is happening to our children on these islands and do something regarding further investigations into their deaths. Theresa May this needs to be looked into NOW before any more lives are taken".

The petition created something truly amazing in the UK. The families of all of the victims got together and created an online support group called Grieving Together We Want Justice. Together we all chatted about the victims and a lot of alarming similarities in the complaints from each family about the shoddy Thai police investigations. Over the months, some really incredible relationships were formed on that page. They are still there today.

To date nearly 17,000 people have signed her petition. On the 6th of March 2018, I travelled to London to meet the families for the first time and to hand the petition in to No. 10 Downing Street. On the drive into London, I had no idea how it would feel to see the families of the victims for the first time. For almost four years I had done nothing other than investigate the deaths of their relatives and I knew it would be emotional to be in the same room as them. We all met in a pub not far from Downing Street for lunch. I was overwhelmed to meet them all and hear their stories and to fill in the gaps that they didn't know. Information such Montriwat's resort being the one Christina had stayed in, although the business is registered to his wife. This was a surprise to Christina's father Boyne. It was surreal and very sad but also empowering to see the families standing united in their grief and doing something to help each other, themselves, and to warn other young travelers. Pat gave an amazing interview outside Downing Street. She said she was very, very nervous but during her delivery of the speech you would never have known.

CHAPTER 55 – THE KNIVES COME OUT AND SO DOES MY ARREST WARRANT

I first heard about the rape of a young British girl on Koh Tao when I was contacted through the *Samui Times* by her mother. The date was Friday the 13th of July 2018. The date was an omen.

To protect the identity of this young woman, I have changed the names in this part of the book.

Jane's mother, Anne, sent me an email informing me that on the 26th of June 2018, at approximately 1 a.m. her daughter had her drink drugged and was robbed and raped on the island of Koh Tao. Jane told her mother that after the rape she had been afraid to stay on the island of Koh Tao and had taken a ferry to the next island, Koh Phangan, where she had tried to report the crimes to the police. The police in Koh Phangan, according to her, had been happy to take her report of robbery, but had flatly refused to take the report of rape. They told her she had to go back to Koh Tao and make the report there.

I found this rather interesting as the police on Koh Tao and the police on Koh Phangan all work under region 8 and there would be no legal reason as to why the police on Koh Phangan could not deal with both allegations. Jane had returned home to the UK on the 2nd of July 2018, but left a T-shirt with DNA on it in Thailand with her friend John, who remained in Thailand.

Anne told me that she was desperately trying to find any information she could about the crimes and that she kept hitting brick walls with the KohTao police that she described as a 'closed shop'. Anne told me she was in touch with Thailand's tourist police and the British Consulate but was at her 'wits end' as to what to do next.

Anne, during her investigations, had contacted the Fishbowl Bar on Koh Tao where she believed her daughter's drink was spiked and was told that on the night in question the CCTV in the bar had not been working. Anne told me that she had some misgivings about a lady called Sonia Bonny, a singer, who took umbrage with her daughter, but, by coincidence, was the one who picked her daughter up when, after the drugs wore off, she came round on the beach.

I was astonished. Not that a girl had been raped, that didn't surprise me in the least, but the fact she had got off the island alive and with DNA evidence was utterly incredible. Could this be the smoking gun that linked the real killers of Hannah and David to the crime? I was distraught that a girl had been raped, and, once again, tried to imagine what yet another set of parents were going through thanks to Koh Tao let alone the poor victim.

Not for the first time I cursed under my breath about Koh Tao and thought 'here we go again'. I had no idea at that point that this case would prevent me ever returning to Thailand or the only bricks and mortar home I own on the planet.

I quickly scoured the internet for any reports of this case in the local and national press in Thailand and found none. I told Anne that I was mortified about what had happened to her daughter and was of course more than happy to help in any way I could. While I was overjoyed Jane had got home safely and even more so with DNA evidence, I felt it only right to warn Anne that the sad truth about Koh Tao. I explained that I had been trying to find justice for many other families who had lost loved ones to Koh Tao and that we had an online support group she was more than welcome to join. At this stage I did not know if Anne wanted this story in the press, but I let her know I could help her facilitate that if that was her choice.

I could not speak to Anne for as long as I wanted to as I was off to London to cover the protests about Tommy Robinson being in jail for a small online news publication I had started in the UK. I spent the day wondering how Jane had got off the island alive and why the police on Koh Phangan had refused to take her report about the rape. Why had they not taken her to the hospital and offered her a rape kit and some kind of medical attention? I wondered if she had been attacked by someone not connected to the powerful local families and that is how she was able to get away, or was it that Koh Tao could simply not survive the death of yet another young and pretty tourist.

I made a few calls to contacts to see what we could find out.

I got an email from Anne asking me if the T-shirt with the DNA on it should be brought to the UK or handed over to the Thai authorities. I quickly replied that under no circumstances should she hand it over to the Thai authorities. I worried that if the DNA belonged to anyone of any influence it would never be seen again. I asked Anne to get as much information from Jane about the night of the incident as she could. Anne started to research the goings on in Koh Tao and was horrified with what she had found online.

The events of that night started to become clearer when on Monday, the 16th of June 2018, I got an email from Anne who told me that reluctantly Jane had given her an account of what went on.

Jane said that she had been staying on Koh Tao with a group of friends from London. They went to the Fishbowl Bar and the Leo Bar. The last thing she remembered was getting a drink and then suddenly feeling very tired. Jane's friend, John, offered to walk her back to her room. The next thing she remembers is waking up on the beach naked from the waist down with a man smiling at her. The man walked off and left her on the beach.

Anne told me the T-shirt was due back in the UK on the 20th of August 2018 and that Jane had confirmed she had not been in the AC bar, a question I had posed earlier. Jane later confirmed that it was in the Leo Bar, not the Fishbowl Bar, she was in when she believes her drink was spiked.

The tourist police had been back in touch with Anne and told her the police reports and the T-shirt with the DNA should be sent directly to them. Thankfully the T-shirt was still with John who had gone back to Koh Tao after Jane had flown home. He had tried to make the rape report on Koh Tao, as suggested by the police on Koh Phangan, but had been told the report had to be made by the victim and not her friend.

I spoke to the Rape Crisis Organization in the UK and then my lawyer in Bangkok. He asked me to find out if, other than the rape, the victim had been attacked or physically harmed, if she had had any treatment on the islands, if he had had a blood test to confirm that she had been drugged, if she had a description of her attacker, such as his nationality, height, and weight and if she had visited a hospital who could confirm she had been raped. Jane had not been offered any kind of medical help in Thailand and had not been harmed other than the rape.

Rape Crisis England and Wales advised me that Jane could approach an Independent Sexual Violence Advisor who would be able to give her support and guidance. I passed the information on to Anne.

Anne told me that when John had gone back to Koh Tao to report, the rape surprisingly the police went to the bars in question, but only to find the CCTV footage had already been erased. Anne also told me the horrible truth that it had been an anal rape. I cast my mind back to the fact that

Hannah had also allegedly been anally raped. I found it hard to even imagine the young girl's pain and humiliation, both at the time, and during the subsequent examinations in the UK.

Jane's rape crisis team had advised her to take the T-Shirt, that was now in the UK, to The Haven. The Haven is one of a network of specialist sexual assault referral centers (SARCs) located across London and open twenty-four hours a day.

A trusted contact of mine suggested that Jane should go to her local police and insist that they file a complaint with Interpol. I was told it was likely the police would not want to do this but it would be possible for them to do if they were pushed. I was also advised that she should contact the UN, UNIFEM, and the United Nations Development Fund for Women, and file a complaint with them. It was suggested she should speak to Pavena Hongskull, the former government minister who had helped abused women, that she should file a criminal report in Bangkok at the Court, not via the police, and file a complaint with Ministry of Justice Rights and Liberties in Chaeng Wattana.

Jane made an appointment with her local police and went along with the support of a lady from The Haven. On the 31st of July 2018, she made her statement to a policeman named Kevin Brown and he took possession of the T-shirt. Brown told Jane that he would hand the T-shirt to his superiors and if he thought she should take the matter further, he would get back to her.

Anne forwarded an email that had been sent to Jane from Lucy Tyrell at the Foreign Office who had asked her to send a copy of the Koh Phangan police report. She said she wanted to approach the police in Koh Pangnan to discuss the case and to see what was reported at the time. She also asked for details of the police reports that had been made about the case in the UK. She went on to say that she had approached by Jess Mackey at Kings College Hospital requesting her assistance with a rape case. Lucy said she believed it was the same case but would need the authority of Jane to discuss it with Jess Mackey due to data protection.

It was not long before Lucy Tyrrell was in touch again, this time asking Jane to confirm that it was police officer Kevin Brown who she had made the UK police report with, and, if so, she would contact him to find out if the report had been transferred through to Interpol. She said the British Embassy in Bangkok would then register their interest with the Thai authorities and find out if an incident report had been received. She went on to say that they would also request confirmation as to why Jane was unable to report the rape at the police station in Koh Phangan, and let Jane know the outcome. Lucy told Jane that she needed to be aware that the police had informed her that it would not be possible for Jane to file a report for the rape now she had left Thailand and wondered if she had considered seeking help from a Thai lawyer who could perhaps make representations on Jane's behalf. She sent a list of Thai lawyers that is standard for the British Embassy.

With little to no information coming out of Koh Tao, Anne and I decided to go public with an open letter, from Anne, to all of the UK and Thai news publications I was in contact with asking for help investigating the case.

The letter explained that Jane had been working at an orphanage in Sri Lanka, a post that she adored. After leaving Sri Lanka, she met up with some friends who were travelling to Thailand and the group ended up on Koh Tao. On the night of the 25th, early morning of the 26th, she had been in the Leo Bar where she and her friend John had a drink that made them both feel very drowsy. They left the bar to go back to the hostel. Jane woke up at 5 a.m. to find she had been robbed and anally raped and remembered an Asian man smiling at her before he walked away. John had also woken up on the beach some distance away from her. Jane got up and, as she walked, saw a French girl who had acquainted herself with Jane's group. The girl took Jane back to the hostel. Jane was slightly wary of this woman, a singer from the Fishbowl Bar, because it was thought she had stolen from the group. Jane did not want to report the crime on the island of Koh Tao because she was too scared and as the ferry to the next island was already booked, she decided to report the crimes there. The open letter explained that the police on Koh Phangan would not take the report of a rape and ended by saying that Anne was in touch with me, was aware that Koh Tao was run by influential families, and requested the media look into the case.

We decided that once again it would be the *Samui Times* that broke the story of Jane's horrific ordeal. I wanted to interview Jane, but she was not up to it. Anne requested that I run the story without her daughter, the victim, being named. I respected her decision and got Anne's approval on the story before publishing. I relayed the story in my paper and asked for anyone with any information to contact me; nobody did. However, Anne sent the article to a friend of hers at the *Sunday Times* and on the 21st of August, the British press took up the story that first came out in the *Daily Mail*.

Hoping to get some information out of people in Thailand, I put Anne in touch with a publication in Thailand called *Khaosod* which ran a story about the rape on the 24th of August. I read an article in their publication that worried me; I knew something was up, the press were starting to backtrack. The headline in the paper said that a British tourist had filed a complaint about theft but not rape. The police had flatly denied allegations that they had refused to take a report of the rape and were slamming the press for suggesting such a thing. Capt. Krissada Thongsakul, an officer on Koh Phangan, told the news publication, by phone, that she had never mentioned a sexual assault and had only filed a report about missing belongings when she visited the police station with a male companion. He listed those items as a mobile phone, a credit card, and 3,000 baht. He went on to say that she had made the report at his police station rather than Koh Tao because she happened to be visiting the island. He recorded her report as being made at around 1 p.m. on the, 27thof June. It was not going down well that Anne had made statements to the press bringing attention to the fact that this was the same beach where Hannah and David had been found and was accusing the Thai police of a cover up.

I passed the article onto Anne who made this statement for me to send to *Khaosod*:

"Jane left Koh Tao and reported the rape and theft to the local police on Koh Phangan. They refused to take her statement regarding the rape as Koh Tao was not in their jurisdiction. They were happy to take a statement regarding the robbery. When she came home, she was examined by a doctor and is under the care of a local rape crisis centre. To disregard my daughter's rape is abhorrent, and I would recommend that no one travels to any part of Thailand until this despicable business has been dealt with. We have given a full statement to the UK police, who are also in possession of the DNA".

This, to me, was yet just another prime example of the utter corruption in Thailand, and how police would make statements to the press that were as far away from the truth as you can get. The police were happy to lie with impunity to try to preserve the reputation of the islands, and when that failed, they would blame the press for giving them a bad reputation, rather than identify, and deal with the perpetrators of the crimes to improve the reputation of the islands. With visions of rapists and murderers being free to roam the islands I was fuming and knew we now needed to prove Jane was raped and publish the medical records to prove it.

Anne had contacted the Fishbowl Bar herself. They had emailed her back apologizing for what had happened to Jane and pledged to do anything they could to help. The told Anne they were the only bar on the island who used Western security and that they had a CCTV system that covered most parts of the bar. Ferando Aquiyama, who sent the message, said he was not on the island but would hand the details to his business partner and asked for more details so they could help.

Later on, he contacted Anne again and said he had been in touch with his business partner who was as shocked as he was. He had spoken to the bar manager who told him the police had been to the bar to see the CCTV footage. Unfortunately, on the night in question, it had not been working. He went on to say that a French traveler named Sonia had sung a few songs with their band in the bar that night, but as there was no proof she had been involved in anything malicious, there was nothing they could do. He said while they did all they could to keep their customers safe, there was little they could do for them once they had left the bar and that there were some 'horrible people in the world' and that it was a real shame that things like this happen.

The article in *Khaosod* had misquoted the name of the bar Jane had been in. Having briefly worked for that publication, as an editor, I believed my past working relationship with them warranted me asking them to correct their mistake. I was a little perturbed that when I contacted them, they as good as accused me of making the entire story up. They suggested getting Anne to contact them directly, which she did, and went so far as to tell them that Jane had seen medics at the Sussex Hospital near Gatwick Airport, had seen her own GP at the Cator Medical Centre, and was under a support worker at the Haven Rape Crisis Centre in Camberwell, and had made a statement at the Lewisham Police Station.

I was told by some friends in Thailand that the police had gone on national television accusing me of making up fake news. They were also accusing Jane of making the police report for nothing other than claiming on her travel insurance. Also featured on the news report was a woman called Wan Vivienne, the owner of the bungalows that Jane had stayed in. She stated that she did not believe Jane had been raped. I found this odd as Jane had told her mother that the same woman had encouraged her to report the rape when she was packing up her room in preparation for leaving the island. It then transpired that after Jane left Thailand, the same Wan Vivienne had found her on Facebook and had been sending her messages telling her to stop talking to the press.

Anne also confirmed that the stolen mobile phone was not insured. There would be no reason for Jane to report the theft to make an insurance claim which totally contradicted the claim made by Police Super Int. Pol. Col. Sathit Kongnian during a video conference with Pol. Maj. Gen. Apichart Boonsrirote, commander of the Surat Thani provincial police.

Meanwhile, Anne had been speaking with David at CSI LA who put her in touch with a well-known Thai journalist, Suthichai, who went against the grain in Thailand and did not peddle the Thai police's versions of stories about crime. Incensed about what was going on in the news in Thailand, Anne agreed to do an online interview live with him.

The interview started with Suthichai stating that there were a few questions he wanted to ask Anne to clear up the confusion with the case related to her daughter and the island of Koh Tao. Suthichai was interested to know why it had taken so long for the incident to hit the press. Anne explained that she had spoken to several journalists during her investigations, and when she made the decision to go public, she had chosen my publication. Anne confirmed that Jane had tried to report a robbery and a rape and that the report had been encouraged by the owner of the bungalows where her daughter had stayed. Suthichai confirmed that according to the police report 4 debit cards, an iPhone 7 and 3,000 baht were stolen. During the interview, Anne made mention that Jane's travel companion, John, was not her daughter's boyfriend and he had been told, on his return to Koh Tao, that he could not report the rape as he was not the victim. Suthichai confirmed that the police had said that there was CCTV from June 28th until July 4th which was kept for two weeks before being taped over. Anne said that this could not be true as John was back on the island before it would have been taped over. Suthichai then asked Anne what she suspected. She said, "I am happy to tell you what everyone else is afraid to say. The island is run by two mafia families who enjoy spiking drinks and raping and murdering tourists" She went on to say that her daughter is a victim, but also a survivor, who was in possession of a T-shirt containing the DNA of her rapist.

Suthichai then stated that the Thai police had agreed to re-open the case for a period of one week if Anne or Jane were prepared to travel to Thailand. They had three months in which to do this. Anne confirmed that she would not allow Jane to travel back to Thailand but would be happy to go back and do it herself as the embassy ambassador, and vice, had told her they would ensure her safety. Suthichai asked Anne if she had the full backing of the Embassy. Anne said they were in touch with her. Suthichai then mentioned that it had been said in the press that Jane had not been raped but was simply trying to discredit Thailand and Koh Tao in the UK papers. Anne said this was ridiculous. She had met some friends in Phi Phi, Thailand, where she had an amazing time, and that she had been loving Thailand. What had happened was a disaster that had changed her life. She had no reason to discredit a beautiful country with only a minority of people who discredit it and disgrace it with their crimes.

Suthichai said that Koh Tao had a very bad history of death and murders and that the Thai people also wanted answers to what was going on there. He asked Anne if she had enough evidence to go to Thailand and prove what happened. She replied she had the T-shirt and her daughter's statement but up against the police, she and the Embassy had their hands tied if the police refused to believe what had happened to her daughter. Suthichai ended the interview by showing Anne one Thai language and one English language newspaper covering the case and said that he would try to get to the bottom of it. If she had any further comments or questions, she should contact him.

I was so proud of Anne for speaking out and sent her this email:

"You did an incredible job. The police have announced themselves as totally incompetent and utter liars. We have been trying to break this rape/murder ring for years. I think you made more progress in that interview than we ever did. People are finally listening and due to the UK press coverage, people won't go to Koh Tao, so without a doubt you have already saved lives. What happened to your daughter is horrific. I hope we can save the lives of the poor innocent men who sit on death row who will pay for these bastard's crimes with their lives. We have a real chance now because of you and your bravery, determination, and the decency you have shown. I can't find words to thank you for that. I visited them 3 times a week for 18 months and took care of their mothers for 3 months while they were in Samui. They all thank you for shining a light on that island, one of the darkest spaces on this planet."

As Suthichai told Anne, the news was indeed featuring in the Thai press, but, horribly, the Thai press were publishing Jane's full and real name. I was absolutely disgusted as my own publication and the British press had protected her anonymity. Things then got even worse when the *Bangkok Post* also disturbingly published a story that the police were going to issue a summons for Jane and John to go back to Thailand. I tried to reassure Anne that this would be impossible without an extradition order. They had committed no crime; it would never happen. However, within a couple of days it was me who started to worry.

News started to hit the pages of the online Thai newspapers that there was a warrant out for my arrest in Thailand for reporting fake news. Messages started to pour in from my friends in Thailand who had seen the police searching Koh Samui for me in a news report on Thai television. Oddly enough, the report showed the police were looking for me at some rented accommodation in the south of the island. They interviewed my so-called landlady, who told them that I had rented a house from her and had left the island four years previously. This was ridiculous. I had not lived in rented accommodation in Thailand for over 14 years. I had my own house and had never seen this woman or her rented accommodation before in my life. I was aghast. The Thai authorities were about to issue an arrest warrant in my name for publishing fake news. The news I had published was not fake. The news reports about me renting a house on the south of the island from a woman I had never met were utter lies.

I was starting to get quite concerned. I kept my eyes on the Thai news and was appalled to read that the police were indeed seeking a warrant for my arrest to charge me under cybercrime laws for defaming the island's reputation. Tourist Police Deputy Commander Maj. Gen. Surachate Hakparn, said that the police had concluded that the reported assault of a British woman did not take place. He would like to insist that the police would never protect any crime or negligent official. He went on to say that in their work the police have only one goal and that is to seek truth in order to defend Thailand's reputation.

The Thai press articles, did however, make mention of the fact that I maintained that my news agency had investigated the claim with due diligence, but it did little to reassure me. This was not fake news, and I found the allegations that it was hurtful. Later, Hakparn said that he would also be issuing an arrest warrant for CSI LA David, as he had made the same allegations about the rape on his Facebook page, and, furthermore, would hold anyone who shared that content liable as well.

It transpired that Maj. Gen. Surachate Hakparn and his crew had flown down to Koh Tao in helicopters and had a look around the island and decided that the rape had never happened. I found this as further proof of the utter lack of proper police investigations. I am not sure what they were hoping to find in way of evidence all this time later. Their basis for saying the rape never happened was because on the night in question it was high tide so there would be no beach and it was a night that the football World Cup was televised. I had spent many years on the islands and knew very well that there was never a time when there was no beach due to high tide. A quick look at the tide tables confirmed that there was no high tide the night that Jane said she was raped.

Something big was happening. This was not normal. Once again, I thought about the DNA on the T-shirt Jane had. There had to be a reason the police in Thailand were acting this way. Accusing me of publishing fake news could only be a tactic to discredit me and my report.

The news reports were coming in thick and fast. One publication, *Ucanews* made this report that told my side of the story:

"The British editor of a small Thailand-based online publication says she was surprised by the arrest warrant issued for her by a Koh Samui Court over her website's coverage of the alleged rape of a young British woman on neighboring island Koh Tao.

"I really don't know why [they decided to come after me]," Suzanne Buchanan, editor of the Samui Times, told ucanews.com.

"Many news publications in Thailand and around the world have reported on the disproportionate incidents of tourist deaths on Koh Tao. It seems very strange to me that this time the authorities are going after the Samui Times. I think the authorities are upset with negative publicity for Koh Tao and wish to silence the small publications who report on it".

Local authorities, she added, may be "Unable or unwilling to go after larger publications who can fight back, or maybe they just want to show they are taking action and feel that the smaller publications are easier to intimidate".

Police in Surat Thani have accused Buchanan of violating the country's Computer Crime Act by publishing claims by a 19-year-old British tourist who says she was drugged and raped during her recent stay on Koh Tao, which is popular with backpackers.

Local police have had another arrest warrant issued for the U.S.-based owner of a popular Facebook page who has also been reporting on the case. They say they found no evidence to indicate the tourist had been raped.

Maj. Gen. Apichart Boonsriroj, commander of police in Surat Thani province, has submitted a report saying the rape as described by the woman did not take place. Controversially, his office has breached confidentiality rules by publicly identifying the alleged victim.

Thailand's draconian cybercrime laws prescribe severe penalties for spreading false information online. If convicted, Buchanan, who is back home in the United Kingdom, could face up to five years in prison if she ever returned to Thailand.

Critics of the law say it is routinely used by officials to try and silence criticism or negative publicity.

"It's almost a reflexive reaction [on the part of some Thai officials] to want to shut up the media rather than deal with problems", said a veteran Thailand-based foreign correspondent who asked to remain anonymous for fear of having his media accreditation revoked.

Buchanan echoes that view. "I feel sorry that they have taken this action instead of investing their energy in solving the obvious problems on Koh Tao", she said.

"The latest rape is not a fake story. The girl in question cut her trip around the world short by several months, returned to the U.K., where she saw health professionals and is being taken care of at a rape crisis centre".

The case has received widespread coverage in the U.K., where the woman reported it to police and provided them with what she said was DNA evidence of the crime. Her mother is reportedly planning to fly to Thailand to ask police to investigate further.

"I find it unfathomable that anybody [in Thailand] could think the Samui Times made this all up," Buchanan said.

In recent years, several foreign tourists have died under suspicious circumstances on Koh Tao , which has been dubbed "Death Island" by foreign media.

I was contacted by several news groups, all wanting to know what I thought about that fact that I was now virtually a fugitive.

As if it was not enough to be going after me and CSI LA on the 28th of August, I read the diabolical news that the Thai people were planning on asking Jane to go back to Thailand to face charges. An article in the *Bangkok Post* confirmed that Pol. Col. Wichob Kerdkliang, deputy commander of Surat Thani police, had stated that his office was drafting the summons for the woman and her male travel companion. He said, "The case being concluded depends on the cooperation of the person concerned. Please understand the duties of interrogators and the impact on residents of Koh Tao and Koh Phangan".

The UK's *Sun* newspaper was reporting that the black T-shirt, worn by the British teenager, could boost the probe after traces of foreign DNA, believed to be from the alleged rapist, was found on it and that the item had been handed over to the UK police in a sealed bag and there was a possibility it would be tested in the UK.

With this news, the relationship between Anne and I changed. She was obviously very upset that her daughter's name was in the paper, and this was causing a great deal of distress to both her and her daughter. I understood her distress, but it was not I who had leaked the name, it was the Royal Thai Police. Anne was just as upset that there were reports that her daughter would be sent back to Thailand to face charges. This was something that I could never have predicted. Even I was shocked at this latest development. At this stage in the game, I had thought that nothing that happened in the country that was still my home could ever shock me.

The MET finally seemed to be doing something for Jane. They sent a message to Anne to say the statement she had given to the police in the UK would be translated into Thai and sent, along with the relevant paperwork, to the National Crime Agency, who would then liaise with the Thai authorities for the matter to be investigated.

I had suggested to Anne that if she had to hand the T-shirt over to anybody it would be a good idea to keep part of it. I had an idea that if the DNA on it belonged to anybody of influence there was a good chance it would be destroyed, rather than being used to identify the perpetrator. Sadly, the MET went on to say that the T-shirt had been seized as evidence and could not be tampered with. This worried me as I thought it was really important for us to keep hold of at least some of the DNA.

The following day I got a message from Laura Witheridge, the sister of Hannah Witheridge to say she wanted to get a message to Anne. I sent her an email to ask permission to give out her details. I had no idea what the message was about. Anne agreed to me giving her contact details to Laura.

Anne asked me if I was safe in the UK. I told her that I hoped so but was not sure what would happen if they moved to extradite me back to Thailand to face the charges. I spoke to my lawyer in Bangkok who assured me that this could never happen. In order to move to extradition, the crime committed has to have been a crime in both the country issuing the order and the country in which the perpetrator lives. As I was in the UK, where reporting on the truth is not illegal, I had nothing to worry about. This did stop me worrying or having dreams about waking up in an overcrowded Thai prison cell. My parents were losing sleep over the arrest warrant and no amount of me reassuring them made a lot of difference. My mum was cross that I had written the article and put myself in danger. I could only repeat that nobody could have predicted the insane outcome of doing that by the Thai police and the Thai authorities.

I confided in Anne that I was perplexed about why the Thai authorities were so upset by this case. I wondered who the DNA might belong to and if there was any link between this sample and the Hannah Witheridge and David Miller cases. Anne had other ideas. She thought it could have been prompted by her mention of the mafia during the Suthichai interview, or even Suthichai giving her airtime.

However, it was not just Anne who got airtime. On the 30th of August 2018, Pol. Lt. Gen. Hakparn, did his own interview on a popular TV show.

During the interview, he said that he had been instructed to go to Koh Tao by Deputy Prime Minister Prawit Wongsuon. At the time of the interview, he said that the investigation into the rape had been concluded. He confirmed during the interview that this had been the first job that had been assigned to him by Deputy Prime Minister Prawit Wongsuon.

The interviewer asked Hakparn if he thought that the rape allegation case had been closed too early, to which he replied:

"Ok so today we went to the south with the police chief and forensic team to check the area and to conclude and clear the case. With all the evidence we have gathered at this point of time we can say that the alleged incident never happened, the rape never happened there is no evidence".

"Last Tuesday we went there, we sent some of our forensic team early, they did not find DNA or semen and there was no report at the hospital. Our team also went to the alleged place that the incident happened, they did not find anything. We interviewed the hostel owner as well as other witnesses, but they did not see anything, we interviewed about ten witnesses, none of them saw anything".

"Because we did not find any forensic evidence, we could only talk to people on Koh Tao. Our number one witness is the hostel owner. She told us that Jane was sharing a room with four male backpackers. She was the only female in a hostel room with four men. She went on to tell us that on the morning of the rape she found Jane sitting outside the bungalow crying. She asked her why she was upset. Jane told her that the previous night she was drunk and accidentally had sexual intercourse with her friend [name withheld in this publication], who was not her boyfriend, she felt very bad about this. The hostel owner immediately advised her to go and report the rape to the police. The hostel owner told us that Jane did not take her advice and was only interested in getting to Koh Phangan in time for the Full Moon Party. Jane said that she had friends meeting her there for the party and they would not be able to have fun unless she arrived on time, she said she also had to meet her boyfriend there".

Hakparn then told the interviewer that he and his team did try to simulate the rape crime scene. However, when they checked the dates, they noted that that night was a high tide and there would have been no beach, so it was not possible a rape occurred on the beach. He went on to say on the night in question the World Cup football was being played and the bars were packed so if anything had happened on the beach somebody would have seen it. He also made note that there were many police in the area that night. At this point, the interviewer asked if this was the final conclusion and how can that be clear when the police were still waiting for evidence from the British police. Hakparn said that Jane's mother said there was DNA on the T-shirt and the Thai police had to wait to see if that DNA was from an Asian or a Caucasian. He went on to say that either way they had to find out if the semen was from consensual sex or from rape.

The interviewer asked if it was possible to find out if it was rape or consensual sex from semen. Hakparn said that last year there were three false accusations of rape on Koh Tao and earlier this year a girl reported that she had been robbed but it turned out to be a false accusation. Eventually the girl admitted the accusation was false and she was now prohibited from entering Thailand. She said she had done it for the insurance money and Hakparn said she had later been accused of fraud by the Thai police. Eight minutes into the interview, Hakparn said the case now was about waiting for more information from Jane. He said the best thing to do would be for the British Consulate to contact the Thai police with the medical reports from the UK adding that that even though the investigation had now been concluded, he would investigate further if Jane or the UK authorities could provide more evidence.

Hakparn said he would like to talk to Jane, and he would like her to take the medical report to the police. Once the UK has provided DNA evidence, he would check it in his computer. He said if he believes the evidence from the UK, British Embassy, or Jane, he would like Jane to come to Thailand. He went on to say that if Jane was unwilling to travel to Thailand, he would be prepared to travel to the UK to meet with her. This was an interesting statement as he had previously announced that if Jane refused to return to Thailand, the case would be closed.

The interviewer asked what the situation would be if Jane and her family did not trust the Thai police and what would happen if they refused to provide the DNA evidence as they were aware that DNA evidence had been lost or 'used up' in other cases, such as that of Hannah Witheridge and David Miller where DNA samples were unavailable for retesting. Hakparn said that in the past there had been problems of that nature, but in this case, he wanted to forget the past and focus on the future. He said he did not want to talk about past cases anymore, but only on this case and future cases and he would not discuss anything that has happened or any DNA that was lost or used up to prevent further testing in the past.

Hakparn said it was important to set a new standard so tourists could trust the Thai police. He said this case is a big gamble, a big bet on the reputation of his country. He said if this case is real then he would do a proper investigation. He said he is not trying to protect his own police force, but the reputation of his country. He said that if this case is fake, then those who are responsible for spreading lies will be prosecuted. He is angry with the British female editor of the *Samui Times* who broke this story. He said he knows who this woman is. He said she has published photos of Koh Tao residents and used them as a logo on her news. He said in view of this reporting, there is a warrant out for the arrest of the editor of the *Samui* Times and she will be arrested and tried for computer crimes which are illegal in Thailand.

The interviewer asked why the mother of Jane does not trust the Thai police. Hakparn said that Jane left Koh Tao without reporting the rape, she did not report the rape on Koh Phangan, and she left Thailand without even reporting the rape to the British Embassy and that made him very suspicious. "Why did she just fly away from Thailand", he said. "We have sent 100 officers to Koh Tao and we can find no evidence the rape two months ago. We have told the British Embassy and shown them we are serious about this crime, but 100 officers did not find any evidence. It is our job to find the truth and we think the British Ambassador is impressed with our performance. We want to give Jane a chance to show us her evidence as we have found none".

"Right now, we are trying to find the Iphone", said Hakparn. "Our team is still on Koh Tao, they are looking at CCTV footage, some of the cameras were actually working, so now we are looking into that. But so far, based on the footage we can say nothing happened".

By the 3rd of September 2018, the Thai authorities had decided that it would be better to ban Jane from entering the country than to try to get her back to face charges, probably because they had been advised they could not press charges against her.

On the 4th of September 2018 I got the news that 12 people were going to be arrested for sharing the story from CSI LA Facebook page. Late that day, it was confirmed in the press that 9 people from all over Thailand had been arrested and taken to the prison on Koh Samui. I could hardly believe it. I got a message from one very distressed western man whose boyfriend had been arrested.

"Hello Susan, My name is Max, and my boyfriend share the post about your story on Facebook. And now he is in jail... Your story destroy our life too because he supports you... I want to help him and I don't know how. I'm French and I think it will be complicated for help him. It's insane..."

I was completely horrified that anything I had published could ruin anyone's life and got onto David from CSI LA straight away. He told me that he had organized a free lawyer for all those who had been arrested for sharing his post on Facebook. I immediately got back to Max:

"Hi Max. The arrests were made for sharing the content from the CSI LA website. Nobody has been arrested for sharing the *Samui Times* news. We have a lawyer who can help you. He is doing all cases free of charge. Would you like me to give you his details"?

Max told me that he understood that it was the CSI LA post that had been shared that had caused the arrest and that his boyfriend had been taken by the police two days earlier. He said he didn't know if he was being held at the Samui police station or at the prison and was getting very little information as to his welfare. He said he would like the details of the lawyer whose name is Winyat.

David from CSI LA and I were in constant contact over this matter. David put this information on his Facebook page to help those who had been arrested.

"To the page followers who have been arrested for sharing information from the CSI LA page, please contact Ms Vinyat on this telephone number. (Number withheld in this publication). Ms Viyet will provide you with a lawyer to help you win your case. Take it easy. The prosecutor wants to silence society".

I told Max that we had contacted human rights organizations about this case and sent him a link to a news article in *The Nation* that confirmed this to be true.

Max told me that he thought the whole thing was completely insane and would stay in touch with me and let me know how his boyfriend got on in the court. I told him that the reports about the rape were not fake, and we would do all we could to support him and his boyfriend. I also mentioned that we had taken the case to Interpol and told him to try not to worry. A few days later he got back to me and said that all of the men who had been arrested for sharing the post had been taken to Koh Tao to be questioned by the Royal Thai Police Technology Crime Suppression group. I told Max that I thought that the DNA Jane had must belong to somebody of significance for this to be happening.

My head was spinning. I was trying to be kind to this man who was obviously going out of his mind with fear, but truth be told so was I. I was terrified as to what might happen to these men on Koh Tao. I was getting very little sleep and wondered what on earth I had set in motion. Max told me he was very worried that those who had been arrested would be held for a long time and had been told that his boyfriend was facing five years behind bars just for sharing the CSI LA post. I tried to reassure him that if Interpol could prove that the rape allegation was not fake, and therefore the news was not fake, then the police would have to let them go. This did nothing to reassure Max who told me that his boyfriend was being charged with speaking badly about Thailand and was being accused of being in opposition to the government. I asked Max to speak to the lawyer that David from CSI LA had provided. Max told me that his boyfriend had already spoken to a lawyer who had told him what to say but he was still behind bars. I suspected this was a way for the government to try to stop journalists releasing stories about Thailand; they could not hurt me or David, but hurting others would put us in a position where we had to back off. This whole thing was turning into a really macabre game of chess and one that I wished I was not playing.

On the 7th of September 2018, Max told me that he had paid sixty thousand baht to get his boyfriend out of jail. The court case would be on the 18th of October 2018. Max told me that his boyfriend was not hurt on Koh Tao. I was very relieved to hear that. Max told me all of those who were arrested would go to court on the same day and he was very worried that the country would try to make an example out of them to deter other people from sharing anything online. I had to agree with him. I told Max in my opinion it would be better for him and his boyfriend to go and live in France and not risk a five-year prison sentence. He said that his boyfriend wanted to stay in Thailand to fight the case. Max and I agreed on one thing, fighting the government and the court was a risky move. Max was worried that if they moved to France, the Thai people could force his boyfriend to go back to face charges. I explained that the extradition treaty would not allow this as sharing a true story on your Facebook page in France is not a crime. But this would mean that his boyfriend would not be able to return to Thailand and that was a sacrifice his boyfriend was not prepared to make, even if he did have to spend five years in a dirty prison cell. The downside of this strategy, however, would mean that he would struggle to get a visa to go even on holiday outside of Thailand afterwards because he would have a criminal record.

I got the email address of Brian Davidson, the British ambassador in Thailand, to try to find out what the British Embassy knew about my arrest warrant and, if there was going to be an extradition order to send me back to Thailand to face charges. Brian Davidson did not get back to me but his colleague Andrew Dalton, the country casework manager for Thailand, sent me an email on the 18th of September 2018. In it, he explained that he was a consular case manager for Thailand working from London dealing with UK contacts in cooperation with the embassy in Bangkok. He said he had seen reports in Thailand with regards to my arrest warrant and was working with the authorities to confirm them. He said he appreciated how I must be feeling at this distressing time and said his organization was fully aware of "*Lèse-majesté*" which in Thailand classes criticism of the monarchy in any form as a crime and was aware of cases where this has been interpreted broadly. He went on to say he was aware I was in the UK and asked me if I was planning on returning to Thailand.

I called Andrew straight away and he told me that he had not seen the arrest warrant and did not know what it was for but would try to get a copy of it. He advised me not to travel to Thailand as I would be arrested. I asked him if it would be safe for me to travel to other countries in Asia. As he did not know if there was to be an extradition order, he was not prepared to say if it would be safe for me to travel there. He was very vague about everything and was not prepared to say anything on the phone that could be used against him at a later date. He did say he thought it was unlikely that the UK would agree to extradite me but was not prepared to guarantee anything and advised me to speak to a lawyer.

Anne's husband heard from Interpol who confirmed that there was a deadline for the case and Jane would need to see the Thai police before the 25th of September 2018. He went on to say that the Thai police had offered to send a delegation from Thailand to speak to Jane in London before the deadline.

The following assurances were given by the Thai Police on the conduct of any discussion with Jane:

- A female Thai police officer who speaks English will be part of the police group deployed to the UK.
- Jane can chose where/time of day the Thai police meet with her. A police station is suggested as an appropriate controlled environment.
- She can have any other person present if she wishes.
- A safeguarding officer has been allocated by the Met Police who could also be present.
- Jane will not be left alone with the Thai police at any time.
- The Thai police will not visit her at home or have her home address.

- No photographs or video will be allowed to be taken by the Thai Police.
- No media will be allowed to be present.

He finished by saying he would be grateful if Anne could let him know Jane's wishes so he could update Interpol and said that if Anne's husband had any additional questions or reassurances that Jane would like in place then he would only have to let him know.

The Thai press was suggesting that Hakparn would be coming to the UK to interview Jane. I was blown away that the Thai police were going to spend money flying their officers over to the UK. Hakparn was still maintaining in the Thai public press that Jane was lying, and I was publishing her lies. If he was so sure there had been no rape, then why was he investing time and money in an unprecedented move by the Royal Thai Police in flying them halfway round the world? I was more convinced than ever that they wanted the DNA and it would somehow impact on the case of Hannah Witheridge and David Miller.

Anne got an update from the British Embassy:

"An update from today is that I am now speaking directly with the Thai police in my Consular role to help facilitate the meeting in London, should Jane wish to continue with arrangements. We stand ready to facilitate the visa applications from the Thai police if you ask us in order to allow them the travel to the UK.

Some points for Jane to consider

The Tourist Police visiting the UK to interview Jane would be an exceptional measure, but one that the Thai Police inform us they are keen to take. The understanding we have is that as a result of the meeting any statement or evidence taken from Jane in the UK may run the risk of not standing up in court. We suggest that you take legal advice on this question. We can provide you with a list of lawyers in Thailand, some who specialize in assisting victims of crime and offer some advice for free. I will speak to the Thai Police again tomorrow and update you further. If you feel able to discuss these issues with Jane in the meantime I would be grateful".

Anne asked me what I thought. I was getting pretty sick of the British Embassy fobbing us off with their list of lawyers who we didn't know, let alone what their prices were. I told Anne that I would recommend she use my lawyer as he was not corruptible and suggested that the very fact the police were prepared to fly to the UK flew in the face of the allegations that no crime had been committed. I felt that if Anne let the Thai police come then they would have to admit a crime had been committed and Jane may have a chance to see justice and my arrest warrant would have to be quashed. I finished by saying that it was her call, and I did not expect Jane to go through with it just to sort out my arrest warrant. Anne said she had no intention of backing out and had asked a different investigation unit to come from Thailand as she did not trust the tourist police. She did however, mention that if the case got thrown out, she would be concerned that Jane might be arrested. I reassured her that the Royal Thai Police had no jurisdiction in the UK and would be in no position to arrest her on British soil.

On the 19th of September 2018, Anne mailed me to say that the Royal Thai Police would send three female officers who were not part of the tourist police to interview Jane. The interview date was set for the 3rd of October 2018. Anne said she was feeling very low that the T-shirt had not been tested for DNA and was starting to worry that this would not happen before the police took it away. She had contacted a law firm who specialized in human rights to ask if they could have a private forensic test done on the T-shirt prior to the interview with the Thai police.

In the meantime, David from CSI LA had got hold of Pornthip, Thailand's leading DNA expert who also testified at the Hannah Witheridge and David Miller case. Pornthip, who we believed to be incorruptible, said she was prepared to test the DNA in Bangkok. I could tell Anne was suffering from the stress of all of this and offered to add her to our online support group. Unlike the other group members, her child had not died but she had been badly affected by her experience in Thailand and all of the other group members agreed that she needed our support.

Back on the 9th of September 2018, Anne asked Derek Johnstone, the vice consul at the British Embassy, to communicate with her husband as on that day Anne was otherwise engaged. In another crazy twist after this had happened, he took it upon himself to refuse to discuss anything with Anne, a decision he confirmed with this email:

"Dear Anne,

I finished work yesterday at 4 p.m. and have only just come back on duty now. As discussed previously there is limited information I can give you in relation to this investigation but I can assure you that the MET will ensure protocols for this kind of investigation are followed correctly. I have been informed that Jane's father has been nominated as a point of contact for Jane, and I am in direct contact with Jane myself, therefore further updates will go through them".

Anne was furious and responded

"Dear sirs,

As you can see from the emails below, my asking you to speak with my husband regarding this rape case, was not handing it over to him, just at that time I had so much going on. For you to then instruct the UK police not to talk with me was atrocious.

I am very concerned that this was because I had the Thai tourist police on a back foot and it was easier for you to be in touch with my husband who was less interested in the history of Koh Tao, meaning, he has only our daughter's interests at heart.

We both have Jane at the foremost of our concerns, however, I do question your position regarding diplomatic relations;

Why are the press in Thailand able to continue to use our daughter's name?

Why is Surachet Hakpul allowed to continue with this investigation when he dismissed it so rapidly, called our daughter a liar, arrested 12 people for sharing the news our daughter had been raped, went to the wrong scene of the crime a whole month after the rape had happened, said it was high tide when it was not, said she was barred from Thailand, and now she's not.

He is parading around now and should not be. Why are you letting all of this happen?

Why are you not making statements?

Please let us know who you put in charge of Jane's interview on 3rd of October 2018, who promised he would make sure that the DNA on the t shirt would be reported to us and him? Detective Sergeant Dipesh Danatti.

Why have the MET agreed not to talk with the press and yet he can say whatever he wants?

Also, why on earth are you allowing him to have an arrest warrant out for Su?

I expect a reply dear sirs,

Kindest regards,

Anne".

The police officers flew over from Thailand and 'interviewed' Jane. During her 5-hour interview, that was more like an interrogation, Jane agreed for the T-shirt to be handed over and just like that our evidence disappeared on a plane to Thailand. Months later, the only news Jane got was that the DNA was Asian but didn't match anyone on their records and just like that the case was closed.

On the 5th of October, I sent Andrew another email after the Thai police flew to the UK to speak to Jane. Surely if the Thai police had flown to the UK, they could hardly still stand by their decision that there had been no crime. If this was an admission that there was a crime, then how could they still be accusing me of making up fake news?

"Hi Andrew,
I hope this email finds you well.
I was wondering if you have any update on the situation now the Thai police have visited the UK.
If not, could you please advise how I find out if there is actually a warrant out for my arrest and if so, what sort of travel restrictions this puts on me in terms of traveling to countries who have some sort of extradition treaty with Thailand where I am likely to get 'picked up' at an airport".

He responded by saying he was sorry he had not got back to me sooner. His colleagues in Bangkok had been in direct contact with the Thai police and they had informed him that there was indeed an arrest warrant in place for me. He went on to say he had not been provided with more details and it was unlikely he was going to get any further details. He mentioned that he was sure that I was aware that the embassy doesn't investigate or interfere with criminal investigations in another country just as they would not expect anyone to interfere with theirs. He finished with a link to a list of lawyers in Thailand and said he hoped his message made sense.

This made no sense to me. The arrest warrant made no sense. The fact that the British Embassy, who are supposed to take care of British subjects, could not get involved in finding out what would be likely to happen to them if they travel to Thailand or any of the surrounding countries made even less sense to me. I mailed him back:

"Hi Andrew,
Do you know what they are accusing me of? Arrest warrant for what"?

His email back to me was just as vague as the previous one.

I gave up with the British Embassy after I called Andrew who confirmed that I would be safe to travel to other countries in Asia and then called me back ten minutes later to say he could not confirm that and once again told me to contact a lawyer. I asked him which countries had an extradition treaty with Thailand and he told me he could not give me that information. Interestingly, not long after these conversations, I got an email from the British Embassy in Wireless Road in Bangkok inviting me to attend a press conference. The British Embassy Bangkok had organized this conference in order to expand professional collaboration between the British Embassy, Thai social workers, and Thai social services providers. The aim was to develop child protection services including knowledge exchange between service providers in Thailand and in the UK.

This invitation was not unusual as they liked me to publish information for them, free of charge, in the *Samui Times*. However, I was less than impressed that they expected me to attend, bearing in mind I would be five years late having to serve time for a crime I did not commit in a Thai jail in order to get there. I sent an email back that simply said:

"As there is a warrant out for my arrest in Thailand you can't help me with, I don't think it is very likely I will attend".

Incredibly, as I had not attended, the British Embassy took it upon themselves to send a press release covering the press conference to publish for them. I mailed them back again.

"I would be grateful if you could sort out my unjust arrest warrant or at least find out what it is for! Incredibly, you want me to help you by publishing your press release but are totally unwilling to investigate charges against me relating to the publication you want free advertising in"!

Unsurprisingly, I did not hear back from them.

The sad fact was that it was over. We had lost the DNA; the case was closed. My arrest warrant was and still is in place. Anne and her husband got no justice for Jane who continues to struggle with not only the trauma of what happened to her in Koh Tao but the circus she was put through that turned out to be fruitless on her return. Like the other victims' families Jane and her family are left with a world of hurt to deal with and no conclusion or line in the sand they can cross over to try to get some closure. The case closed with one last article. This time from the *New York Times* who contacted me for information I was happy to give. I felt frustration beyond belief and for the first time started to give up hope entirely for Zaw Lin and Wai Phyo and for ever seeing the island I still considered being my home ever again.

I had no idea what I could to do help Zaw Lin and Wai Phyo anymore other than to continue to write to them offering words of support. Because Wai Phyo did not write to me very often, I focused my attention to writing to Zaw Lin. I told Zaw Lin that he must use his time in prison to get an education, the kind of education his family had not been able to provide for him. I wrote him very long letters about history and tried to fill his mind full of knowledge to take his mind off his dire predicament. Despite having no faith that Zaw Lin would ever leave prison, I talked endlessly to him about the things we would do when he was finally free. One passage from one of his letters read:

"I know you will have a lot of things to show me and I will certainly come to visit your county when I come out of the prison and will be a great day!!!! I can't stand it. I just want to sit and talk and laugh and laugh each other like we did in Koh Samui".

I cast my mind back to our prison visits when I was in Samui and Zaw Lin was in the Samui Provincial Prison and found it incredible that either of us was able to laugh really. I guess at that time neither one of us ever really thought in the bottom of our hearts that Zaw Lin and Wai Phyo would still be incarcerated years later and I would be living in the UK. Even though I was well aware of the precariousness of their situation and the level of corruption that was ingrained into the system I think somewhere deep inside, we thought that justice would prevail or our endless efforts to find the truth would eventually bear fruit. There were so many people looking into the case and the glare of the world's media had been on this case, it never occured to us at that time that the situation may never be resolved. For many years I had to do my best to not let my mind wander across the moment when I was told the B2 had been executed and it was all in vain. I tried not to think about how I would feel. I had no idea how I would be able to walk through my life knowing that such an injustice had occurred. I would have always wondered if I could have done more. Zaw Lin especially has given my life the sort of purpose that I never dreamed it would have. I sometimes feel guilty for giving him hope in my letters to him, but what else is there other than hope?

CHAPTER 56 – THE SUPREME COURT APPEAL VERDICT

At around 3 p.m. on the 28th of August 2019, I got a message from a friend that the verdict of the Supreme Court of Thailand in the case of Zaw Lin and Wai Phyo was due the next day. I stared at the message in disbelief. A black feeling that had come to be all too familiar to me over the last five years descended on me once again.

My head was all over the place. I had a two-hour meeting to attend at work I could not get out of. I had no idea what happened in that meeting. I thought of nothing other than how excited Zaw Lin must have been feeling having had a letter from him the week before telling me the appeal verdict was due back anytime and he could not wait for the world to know he was innocent. I didn't share his optimism that this would be the outcome. At 5 p.m., I got out of my meeting and called my parents to tell them and then I went to the church. The verdict was due to be read at 4 a.m. UK time the following morning, 10 a.m. Thai time.

I had no idea what to do with myself, so I sat on a pew in the church and asked God for help. I am not in the least bit religious and do not believe in God. However, knowing that Zaw Lin did, I asked God to help him or at least give him some strength. I lit a candle for each of the B2 and drove home to my house that is in a very remote location. Having had more death threats from Thailand, the local police had instructed an alarm company to give me an intruder alarm that would alert the police straight away if anybody entered my property and did not put in the code. I typed in the code, sat down, and then plugged in my personal GPS panic alarm that would alert the police to my location should I feel at risk and checked the indoors panic alarm was working and in place. I checked my CCTV was working and checked that my video doorbell was online, my daily ritual, before sitting down to find support from my friends online. I knew there was not a hope in hell of me getting any sleep and decided to sit it out and wait.

At 4 a.m., I asked Htoo Chit, who I knew would be attending, to give my love to the B2 and asked Andy if he was there. He did not say if he was or was not but when I also asked him to give my love to the B2, he told me not to worry and that they talked about me all the time. It turned out Andy was not there. My mind wandered to visions of me kicking him off the side of a cliff. Four a.m. came and went, as did 5 a.m. and 6 a.m. Then just after 6 a.m., Evelyne sent me a message to say how sad she was. The Supreme Court had upheld the verdict and the death penalty. I was devastated but not surprised.

The B2 had been taken to the court close to the Bangkwang Central Prison in Nonthanaburi, where they are held on death row, and had heard the judgment by video link. Htoo Chit told me that at the end, having been told their last appeal had failed, Zaw Lin had asked the judge if he would kill them by injection. I was beside myself. All that remained in the way of hope for the B2 was a petition to the king, to ask him for a pardon, that would result in a life sentence for the B2 instead of execution. I did not hold out much hope. The judgment had come through on Friday morning for me. I spent the entire weekend trying to find out what we could do for the B2. I spoke to lawyers to find out if we could demand a retrial, if there was any court in Thailand that could be asked to do a judicial review. I racked my brains and answered hundreds of messages I got from friends and supporters of the case who contacted me to say how sorry they were. My Facebook page was awash with comments from all over the world and, amazingly, quite a few from Thailand from people who no longer gave a damn if they got into trouble for expressing their horror at the judgment.

On Sunday afternoon, I wrote to Zaw Lin. It was a hard letter to write. How do you console anyone who is facing death by lethal injection, after they have had to walk back into a prison they thought they were walking out of for the last time, knowing they would never walk out or see the outside world again.

All I could do was tell Zaw Lin that he must not give up, that we would keep trying and that he needed to stay strong and eat and stay healthy and have hope and that he would see his mother soon. I told him the world believed him and that hundreds of people had expressed that to me and as long as there is life there is hope.

Two days later, I sent him a strongly worded letter asking him if he had any more information from the night of the murders that he was now prepared to give me and asked him if he had been forced to give semen to anyone. I told him to grill Wai Phyo as to anything he might be able to give me in the way of information that might help me save their lives.

It was only a few days later I got a letter from Zaw to tell me he had lost his appeal. He was very upset and that nothing was going right for him. I thought it was the biggest understatement I have ever heard in my life.

I hoped at this stage that the families of Hannah and David would step in to ask that they not carry out the death penalties when the unthinkable happened. We found out that Laura Witheridge, the sister of Hannah Witheridge, had died in hospital, just five years and one day after her sister died on Sairee Beach in Koh Tao. She was 30 years old.

I stared at the walls of my house in stunned silence before bursting into tears at the thought of her shattered family. I got the impression that we were all living under some kind of curse. The curse of the turtle. I shivered at the thought that I actually have a tattoo of that island on my back.

CHAPTER 57 – NEW YEAR 2020

During one visit to Zaw Lin, despite Andy's pleas for me to never mention the case, I asked him what happened that fateful night. He gave me a detailed account of his movements. In 2018 I sent him a list of questions asking him to detail what happened. This is his response. It had not changed at all over the years. I can only assume he either has an incredible memory or he is telling the truth.

My sister Su,

1. On that night I couldn't recognize anyone because there were too many people and it was very dark on the beach.

2. I did not know anyone who was on the beach that night.

3. Me and Wai left the beach about 26.00 a.m.(sic)

4. Wai and I did not share accommodation on Koh Tao. I used to work at Brother Bar from about 4.p.m. until about 10.p.m. Wai worked the same shift at the Safety Stop Bar. I want to give you the details about what happened that night. After I finished work, I took my guitar and went to see my Burmese friend, named Mau Mau, who worked at the AC2 restaurant as a waiter. AC2 is next to the AC Bar. I waited for him to finish work with Wai Phyo who joined me there. At around 11.p.m., when Mau Mau left work, the three of us went to a nearby 7 Eleven store on my motorbike. After we brought the drinks, we took my motorbike to a restaurant called Inter'. We went down a small path to the beach and

sat on a tree branch. Here we played guitar and sang, as we often did after work. At about 12.p.m., Mau Mau told me he wanted to go and see his girlfriend and asked to borrow my motorbike. I let him take it and he left, leaving me and Wai Phyo with no transport. We continued to play guitar, drink and smoke cigarettes. After a while, Wai Phyo and I moved to a new spot near Mayer Bar, close to where we first sat. From that area we could see people dancing around a fire and swimming in the distance. By 2.a.m., we were tired. It was too far to go back to where we lived, so we walked to the room of Mau Mau, which was very close to AC2. We lay down and slept. I do not know if Wai Phyo went back out that night. I woke up at around 8.a.m. the following morning and noticed that Wai Phyo was sleeping and my motorbike keys were on the top of Mau Mau's desk. I did not see Mau Mau. I took the keys and drove back to the area I lived with Wai Phyo. I dropped Wai Phyo at his room and went back to mine. I changed my clothes and went to work.

My sister Su, I miss you so very much day and night, I love you like my big sister.

Zaw Lin.

On the 1st of January 2020, I closed the *Samui Times*. I was tired of death threats and tired of Thailand, although I still miss it as my home.

I continue to write to Zaw Lin, but they are not easy letters to write. All the time I had been visiting Zaw Lin and writing to him, there had been hope; hope for the trial, hope for the first appeal, and then hope for the second appeal. It is hard to know what to say when all hope is lost. The only possible chance now for he and Wai Phyo was for a pardon by the king of Thailand to commute their death penalty sentence to one of life in prison. It is hard to imagine in the bowels of the Bangkwang Central Prison AKA the Bangkok Hilton that there is any chance of anything that resembles any kind of life whatsoever.

Not long after the final appeal failed, a request for clemency was submitted to the king to ask for a pardon; the B2 never heard back from it.

Andy, who is now living in Katmandu, told his Facebook page readers that he had raised a great deal of money for the mothers to travel to Thailand to submit the appeal. The mothers managed to make it to Thailand along with the brother of Zaw Lin to visit the B2, possibly for the last time.

It was two months before I got a letter from Zaw Lin, who explained that now his case was over, he is only allowed to send two letters a month at his current prison category. That will change in five years' time when, like the other prisoners, he will be allowed to send three a week.

In a letter to me, Zaw Lin said that he hopes for a transfer to his own country under the Thai-Burmese treaty and hopes that once back on home soil he will find his release. I have not found any evidence that such a treaty exists.

It is incredible to me that he still finds hope to hang on to. Of all the letters he has sent to me over these incredibly hard years holed up in a filthy, hot prison, he has only sworn once and that was when he told me that his DNA being on or in Hannah was "bullshit". In a letter to Evelyne, Wai Phyo told her he is becoming mentally ill being incarcerated for crimes he did not commit.

The correspondence with ILAC and APLAC and BLQS got nowhere.

At the start of 2020, my relationship with Ian Yarwood broke down. Ian continued to drum up support for the B2 with his Facebook page 'Koh Tao Death Island' and his YouTube channel.

Robert Holmes was never heard of again.

Jonathan Head was arrested in Thailand in 2017 and faced a criminal defamation trial brought by a lawyer who featured in an investigation about foreigners being scammed of their retirement homes. The charges were later dropped.

The cloner of the Facebook accounts turned out to be Jim, the very man who said he was helping me. I am aware he has made threats to hurt me.

Since I moved to the UK, I have received dozens of death threats that continue to this day for my involvement in the case.

Andy Hall continues to fight for the rights of migrant workers on his Facebook page.

The families of the victims of Koh Tao still have no answers.

The petition to 10 Downing Street failed.

The execution of prisoners in Bangkwang resumed in 2018 after 9 years when Theerasak Longgi, 26, was executed by lethal injection. Human rights group Amnesty International condemned this action as a 'deeply misguided' effort to reduce crime. He had been found guilty of murdering a 17-year-old boy in 2012. He was the seventh person to be executed by lethal injection since Thailand introduced this method in 2003 to replace death by firing squad.

In 2019, after years of being shut, the AC Bar reopened.

Some friends on the islands in the Gulf of Thailand told me that tourist numbers were at an all-time low and many hundreds of businesses had shut down. The Tourist Authority of Thailand put this down to the strong baht.

In February 2020, the body of a Caucasian man washed up on the shores of Koh Tao and an appeal went out to find out who he was. News reports later emerged stating he was a Thai fisherman. I saw the pictures of the corpse; he was undeniably Caucasian.

In 2020, Hakparn, who issued my arrest warrant, survived an assassination attempt after stepping down from his high-profile role and being moved to an inactive post. It was reported that he then moved to India. An article in the *Bangkok Post* on the 17th of March 2021 it was announced that he would be returning to police headquarters in a newly created position.

A video taken by two fishermen from their boat of the murders of Hannah Witheridge and David Miller has never been found despite our efforts to locate it.

My online petition to try to save the B2 by appealing to the king was signed by only 6,000 people despite being read by over 50,000 after they lost their last chance of freedom.

On the 15th of August 2020 news broke that Zaw Lin and Wai Phyo had had their death sentences commuted to life by Thailand's king to mark his 68th birthday on the 28th of July. I slept well that night, and for the first time in years, the first thing I did when I woke up was not check the news to see if they were still alive.

In March 2020, the *Samui Times* was taken over by a Thai news publication called the *Thaiger*. My articles about the case have been removed.

In August 2021, I started filming with a company called Blast! Films who are commissioned to make a three-part documentary on these events for SKY Crime. We hope it will bring new information forward to finally exonerate the B2 who, at the time of writing, have now spent over seven years in prison in Thailand.

In February 2022 a Canadian lady called Carla Bartel got in touch with me. She told me "I visited Koh Tao in July 2013. One evening, a travel buddy named Sam and I were sitting along an ocean run-off on Sairee Beach. Two men ran up from behind wearing *V for Vendetta* masks and smashed a rock on Sam's head. We were both able to escape the situation with our lives. A little over a year later, the bodies of Hannah and David were found just below where we were sitting that night".

I am still in touch with the families of the victims of Koh Tao.

To the best of my knowledge the Miller family still believe justice has been done and Zaw Lin and Wai Phyo are guilty of the rape and murder of Hannah Witheridge and the murder of David Miller.

It has now been over five years since I stepped foot in my house in Koh Samui; I know I will never see it or my belongings again.

I continue to try to find the truth.

I will never give up.

All it takes for evil to triumph is for good men to do nothing.

This book is dedicated to all of those who lost their lives in Koh Tao, their loving families, and those wrongfully convicted for crimes they did not commit.

PHOTOS

More can be seen at: wbp.bz/curseturtlegallery

Me in Koh Tao circa 2002

Wai Phyo

Zaw Lin

Koh Samui Provincial Court

Beautiful Koh Samui

Fleeing Thailand

The mothers visit their boys in Samui prison

Saying goodbye to theB2 at the Bangkok Hilton

The mothers pray for their sons in the temple

B2's mothers at the temple

Ben Harrington

Nick Pearson

Christina enjoying time with her mother

Luke Miller

See more photos and other material online at:

http://wbp.bz/curseturtlegallery

*For More News About Suzanne Buchanan,
Signup For Our Newsletter:*

http://wbp.bz/newsletter

*Word-of-mouth is critical to an author's long-
term success. If you appreciated this book please
leave a review on the Amazon sales page:*

http://wbp.bz/curseturtlea

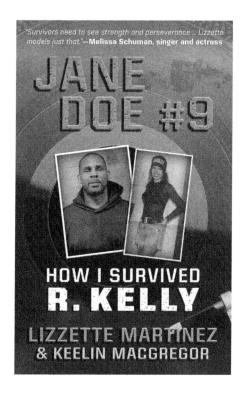

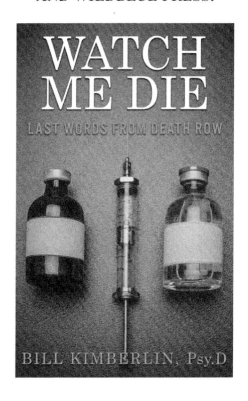

Printed in Great Britain
by Amazon

12599452R00220